ELDER INTERVENTIONS

A Guide to Caring for the Elderly with Emotional and Behavioral Problems

---

Thomas Krajewski, M.D.

Bloomington, IN Milton Keynes, UK

authorHOUSE

AuthorHouse™
1663 Liberty Drive, Suite 200
Bloomington, IN 47403
www.authorhouse.com
Phone: 1-800-839-8640

AuthorHouse™ UK Ltd.
500 Avebury Boulevard
Central Milton Keynes, MK9 2BE
www.authorhouse.co.uk
Phone: 08001974150

First published by AuthorHouse 2/16/2006

ISBN: 1-4208-8212-0 (sc)

Library of Congress Control Number: 2005907985

Printed in the United States of America
Bloomington, Indiana

This book is printed on acid-free paper.

ELDER INTERVENTIONS

EDITORIAL STAFF

Executive Editor   Jack Krajewski

Staff Editors   Lynn S. Dopkin
Ellie Krajewski
Anne Krajewski
Kevin L. Laser, MD

SPECIAL NOTE

The author has made an extensive effort to ensure that the information contained herein is accurate and conforms to the standards accepted at the time of publication. You are advised, however, to discuss the information obtained in this book with a physician, nurse, pharmacist or other health care professional.

To Ellie, who did not let her flame go out

and

Anne, Tom, Jack and Laura

who are truly starting to glow.

Special thanks to Hon, an inspirational

lady I am proud to call mother.

This book is especially dedicated to those who truly

care for and about the elderly.

TABLE OF CONTENTS

INTRODUCTION

This is not just another book about Alzheimer's disease. There are many fine books that discuss Alzheimer's as well as other dementias, but only a small portion of those books, usually a chapter or so, deal with the behavioral and emotional problems related to the dementias. This book will deal with the difficult behaviors and emotional states that are seen in the elderly population. These problems are the result of a variety of different clinical conditions. This book will take a step-by-step approach in identifying the problem, seeking an evaluation, understanding the diagnosis and finally developing specific plans to deal with the abnormal conduct.

According to the U.S. Census Bureau, the group of citizens that is 65 and over grew by 74% between 1970 and 1999. This elderly population will grow even more rapidly in the future as the baby boomers enter this older age group. In the year 2000 those 65 and older accounted for 13% of the overall population. By 2030 this older group will comprise 20% of the entire population.

At present about 20% of those over 55 will experience a mental disorder that is not a part of normal aging. Most studies believe that psychiatric problems in the elderly are still underreported. Allow me to cite a few examples of mental illness in the elderly. About 11% of adults over 55 meet the criteria for anxiety disorder. The number of older individuals with depressive symptoms comprises up to 20% of the over-65 population. About 2 million persons in this older age group have a diagnosable depressive illness. Between 1 and 5 percent of persons 65 and older abuse substances, and up to 15% of those seeking medical help have alcohol related problems. The highest rate of suicide is in this older age group. As you can see, millions of elderly people are affected by non-Alzheimer related mental health problems.

It is estimated that at least 4 million people in the U.S. suffer from Alzheimer's disease or some form of dementia. Nearly 10% of the over-65 population and up to 50% of people over 85 have some type of dementia. Approximately 9 million Americans have a family member with Alzheimer's.

Many people who have these various forms of mental illnesses have associated behavioral problems that are troubling to their families, friends and society in general. This book was written for these individuals, as well as the affected elderly person.

About 15 years ago I was asked to write a book based on a series of lectures that I had produced for mental health professionals. Unfortunately, at the same time, my wife was diagnosed with leukemia, and given only a 10% chance for survival. Though my life had taken a different focus over the next several years, I continued with my lectures regarding the behavioral problems of the elderly. My wife survived, as did my desire to write that book.

During my talks about the behavioral problems of the elderly, I was often asked to provide handouts or flyers to the family doctors, nurses and other caregivers who attended my lectures. It was fairly common for them to ask permission to duplicate these handouts, so that they could give them to patients and their family members.

As time went on, I was asked to speak to lay groups regarding the same issues. Family members, too, would often ask me about articles or books that would provide them with solutions to the problems they encounter on a daily basis with their loved ones. Unfortunately, many of the books available were directed toward professionals and often did not provide easily understandable techniques that the general public could use to help their loved ones with a variety of behavioral problems. These problems would include wandering, memory loss, assaultive behaviors and a variety of other issues that would disrupt the ability of their family member to remain independent and functional.

Hopefully, this book will guide patients, as well as their significant others, in a logical fashion to identify problems and patterns, set realistic goals, develop interventions and then adjust goals and interventions to achieve a successful outcome. I did not wish, however, to simply produce a textbook for the lay public. Rather, I wanted to write this book in a style that the reader would find not only informative, but also enjoyable. Therefore, I have added numerous examples and anecdotes to make the text more interesting. Of course, the names of the patients have been changed for confidentiality reasons. To some extent it is difficult to take such a depressing topic such as elderly behavioral problems and write about it in a captivating fashion. Yet, I hope this book meets that objective.

I sincerely hope that the readers of this book include those individuals who came to me at the end of the lectures and asked for more information to help their loved ones. These folks presented a variety of straightforward questions as to how they could help family members, neighbors and associates who were having problems maintaining their behavior within social norms. It was not unusual to hear about problems that I had never encountered. One time, I was asked to help a patient who had been writing on the wall with crayons. This person seemed to be functional in every other parameter. The family was embarrassed to ask their relative why she was doing that, and felt it was a sign of some serious psychiatric problem. After taking a careful history, it was clear that this patient might have been having some problems with her vision. After a thorough medical evaluation, it was found that the patient had difficulty seeing. When I asked the patient why she was writing with crayons on the wall, she stated that she thought she was writing on a large notepad. Apparently, at one time in her life she did have a large notepad on her refrigerator. Once the family realized that this was not a psychiatric disorder, they were relieved. The patient stopped writing on the wall after she had some corrective eye surgery.

While all of the problems faced by the elderly do not have easy answers, as in the above example, many complicated issues can be divided into simple ones. This, then, simplifies the interventions, which will often lead to a successful outcome. This book will provide an outline the reader can use to face and tackle these difficult issues.

The initial portion of this text will deal with the task of developing a positive relationship with the identified individual, thereby initiating the evaluation process. The middle of the book will address the potential causes of the behavioral problems and some readily available solutions. The final phase will assist the reader in developing plans to address the more complicated problems on a continuing basis, as well as considering the options available to the caregiver to minimize the chance of burnout and increase the chance of a successful outcome.

There is no doubt that dealing with an individual who is cognitively impaired and "acting out" is often an embarrassing and challenging situation for any family. I want you to know that this is not an uncommon situation. There are hundreds of thousands of people dealing with such issues everyday. Many of these people become very frustrated and are looking for help. This book was written for them as well.

Also, there are a number of people in the community who deal with these problems on a daily basis because it is their job. These are the volunteers or paid professionals who encounter these impaired elderly persons every day and, sometimes, in spite of their training, are exposed to situations that are not only complicated but also frustrating. They feel that they have done everything they can do, but have failed. This book was written for them.

Numerous family doctors and other health care professionals have asked me to provide them with handouts or brochures that they can give to family members who are experiencing problems with their loved ones. Often, because of their busy practices, they do not have the time to go into the detail needed to develop a plan to decrease or eliminate these behaviors. In addition, when they do take the time to help families with these issues, these physicians often become frustrated because the solutions require time and consistent effort. In this day of managed-care, doctors are rarely reimbursed for the additional time needed to handle complicated behavioral issues. It is much easier to educate a patient or their family by giving them something to read that is simple and direct. Family members and patients can use this information on their own to develop plans, which can be further elaborated by consultation with their doctor. Hopefully, these family members and health care providers will find this book to be helpful.

When you read this book, I hope you will come away with one very important message. Elderly people with emotional and behavioral problems can be helped. These maladies are not an automatic part of growing old. We tend to view the elderly as broken-down people who are merely waiting to die. We must not discard our older folks as we do other items in our throwaway society.

Far too many times, I have heard the comment, "Well, they're just getting old." This seems to be the common phrase used to explain away the various difficulties the elderly suffer in their later years. In our culture, we seem to believe abnormal, inappropriate or confused behavior is a normal part of growing old. The result is that these people, because of their age, do not receive the necessary evaluations and services that would help them resolve their problems. I have even heard these words uttered by emergency room staff when an older person comes to the hospital in a confused state. It is extremely important for any such person with behavioral and emotional issues to be thoroughly evaluated.

A similar situation even occurred in my family. One of my relatives was in the late stages of Alzheimer's disease and started to decrease her dietary intake. This individual became more confused and lethargic over the next several months to the point where all she would do was sit and stare or fall sleep. The staff caring for her said that this was the final stage of her illness, and the end was near. Family members were preparing for her to die in the very near future. Fortunately, she received a medical evaluation and the laboratory reports indicated that the patient was chronically and severely dehydrated. Over the next few days, she was given intravenous fluids, and by the end of the week she became much more alert and communicative. In fact, this individual continues to be demented but still sociable and clearly very much alive.

Based on my experience, I estimate that there are thousands of elderly individuals every year who do not receive the adequate care that would result in a quality life during their remaining years. I hope that this book will convince the reader of the absolute need for a thorough evaluation, so that these older folks will receive the treatment that they deserve.

Finally, I would like to spend a little time talking about the problems that require intervention. It is amazing how many times families come to me talking about behavioral issues that concern them, but after some education, they realize that these behaviors are not outside of the general norm.

Harry came to my office, escorted by his family, who stated that he was behaving in a way that they had never seen. Harry, an 82-year-old active man, had been courting a 77-year-old woman in his neighborhood. He was holding hands with this woman, and at times, according to the family, was even kissing her. The family became most concerned when Harry and his girlfriend were found cuddling on the couch while watching television. Harry's romantic actions were quite upsetting to the family. Harry had been somewhat quiet and withdrawn since his wife died over 10 years ago. It appeared that the family was comfortable with Harry's behavior over that decade.

During my meeting with the family, I took Harry aside and he told me that his life had been renewed with this recent relationship. He felt more joy than he had in years. I asked Harry if he explained his situation to his family. Harry told me that he had no idea that this relationship was a problem for them. In fact, his family told him that he was coming into the doctor's office to get a physical.

I met with Harry and his family to talk about the issues of romance, love and sexuality in the elderly. We spent the rest of the session talking about the need for open and honest communication in the future. In the end, the family seemed to be comfortable talking about a variety of issues including the death of their mother, his wife, and how his future choices will affect his children, as well as his girlfriend.

While this case had a relatively happy ending, it points out the fact that there are numerous behaviors that are problematic for family members, significant others and other members of the community. Sometimes these so-called problems are merely variants of the normal behavioral patterns of the elderly. This book will discuss some of these issues, and will also attempt to address the clearly abnormal actions that the elderly display that may prove embarrassing to themselves or those around them. It would take an encyclopedia to describe all the possible situations that are clearly outside the realm of what is considered to be socially appropriate. Trust me, I have been in this business for almost 30 years and still hear new stories almost everyday.

Let me mention some common examples that will be addressed in this book. We will be talking about people who are confused, wandering, forgetful, combative, withdrawn, depressed, socially inappropriate, verbally abusive, or people who are acting in a way that can be potentially dangerous to themselves or others.

Even though there may be many different types of problematic behaviors that do not fit into the above categories, the interventions in this book can be adjusted in such a way that a reasonable plan can be developed to minimize or extinguish these acts. I will discuss this in future chapters.

So sit back and relax, as I will take you through the methodical process of identifying and evaluating the problem, and then developing a plan to overcome it. I will do my best to keep the text lively, interesting and perhaps even a bit entertaining. Let's begin.

CHAPTER ONE
Identifying the Problem

Rita was a 79-year-old woman who had extensive burns over 20% of her body. By the time I saw her, the burns were mostly healed, after she had spent the last several weeks in the hospital. Rita had a difficult time remembering exactly what happened the day she went to the hospital. With the help of her family, we were able to piece together what happened. As Rita was trying to cook dinner, she turned her gas stove on and went to answer the phone. After some time on the phone she smelled the gas and went back into the kitchen. That was the last thing she remembered.

Her family was feeling quite guilty because they realized that their mother had been deteriorating for the past several years and they felt they should have done something to prevent this tragedy. When Rita was in her late sixties they noticed that the mother became very forgetful. By her seventies she could no longer drive. She voluntarily gave up the privilege after she was found lost in a high crime area. The family was very supportive of their mother, visiting several times a week. They wanted to keep an eye on her as best they could, in order to prevent her from being placed into a nursing home. They took the approach that, if they could just watch their mother to keep her from getting into trouble, the mother could remain in her home.

Unfortunately, this is a very common philosophy in families with an older person. This family was constantly apprehensive, since they could not always watch their mother. Their guilt was clearly magnified after the mother had her accident. The family then asked what they could have done differently to prevent this situation. How we identify problem behaviors is the general question we will address in this chapter.

Far too often, families wait until something serious happens before they get help. They are either too embarrassed to admit that there is a problem, or their family member who has the problem is unwilling to get help. There are times in which the problem goes unrecognized for months, and even years. Finally, there is the belief in society that these problems are just a part of normal aging and nothing can be done about them. You will find out in later chapters that there are numerous available interventions.

BEHAVIORS REQUIRING PROMPT ACTION

There are two common precarious areas that require prompt intervention. First, there are socially inappropriate acts. This would include conduct such as indecent exposure, grossly rude behavior, screaming, public profanity and other acts that are so outside the realm of acceptable behavior that something must be done immediately. Otherwise there will be a demand that this person be removed from the general community or neighborhood. People do get evicted.

The second problem area includes those behaviors that would make the person dangerous toward themselves, others or property. This would include such acts as assault, property destruction or suicidal behaviors. There are also dangerous behaviors that occur as the result of bad choices. An example of this would be the person who wanders away from home improperly clothed during winter. I am sure that you have heard announcements on the news from time to time about a lost elderly person who was at risk due to severe weather. Another common illustration of such behavior is the reckless older driver who places not only himself, but others at risk. Unfortunately, there are far too many examples of such behavior to be listed in this book. If you are unsure that someone may be dangerous you should have this person promptly evaluated by a professional such as a family doctor or psychiatrist. Remember, it is always better to be safe than sorry.

WHEN BEHAVIOR IS A PROBLEM

Let us take a look at those people who have questionable problems. Identifying people who are just beginning to deteriorate in functioning takes some practice and observation. Jonathan Swift once said, "Vision is the art of seeing things invisible." We see elderly people around us all the time, but are we really looking at them? It is truly important to closely observe our elderly loved ones so that we can identify problems early on, when interventions can be more helpful. Not only do we have medications but we also have behavioral techniques that can prevent or minimize future problems and can improve the quality of their life, particularly if these behaviors are identified early on in the process.

At times we see the elderly as just older versions of their young selves. You see, we tend to overlook or deny any problems when we look at people this way. It is human nature to see people in a positive light. Now I do not want you to give up this positive view, but I do want you to pay attention to any abnormal signs that do not fit with the overall picture of proper conduct.

How many times have you been concerned when you walked into a room to get something and forgot what it was? We assume that this is a bad sign. If this happens only once in a while, do not worry. Believe it or not, this is normal behavior. It is only when a behavioral pattern becomes established that we should become concerned. By a pattern I mean occurring almost every day or even more frequently. If this happens, then the person warrants an evaluation. Obviously there are gray areas in every definition, thus, if you are not sure, have your loved one evaluated.

Memory deficits can cause numerous behavioral problems. Persons who wander may not remember how to find their home. People can forget that the gas was left on. Memory is an important tool in our daily functioning. One of the most disastrous results of a poor memory is also, unfortunately, one of the more common problems. This happens when an elderly person forgets that they have already taken their medication for the day and then take additional pills. This unintentional overdose can cause severe mental as well as physical problems. Delirium is a serious and potentially life threatening consequence of such erratic medication ingestion. Therefore, it is important to have your loved one evaluated if you notice significant memory problems, particularly if the problem arose rather abruptly.

As we age, our senses decline. A friend of mine asked me to see his mother because he felt she was getting paranoid. He knew that we could treat paranoia with medication. When I examined the patient, I noted that she had some cataracts. The patient complained that every night a dark skinned individual was standing in her doorway, spying on her. She spent many nights staying awake, fearing the stranger would appear. I was able to visit her home and see her sleeping area. The door that led to her bedroom was painted brown. She pointed to the area of the door and stated, "That is where he stands at night."

I suggested to my friend that he put a light near the door. This resolved the problem immediately and the woman was able to sleep soundly throughout the night. She said that the light must have scared him away. A few weeks later she had her cataract surgery and no longer needed the light near the door.

If you notice your family member having difficulty identifying elements in their environment, it is time to have them evaluated. They may misperceive their surroundings, as in the example above, or fail to sense important stimuli. It is not uncommon for the elderly to leave the gas on and not even smell it. Do not wait until something bad happens. Identify any sensory deficits early, so they can hopefully be corrected. If the deficits cannot be fixed, a person can often learn compensatory techniques. We will talk about these later.

Memory problems and sensory deficits can usually be noticed fairly early on a person's decline. Some other issues can be a bit more challenging. So how do we identify these other problems promptly, so that we can provide a timely intervention? Remember, when you identify and treat a problem in an early stage, a successful outcome is more likely. So be alert.

TECHNIQUES FOR EARLY
IDENTIFICATION

Look carefully and observe closely. To do this properly you must see your loved one as a person trying to interact with the environment. Notice how elderly persons handle complicated tasks. Do they conduct themselves differently than they did a few years ago? Are they having a hard time performing one or two tasks at a time, when this was easy for them to do when they were younger? For example, a woman who could talk on the phone while watching television in the past now finds it to be too distracting. This could be a new sign of cognitive decline.

I want you to be a cautious detective. Look closely for unusual patterns of behavior. Pay attention to any deterioration in functioning. Are they dressing properly? Is their hygiene adequate? Have they developed socially unacceptable conduct? If they are acting in a manner that is quite unlike them, then further investigation is necessary. This does not mean that they need to see a physician, but it does mean that you need to be even more observant so that other maladaptive patterns may be identified.

Do not overlook the word "cautious" in the previous paragraph. Be reasonable in your examination. One bad act does not necessarily mean that something serious is going on. Before you jump to a conclusion, or begin to worry, look at the big picture. In other words, watch for multiple problems or patterns. Then it would be reasonable to get an evaluation. The only exception to this rule is when the one-time behavior is a dangerous one. Unsafe behavior requires prompt intervention in the form of a thorough assessment and treatment.

It is also helpful to observe other elderly people. Talk to them. Enjoy their company. I once told some medical students that my idea of the greatest toy would be a time machine. The closest that I have come to such a reality is a conversation with an older person.

I once had the privilege of talking to an individual who was ten years old during the great Baltimore fire. He was able to almost transport me to that event by his vivid tale of the heat, smells and sights of that day. The amount of detail that he remembered was exhilarating. To this day, I am not sure as to which one of us enjoyed the conversation more. This is clearly a treasured benefit of my job, as it can be for you as you establish a picture of what is normal conduct for the elderly. Then you can compare this impression to the behavior of your loved one.

GETTING OUTSIDE HELP

If you are not sure that your loved one's actions are abnormal to the point where an assessment is required, talk to someone. The first step would be to talk to other family members. Share your concerns with them and ask them to observe the identified family member. Just asking them to be involved not only provides more eyes and ears to address the problem but also marks the beginning of your new support network. As in the business world, brainstorming amongst numerous individuals can help resolve many problems. This will help you take the right course of action.

If you still feel you maybe missing the early signs of an illness then get a consult. Certainly talking with a doctor would be helpful, but, if you are not ready for that, use other resources. There are many of them out there. First, there are neighbors and friends who may have had similar experiences. People are surprised that these problems are so common once they talk about them with others. You will often find that when you talk about these issues with others they are not bothered by it. Instead they are happy to share their information and experiences, and are comforted by the fact that there are other people who are trying to deal with the same challenges. Now you are really beginning to develop your support network.

Another important part of your support system should be professional organizations that have expertise in the area of the elderly. The Alzheimer's Association is an important resource in this area. You can find them in any local telephone book, for there are many chapters throughout the nation. They are not only a resource for information regarding problems related to dementia in the elderly, but they also provide support groups that will assist you in dealing with these issues.

The Mental Health Association and the National Alliance for the Mentally Ill (NAMI) are other organizations that can provide you with information and support to address problems with a family member. There are other support groups that are linked to other diagnostic categories, which could also provide assistance. These organizations are easily found in a local phone book.

Finally there is an important category of people in the community who may know your loved one. Priests, rabbis and ministers often pay close attention to the elderly in their congregation. They may be the first to notice some unusual behaviors. Neighbors, friends and associates of the identified person are also sources of information. The reason I listed this category last has to do with the fact that while probing these sources for information, you may run the risk of embarrassing your family member. In such a case they may feel that you were talking about them behind their back. This could make it difficult to establish a relationship with this person in the future.

In summary, there are many ways to obtain data to help your family member. The most important way to identify problems in an early stage is to closely observe the situation. Spend time with this person. Take them out to dinner, a show or a family gathering. See how they react in normal situations. You can usually determine problems early on once you see how this person reacts with the environment. Are there any changes in the way they react to situations, as opposed to how they handled them in the past? Is their conduct in any way bizarre? Are they acting in ways that are not in keeping with their past personality?

Observation is the key. But, do not read too much into one small detail. You have to balance the fact that you want to pick up early, and perhaps, subtle signs but at the same time you do not want to overdo it. Look for patterns of unusual behavior. I have found it helpful to have someone else review your information and provide an objective view of the situation. If you have exhausted all of the above opportunities and are still unsure, consult a physician. It is always better to err on the side of caution.

Now that you have identified a problem that needs an assessment what do you do? Before you call a physician or other professional specialists read Chapter Two.

CHAPTER TWO
The Initial Approach

"Doc, I'm not crazy. I have no idea why they brought me to your office. There is absolutely nothing wrong with me. I was tricked into coming." I hear these statements far too often. The message is clear. Family and friends did not properly prepare this individual to get help for their problem. We now have a situation where the original problem that brought the patient in is complicated by the fact that this person does not want help because they feel nothing is wrong with them. This chapter will tell you how to start off in a positive manner with your relative so that they will understand why they need assistance; the result is that they are more willing to be helped.

First, let me give you one caution. If you believe that your family member may be involved in a dangerous situation, read Chapter Seven promptly. The techniques that follow in Chapter Two often take time, which you may not have if the state of affairs is precarious.

Do not skip this chapter even if you feel you have a good relationship with your loved one. Many good relationships have gone by the wayside when you tell your family member that they have a problem. They can become surprisingly defensive, uncooperative and thus jeopardize your chance to lend them a hand. Here is the reality. You may perceive this intervention as a chance to help them and better their future, but they can see this as a personal insult.

Mabel had a loving and supportive family. Her children and grandchildren would visit and take her out almost everyday. She was in excellent physical health and was very active for a woman in her early eighties. Unfortunately, Mabel was involved in four minor car accidents over the past year. She was able to keep them secret from her family because the damage to her car was minimal. One day, a few weeks after her latest accident, she received a letter that was quite upsetting. The letter was from a lawyer and it stated that she was going to be sued for financial damages suffered by her client as a result of one of the accidents. She realized that she had to go to her son who, fortunately, was also a lawyer, and ask him for help. When she told him about this problem, she also provided a history about each one of the collisions, fearing she could also be sued for them. Based on careful questioning he found that his mother had a difficult time concentrating when she was driving.

He tested out this theory by driving with his mother to the market on a couple of occasions. In addition he had his sister ride with the mother to church a few times. After a few trips, there was no doubt that the mother could not pay attention to her environment when driving, particularly if she was driving in a congested area where there were numerous stimuli.

They thought they would have no problem convincing their mother to give up her car keys. After all, she did have four accidents for which she was at fault. In addition, they were able to point out to her during their trips that she was coming close to hitting other cars. Her response was quite unexpected. She felt that the family was conspiring against her in order to take away her independence. Mabel even said that if they were going to take away her car keys they might as well take away her life. She was emotionally distraught and angry with her family over the next several weeks, as they remained adamant about their decision to keep her car keys. It was not until months later that Mabel was able to understand and come to terms with the family's decision. It certainly appeared that Mabel's family did everything right. They were methodical and thorough in their approach. The belief that their mother would act in a logical fashion was their only mistake.

PREPARING THE INDIVIDUAL FOR HELP

Let's say that I'm your best friend, and I told you that you needed to change your outdated hairstyle. It is likely that you would take this as an insult and our friendship may now be a little shaky. Even though I gave you this advice with good intentions, I did not lay the foundation for this suggestion to be acceptable to you. Imagine if you told your loved one that they needed to see a doctor because their memory was declining. They might just focus on the fact that you insulted them, or more specifically, their mental abilities and were oblivious to the fact that you were trying to help them. The remainder of this chapter will help you lay a foundation so that your family member would be willing to seek help.

First, you must have an amicable and trusting relationship with the person who needs help. If for some reason you do not have a strong bond with that individual, you will need to identify another person who does. It is not unusual that your loved one may have a close friend or another family member whom they trust more than they do you. If so, talk with that person and explain to them the need for an intervention. You will need to outline to this friend how you came to your decision that your relative needs help, so that you can convince them to intervene on your behalf. If you cannot find an ally amongst their groups of friends, you may want to check out other resource persons who might be able to meet with this person and convince them to get help. Remember, the clergy can be particularly helpful. The important parameter is that it must be a significant other whom the patient will trust.

A strong and trusting relationship is a start, but you will need more. When it is not an urgent situation, it may be helpful to socialize with your loved one for at least a brief time before you make any type of suggestion. You will need to develop an active line of communication with this person that will result in an open and honest dialogue that has nothing to do with your impending recommendation. As I noted in the previous chapter, it is helpful to socialize with your family members when you are trying to observe them for any potential problems. Therefore, you may have already accomplished this communication objective.

APPROACHING THE IMPAIRED PERSON

The next step will be to indirectly discuss the issue that is at hand. Don't make a recommendation, suggestion or demand but rather, ask the person if they noticed anything different about themselves. Let them talk. Then, ask if they have experienced any difficulties recently. Again, let them talk. If they are able to recognize a definitive problem, then ask them what they would like to do. If you can lead them on by asking questions, they may come to the solution on their own accord.

Here is a sample dialogue.

Son – "Mom, how are you doing? Is there anything new going on?"

Mom – "Everything is about the same. Why do you ask?"

Son – "Well, you left your car keys over our house again, and this made you pretty upset. I just wanted to know how you were doing."

Mom – "I was upset. It seems as though I have been forgetting a lot of things recently. I don't know what's happening to me."

Son – "Don't worry, Mom. I know a lot of people have that problem once they get older. Do you think that there might be something that could help? You read all kinds of things in magazines."

Mom – "I did see something on television recently. It was something about a pill that might be able to help with memory. I don't know whether it would help."

Son – "Do you know where you could get such a pill?"

Mom – "I guess I could give my doctor a call."

While the above is an ideal dialogue, it serves to show how an indirect questioning process can lead to a successful outcome. If you are not exactly sure how to do this, ask a friend or relative to practice a possible dialogue. One of you might even try to be difficult, in order to practice for any potential resistance. If you know your relative, you might be able to anticipate their responses in such a dialogue. Practicing will also help you feel more comfortable when you ultimately have to address your loved one. I tend to try this approach first, and if there are any problems, I will adjust my technique.

Sometimes the impaired person may have their reasons to refuse assistance. Ask them why they do not want help. Listen to them. They may have some rationale that may be faulty or valid. I have heard elderly relatives say they do not want to be a bother to their family or friends. Some people are fearful of doctors. Others may think that if they need some type of mental health treatment, people will think they are crazy. Whatever the reason let them explain it fully because it will give you clues as to what strategy changes need to be made in order to convince them to seek help. Usually a straightforward educational approach can counter their fears or misconceptions.

If the indirect approach does not work, then you can try the "Praise Approach." Speak with your loved one about the positive characteristics they possess. While doing this, bring up some of the difficulties the person may be having. Point out to them that they could have a better life and enhance their positive aspects by eliminating these difficulties. For example, if someone has a history of being a good writer, but is now having difficulty finding the right words, I would point out that there may be exercises or other interventions that could help restore their ability to write. By listing their positive characteristics, you are focusing on the good qualities of the person and they will tend to see your suggestion as constructive. Thus, it will be less likely that they will see your intervention as intrusive or insulting.

Another commonly used intervention is what I call the "Love Approach." This is actually quite simple. I explain to the person that I care about them and I want them to have a rich and happy life. Do not over-exaggerate your feelings but give them the sincere impression that you have their best interest in mind. Give them a number of reasons why you care about them. Then, when you make your recommendation, they are less likely to turn it down because they feel that they might insult the person who truly cares about them.

HELPING THE UNCOOPERATIVE PERSON

I do not want to give you the impression that the standard approaches will always work. Sometimes it is very difficult to convince elderly people that you are making these recommendations for their own good. They may not see the situation in a logical manner. They may become angry with you, or even refuse to talk. What do you do in a situation where you know the person needs help, but adamantly refuses?

You can try what I call the "12-Step Intervention". This is the type of approach that is used in confronting a drug abuser or alcoholic, in order to get them into treatment. You may have heard about this. Essentially you bring together family and close friends to confront the individual about their problem. An important factor in this approach is to use group pressure to get the person help. When they see a number of individuals all making this same request, they just might agree to do it. An important component of this approach is for all the people to present themselves in a loving and caring manner. There is no doubt the person in question may feel that they are being forced to do something, but if it is done in a positive and loving way, they will likely be more cooperative in the long run.

Sometimes you can use a behavioral modification approach. One family told their father that before they could take him on their cruise vacation, he had to get a physical. If you try this approach please use a positive reward. Whatever you do, try not to use this method in a punitive fashion. It often will not work. For example, to threaten to take away a person's car keys if they do not see a doctor will just make them angry and resistant to any intervention.

Bill was a 79-year-old man who became very depressed after his wife died two years earlier, as a result of a stroke. His family was becoming concerned, as he would never leave the house. When he started to lose a significant amount of weight, the family became even more concerned and they wanted to get him help. Bill said that there was no way he was going to go to a doctor and he wanted to be left alone. Indeed, Bill was quite alone. He would spend his days watching television and eating very little. Even his hygiene started to deteriorate to the point where he was not showering for weeks. His family tried every approach they knew, but to no avail. They tried a behavioral modification approach but there was nothing that Bill wanted that they could use as a reward. Though Bill was not immediately dangerous to himself, he clearly was slowly deteriorating. The family called their lawyer. The attorney stated that, since this was not an emergency situation, it could take weeks and even months to get a guardianship and force Bill to get some type of help. Because the family thought they could not wait, they asked the lawyer if there were any alternatives they could utilize. Fortunately, he was able to help them, since he had some experience with the elderly.

He asked the family members to take turns sitting with the patient when he was watching television, which seemed to be about all the time. They were told to take notes related to what he was watching. He told them to observe the channels that the patient preferred, as well as any shows on the channels. After a couple of weeks, the family members shared their notes and it became quite clear that Bill preferred shows regarding animals.

As luck would have it, one of the family members knew a person whose dog just had a litter of puppies. His daughter borrowed one of the puppies and took it along with them when they visited Bill. When the daughter carried the puppy into Bill's living room, she noticed a subdued smile. The daughter did not really say much to her father. She just sat there with the dog watching television. After a few minutes, Bill asked where she got the puppy. The daughter stated that she was watching the dog for a friend and couldn't leave it alone. Bill asked if he could hold the dog, and his smile was no longer subtle.

It wasn't long before Bill popped the question, "Where can I get a dog like this?" The daughter expressed her concern that her father was not taking care of himself and how could he take care of the dog. After some discussion she was able to convince her father to at least go talk with a doctor to see if he needed help. A few weeks later Bill was on an antidepressant, feeling much better and taking his new dog for walks.

In the previous section we talked about observing the situation in order to see if a relative is truly having a problem. Here you see how observation can help set up a plan to convince a family member to obtain help.

Also in the previous section we talked about how to consult other resources in order to recognize any subtle, though abnormal, actions in your loved one. In the above case, the family consulted a lawyer, who had some experience in working with the elderly. If you run into a roadblock trying to convince your family member to seek help, do not hesitate to access those resources. Those organizations have dealt with thousands of cases similar to yours and they can give you a number of different suggestions as to how you can convince your troubled family member or friend to go for help. I cannot help repeating the fact that millions of elderly over the centuries have had significant behavioral problems. Over time, we have developed numerous ways to help them. Remember, you are not alone.

Henry David Thoreau once said, "Time is but the stream I go a-fishing in." There will be times when you have tried all of the techniques in this chapter and still are unsuccessful. Keep fishing. Alter these techniques to fit the situation. Sometimes an intervention will fail only to succeed another time in the future when circumstances may be different. Consult other resources for other suggestions. Most importantly do not give up. I have seen people in my practice who have tried a variety of strategies to encourage their relative to seek help. Sometimes they will try a technique a second time and for some reason it will now work.

Before I end this chapter I want to warn you again that these techniques may take time and are often difficult to use if the person in question is a danger to themselves or others. You can certainly try to use them, but if time is a factor, you should consult Chapter Seven. When there is a question of harmful behavior, you must react promptly and decisively. I realize I am repeating myself, but I need to say that if you are not sure whether the situation is dangerous, act as if it is. I have seen far too many times when the family waited a little too long to make an intervention and their loved one suffered harm needlessly.

Let me summarize Chapter Two. You will need to have a good and trusting relationship with the affected individual. If you do not have such a relationship you should find someone who does. Developing a relationship with your loved one may take some time but is well worth it. Try not to be too direct and overbearing. Lead this person to a physician in an indirect and caring manner. Use loving group pressure, if needed. Finally try to find a positive reward that would motivate the individual to seek help. Let that person know that you care about them and that you want them to live a happy life. Do not forget the numerous resources out there if you get stuck. Do not give up. Remember, keep fishing.

CHAPTER THREE
The Evaluation

I am sure you have heard the story. There is a man standing on a crowded corner in New York, whistling as loud as he could. For a few hours everyone was passing him by, ignoring him. Finally, a shopkeeper on the corner noticed the gentleman and left his shop to go out and ask him why he had been whistling on the corner all afternoon. The man said that he was whistling in order to keep away the wild elephants. The shopkeeper responded that he didn't see any wild elephants. The whistling man then said that's because what he was doing was working. We call this a faulty assumption.

Unfortunately, we have been programmed by society to see the elderly with faulty stereotypical assumptions. We expect that all older people will become forgetful, confused and fragile. There are still many people in our culture who believe that nothing can be done to help these people. While in some cases this might be true, we can delay and even prevent this pattern from happening in numerous others. Please, do not make the faulty assumption that old age is the cause of a problem. You need to make sure the elderly person receives the proper assessment to determine if something can be done to help them. This chapter will outline the process of identifying common causes of problem behaviors. With that information, we can develop a plan to decrease or eliminate these obstacles to a healthy and happy life.

FIRST, A MEDICAL EVALUATION

Now that you have identified the specific problem and your loved one is willing to seek help, take them to see a physician. Specifically, you should try to contact a medical doctor who has some expertise with the elderly. Sometimes, you will see the term "geriatric physicians" used to describe these doctors. However, most primary care doctors or family practitioners are skillful in assessing the elderly. Doctors specializing in the area of internal medicine are also quite helpful in this area. They tend to see a large portion of elderly people in the practice. Even though I'm a psychiatrist I believe that it would be more helpful to have the patient seen by the generalist type physician at this first step. This is true even when the older person has mental-health or behavioral problems. Let me explain this further.

Abnormal behaviors in the elderly are often indicative of underlying physical problems. Even though a psychiatrist is a medical doctor and can perform an assessment, a referral to a non-psychiatric physician is often more acceptable to a patient. I am sorry to say that even in this age of open-mindedness, there still is a stigma attached to mental illness and psychiatry. If an assessment comes to a conclusion that there is a treatable medical illness, then the physicians outlined above should be able to handle any interventions that are needed. If a psychiatrist is ultimately needed for further assessment and treatment, then the general doctor can make a referral. By the time this primary care physician has performed a thorough evaluation, a fair amount of rapport and trust should have developed between physician and patient, so that the impaired individual will willingly accept such a referral to a psychiatrist.

Psychiatrists are usually consulted when a patient requires psychiatric medications or psychotherapeutic interventions to remedy emotional or behavioral problems. In addition, psychiatrists have not only the skill, but also the time, needed to develop a treatment plan with a variety of interventions. This is particularly true when there are both medical and psychiatric factors involved in the case. As you will see in later chapters, these treatment plans may be complicated and require time and adjustments to be fully successful. Psychiatrists have both the expertise, as well as the time, to explore all the mental health issues that may be the cause of any aberrant actions.

CHOOSING THE RIGHT DOCTOR

Now that you understand the options available regarding the type of doctor needed to conduct the assessment, you now must direct your attention to the specific doctor. There are many good general practitioners and family doctors as well as internists. Because of managed-care and other third party restraints such as insurers and governmental programs like Medicare, these doctors are often limited in the time that they can spend with their patients. Yet a comprehensive evaluation requires time. How do you find out which of the doctors available to you will be able to provide such an evaluation? Ask family members and friends about the doctors they see. You can also ask neighbors, friends and associates about their physicians.

Do not forget the people and organizations we have talked about previously. The local city or state medical society will usually have listings of physicians who are specialists in geriatric care. Clergy and health care workers, such as nurses, are good sources of information when searching for the right physician. The local health department or Office on Aging will usually have directories that list doctors who specialize in treating the elderly. Even many local phone books are now organized by categories, and will have a special section for those physicians who work with the geriatric population.

Once you obtain a few names, these are some questions that you will need to consider. Does the doctor have good rapport with the elderly? Does the physician spend a reasonable amount of time during the initial evaluation? A five or 10-minute evaluation will not suffice. Will the physician obtain appropriate laboratory tests or other studies? Will the practitioner, with the permission of the patient, discuss the case with his family or other concerned individuals? Will the physician take time to follow up the patient's condition on a consistent basis? How easy is it to schedule initial and follow-up appointments? Will the patient see the same physician on a consistent basis? Elderly people do far better when they have one doctor managing all of the care, which includes periodic communication with specialists who are also seeing the patient.

Due to time constraints, there are some physicians who will operate within a group practice and their partners will take turns seeing patients. I would prefer not to refer patients to such a practice. Does the physician have experience in dealing with patients with behavioral problems? Some physicians exclude from their practice certain individuals that may make them uncomfortable. Patients with behavioral problems tend to fall in that category.

Most physicians or, more often, their secretaries are readily able to answer many of these questions. If a physician tends to be defensive when asked these questions ahead of time, you may want to look elsewhere. If a relative or friend is seeing the physician you are considering, they should be able to answer most of these questions based on their own experience.

In order to find the underlying cause of an individual's problems, a comprehensive assessment is usually needed. If, by now, you have not realized it, you have become part of your relative's care-giving network. This means you may need to be available to take this person to the physician's office for not only the evaluation, but also for follow-up appointments. You may also be required to assist the patient as they go for laboratory tests or other studies. Do not underestimate your role. A comprehensive evaluation for a complicated problem may be both lengthy and frustrating. Your loved one will need your support during this time to get through this process. If you think you will be overburdened with this task, a later chapter will tell you how to minimize your effort and maintain your sanity in your new role of care provider.

THE PROPER ASSESSMENT

A good evaluation begins with a detailed history of the patient's problem. The history will also include past information regarding any other mental-health or physical problems. The doctor will also ask what type of medications the patient is currently taking. A thorough evaluation includes a history of any family medical or mental health issues. A physician performing a comprehensive evaluation will ask about over-the-counter as well as prescription medications the person has used in the past along with their reaction to them, both negative and positive. This data can give the physician some insight about what categories of medications to use or avoid. A patient will be asked about their current functioning and how it may have changed over the days, months and years. The doctor will usually finish this history with numerous questions about a variety of symptoms that could be experienced by an elderly individual. This is called the review of systems.

The next step in this evaluation is a comprehensive physical examination. This will lead to clues about the underlying causes of the patient's behavioral problems. The examination will assess the patient from head to toe.

The third component of the evaluation would include some general laboratory tests including an x-ray and EKG. A CAT scan or MRI are often performed but are not mandatory in every case. These tests take pictures of the brain in different dimensions to determine if there are any physical abnormalities.

Problem behaviors are usually the result of deficits in the brain's normal ability to handle everyday tasks. An important part of this evaluation is to assess the patient's thinking or cognitive abilities. The standard way to do this is to perform what is called a mental status examination. This exam will test both the short-term and long-term memory of the patient. It will also assess a variety of different areas of the brain that deal with everyday functioning such as numerical problems, abstractions, reading ability, following directions and other tasks that we take for granted everyday. In addition the examination should include questions about the presence of specific psychiatric symptoms, which we will talk about later, as well as an evaluation of the person's suicidal or homicidal potential. It is important that the physician you choose carry out such an examination.

For more complicated cases a physician may suggest that a psychologist perform a battery of neuro-psychological tests. This type of evaluation is often very helpful in the early stages of a mental disorder. These tests typically will identify early states of brain deficits that would otherwise go unnoticed and may be successfully treated at this initial stage.

One day, when I was teaching some medical students how to perform a mental status examination, I told them that they needed to practice the exam on several patients and then report to me their experience the next day. One of the students, who shall remain nameless, gave the exam to three different patients on my hospital ward. He came back the next day telling me that two of the patients were extremely demented, but that the other patient was absolutely fine. I was rather puzzled because I knew all of the patients and they all had severe forms of dementia. The student and I went back to the three patients and I had him ask the same questions as he had the day before.

The student asked the first patient to subtract seven from 100. The response that he got was 491. He then asked the second patient to name the current president. The patient answered George Washington. He then asked the third patient whom he felt was normal to subtract seven from 100. The patient promptly gave the answer 93. The medical student then turned around and said that she seems to be perfectly fine. I then asked the third patient how she figured out that the answer was 93. She said that she merely subtracted George Washington from 491.

The point of this story is that you cannot jump to conclusions and make a quick judgment before you perform a thorough evaluation. It is important to come to a diagnosis, so that the appropriate treatment can be offered. At the same time, however, in this age of trying to practice medicine in an efficient manner, not all tests are required for all people. I do not want to leave you with the impression that every evaluation requires all possible tests. Physicians are quite skilled in determining what tests are needed based on a physical examination, a thorough history and any previous testing results.

In summary, the goal of this chapter was to give you an idea of what type of physician you would need to conduct an evaluation of the elderly individual, and some idea of the components of this evaluation. Expect a thorough evaluation, a specific diagnosis and a detailed treatment plan.

The next several chapters will focus on the diagnostic categories that are commonly associated with behavioral problems in the elderly. They will cover three basic areas, dementia, medical and psychiatric. It is important to understand the causes of certain behavioral problems, so that a specific and effective treatment plan can be developed.

CHAPTER FOUR
Dementia

A physician must make a diagnosis to determine what type of treatment will be provided. While a diagnosis is important for a physician, I believe, it can be, at times, problematic for the patient and family particularly in the case of an individual with dementia.

John came to my office with his younger sister because over the last few months he developed a pattern of losing everyday items. A spry man of seventy-two, John was an active traveler who was on the road more than he was at home. Over the past year, however, his family noticed he was forgetting where he was putting things. His sister brought him into my office soon after he left his overnight bag on the concourse at the local airport.

He had already been evaluated by his family doctor and was found to be in perfect health. After my assessment, I sent him for a MRI, which showed that he had some mild atrophy, or wasting of his brain. The diagnosis was clear. He had early signs of dementia.

I tend to be cautious before I give a diagnosis to a patient or their family. Sometimes, however, the family is already aware of the diagnosis, as was John's sister. During my follow-up session with the family, the sister was concerned about the fact that John, as she had already discovered, was suffering from dementia. She pleaded with me to tell her that he wasn't suffering from dementia. I had been very careful thus far in specifying the exact diagnosis. From my experience I have learned that families fear the diagnosis of dementia or Alzheimer's disease as much as any other diagnosis in medicine. The general population believes that Alzheimer's is a disease that cannot be treated and leads to a rapid decline of the person's functioning.

Finally, I had to go over my findings with the family and patient and tell them the cause of his forgetfulness. Before I used the word "dementia", I told John's sister that he was suffering from an illness, which can be treated with a variety of interventions, such as medications and compensation techniques. In addition, I told her that John could have a rich and full life for many years before her fears would actually come to pass, and even at that stage, there are interventions to make life more palatable.

As we continued our discussion, I discovered, from taking a careful family history, that John and his sister had two parents who suffered from dementia at an early age. While she was 69 years old and showed no cognitive deficits whatsoever, she was extremely fearful that she would soon become demented because her brother and parents suffered from the same illness. After providing a significant amount of education and written information, the sister seemed to be more understanding of the diagnosis. I also screened her for cognitive problems but she had no deficits whatsoever. She left the office on a positive note willing to help her brother maintain his active lifestyle.

The diagnosis of dementia generates all types of fears in patients as well as family members. This is usually based on the cultural understanding of dementia or Alzheimer's disease as well as one's own personal experience with individuals affected with dementia. Since this is such a common and dreaded disease, I believe it deserved its own chapter.

Dementia is very common. There are millions of people in the world who are currently demented to some degree. For example, 5% of the United States population over 65 have severe dementia, and approximately 15% have mild dementia. When you look at Americans over 80, the prevalence of severe dementia rises to 20%. As I stated in earlier chapters, if you know someone in your family that has this feared diagnosis, you are by no means alone.

THE SIGNS OF DEMENTIA

Dementia is a condition in which a person's cognitive functions significantly decline. In general, cognitive functions include overall intelligence, memory, language, orientation, problem solving and specific areas of thinking that impact one's daily living. The patient with this diagnosis has difficulty concentrating and paying attention to his environment. They also have problems carrying out routine activities, which they could easily perform in their earlier years.

While a memory deficit may be the first symptom to surface according to the professional literature, I have found that difficulty concentrating is an underestimated early sign. Patients come to me with the frequent story that they have missed something that gets them into trouble. An example of this is the patient who goes through a stop sign without stopping, even though they had stopped at that stop sign on a daily basis throughout their life. Often they will say that for some reason they did not realize that the stop sign was there. Another example occurs when a person keeps bumping into items in their household because they are just not paying attention. They often complain that they had never been that clumsy in the past.

Memory loss is still one of the first signs seen in the person with early dementia. More specifically, short-term memory problems are the hallmark of this diagnosis. This means that a person will remember the names of their childhood friends or grade school teachers but they may not be able to say what they had for breakfast or where they went the previous day. Demented patients have a difficult time forming new memories. On the other hand, they can recollect thoughts of years ago until quite late into the disease process.

As a person's thinking ability declines their personality can be affected. People who were anxious before they showed signs of dementia now become even more anxious. On the other hand, people who have been independent can become vulnerable and even childlike. We will talk more about this in a later chapter.

There are two major types of dementia. The most common is dementia of the Alzheimer's type. The second most common is dementia related to a vascular disorder. This means dementia that is caused by brain damage, secondary to a lack of blood circulation in the brain. The most commonly known cause is a stroke. Essentially, blood does not travel into an area of the brain, and the brain cannot get the proper amount of oxygen. Brain cells then become damaged. If the cells are in the area of the brain that control cognitive abilities, these abilities suffer. The amount of decline is usually related to the amount of brain tissue that is damaged in that area.

VASCULAR DEMENTIA

The abrupt decline of cognitive ability in vascular dementia differentiates it from the Alzheimer's type. A person who has chronic problems with the blood vessels in their brain is often described as having a step-like decline in their cognitive abilities as opposed to the slow gradual decline in Alzheimer's disease. Also, in the dementia related to vascular problems, we usually have associated neurologic signs such as paralysis and weakness, or loss of sensation in certain areas of the body. We will talk more about this in chapter six.

ALZHEIMER'S DEMENTIA

Dementia of the Alzheimer's type is the most common brain abnormality in the elderly. For example, vascular dementia that we discussed above only accounts for 20 to 30% of dementia conditions.

While dementia has probably been around for thousands of years, it was not until 1907 that a man by the name of Alzheimer described the cognitive decline in a 51-year-old woman. Even over the last century, our knowledge of Alzheimer's dementia is still somewhat limited. We do not know the exact cause of this disease, but we do know that there are certain anatomical elements in the brain that are seen in demented patients. Also, we know that there is a protein on one of our chromosomes that may be related to the development of Alzheimer's. Another area of research that has been quite positive is based on the fact that Alzheimer's patients have impaired chemical pathways in the brain. One of these pathways uses the chemical, acetylcholine, which helps transmit electrical charges in the brain. These impulses in the brain allow us to perform numerous mental tasks. If there is something wrong with this pathway, our cognitive abilities can decline. We will talk more about this later, as it has provided some treatment possibilities.

John's sister had some reason to be worried about her chances of developing dementia. There is some basis that this disease is genetically determined. Up to 40% of patients who have Alzheimer's have family members with that same illness. Being the optimist that I am, I tell the relatives of patients that it is much more likely for them not to develop dementia, given the current studies. At the same time, I inform them about the early signs of Alzheimer's because I find that proper education usually allays their anxiety.

Let us take a look at the various deficits that occur in Alzheimer's disease. We have already talked about memory impairment. Remember, a patient with this illness can remember details of an event that occurred 50 years ago but may not be able to remember where they just placed their car keys. This means that short-term memory is impaired as opposed to long-term memory. There are interventions that we will discuss later that can help people improve their memory.

AUTOMATIC FUNCTION PROBLEMS

We have already talked about the lack of concentration, or the inability of a person to pay attention to their surroundings. One aspect of this symptom, that does not get a lot of press, is what I call our automatic functioning. Usually, when I come home from work, I will take my briefcase and car keys into the house and place them in a certain location. I will then take off my coat and tie and hang them in the closet. Then I usually go to the kitchen for a glass of iced tea and look for the newspapers. When I perform all of these activities, I am not thinking that I put my briefcase on my desk and my car keys on the shelf. I am not necessarily focusing specific attention on the task of putting my coat and tie away. We do similar automatic behaviors numerous times on a daily basis. Essentially, we do not think about these behaviors because they are so automatic that they do not require our full attention. In early stages of dementia and other cognitive disorders this automatic functioning deteriorates.

An impaired individual, according to the above example, will go through all the motions but, because their attention functioning is not 100%, may put their keys in a different place without thinking. Later they can be quite upset when they find out that the keys are not on their shelf, but that during this automatic process they may have put them elsewhere. They may be puzzled and at times very angry as to why they did not automatically carry out their actions the way they normally do. It is not unusual for them to become so frustrated that they take it out on family members and caregivers. This can be quite upsetting for all concerned causing the impaired individual to feel angry, depressed and even guilty.

APHASIA

Another element of Alzheimer's dementia is called "aphasia", which is a disturbance of language. Essentially, it means using the wrong words or being unable to find the proper words to use when one tries to communicate. This can become an issue if the impaired individual uses politically incorrect or profane language. It is not uncommon to hear an elderly man refer to a middle-age woman as "that little girl". Sometimes the person who is speaking may realize their error after they speak, but other times, they may be totally clueless. A patient of mine embarrassed their family because she kept calling her baby granddaughter a "baboon". When the family gently reminded the patient that she was using the wrong word, the patient compensated by repeating the word "baby" over and over in her head, basically training herself to say the correct term. Obviously the parents of the child were relieved when grandma finally got it right.

When a person has aphasia, they may substitute words that sound similar to the appropriate word such as "baby" and "baboon". They may also choose a word that is similar to the word they want, but it may carry the wrong connotation. In the previous paragraph we gave an example of a man calling a middle-age woman a little girl. At its worst, this condition will produce a person who cannot even express a word. Ironically sometimes these individuals might be able to write the correct word but cannot say it or vice versa.

APRAXIA

Apraxia is also a symptom of dementia. This symptom occurs when a person cannot carry out normal movements, even though the person has good muscle strength and sensation. An old professor of mine once said that it is like the brain is trying to put together a model car without the instruction booklet. The person's hands may be working well but the brain cannot give them the proper instructions.

A colleague of mine had a 70-year-old father who was very skillful in working on car engines. He had the job of fixing the broken-down cars of various family members. As he became older, he started to make numerous mistakes. Some of the initial problems caused were minor, but it was not long until he accidentally crossed some wires, causing some serious damage to his grandson's car. While this elderly gentleman fortunately did not hurt himself, he nevertheless became quite depressed, because this was one of the contributions that he could still make to his family and now it was gone.

My colleague asked me to see his father, and after determining the extent of his apraxia, I was able to see that he still had a number of skills left. I was also able to find out that this grandson, whose car was damaged, was actually quite interested in working on automobiles. Thus, I was able to pair the grandfather and grandson together, so that the grandson could learn the skills of the grandfather, and at the same time, correct some of his mistakes. They were able to enjoy this relationship for the next several years. There are many older persons who lose their skills, but with the help of family members and friends, can compensate to the point where they still can see themselves as contributing.

As you can see from the above example, apraxia can, at times, be dangerous, if the person is involved in activities where mistakes carry a significant risk. It is often helpful to get an outside opinion so that you can balance the risk of keeping that person involved in such activities with some help, versus encouraging them to stop it altogether.

PROBLEMS IN EXECUTIVE FUNCTIONING

Difficulties in executive functioning, such as organizing, planning and carrying out an activity, are also impaired in certain types of dementia. If apraxia is the loss of the brain's instruction book to perform a manual job, then the lack of executive functioning is like losing the instruction book to perform a complicated or abstract job.

Lil' was the owner of a dress salon, and for many years was able to organize elaborate fashion shows. She was an independent woman of 72, and, according to her family, always had to be in charge. As I learned from both Lil' and her family, a successful fashion show combined elements of conceptualization, planning, delegation, and coordination of numerous complicated tasks. During some recent shows, Lil' was found acting quite confused, particularly in the area of coordinating the components of the show. On one occasion she was found backstage crying because she had become confused about the order of events in the show, a task that she could have performed perfectly a few years ago.

During the counseling process, the first challenge was to help Lil' give up her need to be in charge. We were able to identify her most competent employee who was willing to take on the task of organizing future shows. At the same time we had Lil's brother, a successful businessman in his own right, convince his sister to take on a new job as consultant to her own company. In this job she trained her second in command to run the shop. This left Lil' with spare time to travel, something that she always wanted to do. Together with her family, we were able to convince her that leaving a positive legacy in the form of a successful shop was a very meaningful enterprise at this stage of her life.

THE BEHAVIOR PROBLEMS OF DEMENTIA

Now that we have described some of the major elements of dementia, let us take a look at some of the possible behavioral problems. A person can become quite frustrated, and even angry, when they begin to notice that they cannot perform the functions they used to accomplish in their earlier years. This can lead to sudden outbursts of anger, which, to an outsider, can happen very unexpectedly. Some displays of anger can include verbal abuse, sarcasm, shouting, profanity and even, at times, physical aggressiveness. Examples of physical aggression include biting, kicking, slapping, pinching, grabbing, choking and striking with fists. Other aggressive acts may include destroying property or throwing items. A demented person can have a difficult time controlling the extent of their anger. Even though these hostile behaviors may seem to occur for no reason a cause can often be found. This topic will be discussed further in the chapter on dangerous behavior.

Other inappropriate acts may include overcompensation. For example, a person who spends hours a day making lists so that they will not forget may be taking valuable time from other needed functions. Another dementia related problem is withdrawn behavior. This can lead to a hermit like lifestyle or to self-neglect. These behaviors may arise out of a person's need to hide their failings from society. Moodiness, apathy, inappropriate humor, poor judgment, rude remarks and inadequate hygiene are other problematic behaviors that often require some type of action to keep them under control.

Many books and articles about dementia talk about personality changes that can often occur. Certainly, there are people who have completely new character traits as a result of their illness. There are also demented individuals who are now expressing hidden traits or exaggerating lifelong characteristics. This will be covered in more detail in the chapter on personality disorders.

Finally, there is a significant minority of demented patients who have some type of psychotic behavior. Up to a third of these patients can display symptoms such as suspiciousness, delusions, paranoia and hallucinations both auditory and visual. These patients have a higher risk of aggressive behavior.

THE CATASTROPHIC REACTION

There is a special syndrome that can occur in a demented patient called the "catastrophic reaction". Essentially, this term describes an agitated state that occurs when a patient comes to the realization that they have significant deficits.

Susan was a copy editor for most of her adult life. She unfortunately suffered from an early dementing process in her mid-fifties. For a couple of years she was able to compensate for her inability to handle her job by outlining her tasks on paper and following the outline obsessively. But even with her cleverness her deterioration one day caught up with her to the point where she had to acknowledge her deficits. This insight did not come easily. On that day she was found screaming and crying in her office, as she was tearing up every paper in sight.

Support and reassurance are keys to overcoming the acute phase of this syndrome. It is essential that further discussions take place after the acute episode that focus on using the person's remaining skills to compensate for any deficits due to the dementia.

SUNDOWNER SYNDROME

Another term that is associated with Alzheimer's is the "Sundowner Syndrome". This is characterized by a period of significant confusion that occurs typically in the twilight of evening when the impaired individual has a difficult time interacting with their environment. Persons who have been placed in a new setting such as a nursing home are at a higher risk for this problem. One of my first patients, Ed, was a perfect example of this syndrome.

Everybody in the family knew that Ed had a mild form of dementia. In spite of this he was able to work at his job with minimal assistance. At home, he was doing well and met all of his needs. About a year after the diagnosis of mild dementia was made, Ed maintained his same level of functioning with one exception. Every evening, at sunset, he would call a family member, in a state of panic. He complained that he was very confused and could not find how to get into the various rooms of this house. He would stand, phone in hand and frozen in fear, until a family member came over to turn on the lights and reassure him. One of the ways we minimized these attacks was to have Ed leave the lights on all the time in most of the areas of the house.

Reassurance and support are obvious interventions in these cases. Keeping the environment simple and well lit can also be quite helpful.

MEDICAL TREATMENTS FOR DEMENTIA

Now that you have some of the basics regarding Alzheimer's disease, let us talk about the available medical treatments. Even though there is no current cure for this illness, there are medications available that can slow down the deterioration. These medications increase a chemical in the brain, acetylcholine, which helps the brain function more effectively. Unfortunately, they usually do not improve the person's ability to function, but they can slow down the process of decline. One of the best ways to look at these medications is that they are able to prevent, at least temporarily, Alzheimer's patients from declining to the point where they require special services such as an assisted-living or nursing home placement. They may delay these interventions by up to two years. There are several medications on the market and you should talk to your doctor as to the right choice for your loved one. As is the case with most medications, the potential for side effects needs to be thoroughly discussed with a physician.

Typically, the severity of the dementia is related to the inability to carry out normal functions. Behavioral problems are more common when the dementia is moderate to severe. So, if you can keep the person functioning at a higher level, you may be avoiding, or at least postponing, any difficult issues that need to be addressed. More importantly, these medications provide the Alzheimer's patient with a better quality of life for a longer period. There are other medications that are used specifically for behavioral problems that we will discuss later.

PREVENTION OF DEMENTIA

Another area that is currently quite controversial is the prevention of Alzheimer's disease. There have been numerous articles in professional and lay journals concerning various vitamin supplements or other homeopathic interventions that could prevent a person from developing dementia. There has been only limited research to test these various options. So far there is no definitive medication, vitamin or dietary supplement that will clearly prevent Alzheimer's. I can only tell you that there are a number of physicians that have been taking vitamin E, or some type of anti-inflammatory medication such as ibuprofen, because there has been some belief that they may be helpful as a preventive medication. Please be cautious in this area. See your doctor first before you try any of these supplements. You may have some type of medical disorder that may conflict with your taking certain drugs.

Do not be fooled by the fact that many of these recommended supplements are natural. Even so-called "natural remedies" can have severe side effects that can cause serious medical complications. I often tell my patients that the foxglove plant is natural, but I would not eat it because it is a source of digitalis, which at high levels, can cause severe toxic reactions. So, please do consult a physician before you try any of these remedies.

In summary, dementia of the Alzheimer's type is the most common cause of behavioral problems in the elderly. Its hallmarks include deficits in memory, language, perception and organization. Though Alzheimer's disease is often related to conduct disturbances in the elderly there are many other medical illnesses that can cause behavioral problems, as you will see in the next two chapters. Even more importantly, these problems can be remedied or even prevented since those medical illnesses are often very treatable.

CHAPTER FIVE

Delirium

Delirium is an acute state of confusion. It is an illness of extremes. On the negative side, it is often associated with severe medical illness and can lead to death. The positive aspect is that it can be readily treated and prevented in most instances, if discovered in an early stage. Even though some of my colleagues may disagree with my description of this condition, I often refer to delirium as an acute dementia. It is a dementing process that occurs quite rapidly and can cause symptoms similar to those of Alzheimer's disease. In fact, late stage Alzheimer's looks very similar to delirium. The chronic process of Alzheimer's may take several years, but delirium can occur in several hours or days.

Like Alzheimer's disease, delirium is a common cause of behavioral difficulties in the elderly. Delirium is the most common serious mental disorder seen in the general hospital population because it can lead to death. Some studies show that anywhere between 10 and 20% of hospital admissions of elderly patients are linked to a delirious state.

THE SIGNS OF DELIRIUM

A delirious patient like a demented patient may have numerous cognitive deficits, however, they also have what is termed a "clouded consciousness". This means that they are not fully aware of their environment and cannot focus their attention. The severity of these symptoms usually fluctuate over short periods of time. For example, persons with delirium can be very confused for a few hours and then, all of a sudden, are back to normal for a brief time. They can flip back to a confused state just as quickly. At times they can have rapidly changing episodes of anxiety, hallucinations, nightmares, restlessness and agitation. Behavioral problems are often seen in delirious patients as they respond to their impaired perception of the environment. For example, patients can attack nursing staff because, in their delirious state, they believe that those people are strangers who are trying to kill them.

Even in mild cases of delirium a patient may not recognize the people around him. They may not know the day, the date or where they are. Only in severe cases of Alzheimer's would orientation be so impaired.

It is important to remember that delirium, as opposed to dementia, usually has an acute onset of hours or days. Dementia, on the other hand, is a chronic process of deteriorating cognition over months or years. In other words, delirium is a quick cognitive decline and dementia is slow. Therefore a delirious patient could have an abrupt impairment of speech recognition, incoherent communication, problem solving difficulties and other significantly impaired cognitive abilities.

One of the most dramatic elements of delirium is the already mentioned inability of the delirious patient to recognize his environment. They may see or hear things that are not there, in other words, hallucinations. They may have beliefs that are quite outlandish and simply untrue. These are called delusions. Behavioral problems are often seen in relation to hallucinations and delusions because patients feel threatened by them. It is not uncommon to see delirious patients express unwarranted anger or fear. Therefore, they may act out aggressively in order to protect themselves from these falsely perceived threats.

MEDICATION AND DELIRIUM

One of the most common causes of delirium is medication. Patients who are taking multiple medications are at much higher risk of having a delirious state. Up to 20% of hospital admissions in the elderly are due to delirium.

Martha was a 77-year-old woman who had hip replacement surgery. The evening after her surgery she was resting comfortably in her hospital room, when all of a sudden she started to scream that men were coming through the window and trying to attack her. The nurses quickly ran into her room, turned the light on, and tried to reassure her that there was no one there. Martha was able to calm down fairly quickly. The nurses then left. A few minutes later Martha started to scream again and told the nurses the same story when they arrived. This time the nurses left the light on. That seemed to work for a while. About an hour later she started to scream again. This time the nurses wanted to call the physician on duty so that a sedative could be prescribed. Fortunately, a family member came to visit and agreed to stay with Martha. By midnight Martha was able to fall asleep and there were no further problems.

This story provides two lessons. First, elderly persons can have severe side effects due to commonly used medications, such as the ones given for anesthesia. Secondly, a calm reassuring approach is often better than automatically prescribing a sedative. Additional medications often can complicate, and even worsen, the clinical situation. Medical and nursing staff should first provide options to family members so that non-medication interventions can be tried first. If you, as a family member or friend, have some information that an elderly person has had previous episodes of delirium, this could be quite useful to the people caring for your loved one. Such data could prevent a future episode. This is particularly true if you have knowledge as to how the previous delirious state was caused or was treated.

Rarely are restraints needed. Sometimes they can make the confused patient even more agitated and at risk of physical harm, particularly if they fight against the restraints. There are gentle interventions that can help reassure and orient the elderly person so as to minimize any behavioral problems. Examples that can be tried include calm verbal reassurance and helping the person correctly interpret the environment. The latter approach includes turning the light up so that the confused person can better see his surroundings, as well as repeated explanations as to what is going on around them. Frequent family visits can help implement these interventions. If possible, try to develop a schedule of sitters, comprised of family members or friends. These people can be most helpful orienting the confused individual.

Posted signs that explain a situation can help the elderly confused person, especially someone who is in an unfamiliar setting. For example, posters with large print can remind the patient that they, not only are in a hospital room, but also the reason why they are in the hospital and the potential day they will be going home. Photos of family members are also quite reassuring. Of course, most hospital rooms have large calendars that orient such an individual to the day and date.

Nurses are typically trained to explain, in advance, what they are going to do for a confused patient so that there is less chance of misinterpretation. This will decrease the risk that the delirious person will feel threatened, and possibly strike out. Family members should do the same.

As an interested party you should expect that the medical staff would try to find the cause for the delirium. Finding this cause and treating it is usually the simplest and most effective approach. In the above case of Martha watchful waiting was an easy and safe intervention that allowed the anesthetic to pass through her system. In fact, this is a common approach to drug-induced delirious states. Sometimes, this approach is upsetting to family members because they perceive it as doing nothing. Please be assured that this is sometimes the best intervention possible.

Doris, an 80-year-old woman, went with her family to her doctor's office because she became very anxious and confused at a local grocery store. She recently had a cold and was taking a number of over-the-counter medications. At that visit her physician stopped all of these medications, and told her as well as her family that the best medicine was for her to go home and rest for the next day or two. Doris, however, was quite anxious the remainder of the day to the point where one of her brothers gave her one of his prescription tranquilizers, which he thought would help. A few hours after she took these pills she became agitated, confused and combative. It took several family members to get her to come into the emergency room.

In our society we tend to expect a medication to be given whenever we visit a doctor's office. In the above example, Doris' family member felt that nothing was being done so he prescribed his own drug. Perhaps Doris' doctor did not fully and forcibly explain the situation, particularly the fact that she should not be given any additional medications. This likely would have prevented the crisis situation that developed.

Since it is quite common to see drug-induced delirium, it is important for family members as well as patients to keep a careful record of the medications that they take. As I mentioned in a previous chapter observation is an important tool. Therefore, when a situation like this occurs, it is wise to gather the medications around the household and bring them in so that they can be used as part of the evaluation. Do not forget to bring in any over-the-counter medications that might be around the home. We often assume that such medications, because they are so easily available, do not cause any severe side effects. Nothing could be further from the truth. There are a number of over-the-counter medications that can cause serious delirious states and related behavioral disturbances. Drugs that can produce drowsiness seem to be common culprits. Elderly persons who already have some type of brain disease or dementia are also at higher risk of developing a drug-induced delirium.

The opposite can also happen. When an elderly person is taking a medication for a long time and then abruptly stops it, there are withdrawal states that can produce a delirium. Though alcohol is not formally considered a medication, there are a number of older people who use this substance to calm their nerves or to fall asleep.

Actually, the use of alcohol is a double-edged sword. You can get a delirious state with the heavy ingestion of alcohol as well as by abruptly stopping its chronic use.

Addictive sedatives and tranquilizers are medications with profiles similar to alcohol. Barbiturates and benzodiazepines fall into this category. Thus, they also can cause problems with both heavy use and abrupt withdrawal. Sometimes the elderly person is not forthcoming about their use of such substances, and family members as well as friends need to be keen observers. Indeed, there are elderly people who will hide these drugs because they are embarrassed to own up to their habit. Family members and friends often have to be very sensitive as well as observant in addressing this problem.

You can always consult with your local pharmacist to obtain specific data about the medications your relative is taking. They can provide you with literature regarding the side effects of medications. Get to know this information ahead of time, so that you can be on the lookout for any potential problems. Remember, it is better to be knowledgeable and observant early on in the process rather than have to deal with a crisis.

Alcohol can be a problem substance, not only by itself, but also in combination with legitimate medications. Remember, as I said above, people on multiple medications have a much higher risk of a delirious state. You must view alcohol as another drug that can react with other medications in an adverse manner. If you suspect that a family member is abusing alcohol, particularly while using other medications, please have that person evaluated by a physician.

Wilma was an 84-year-old woman who told her family that she would drink a glass of wine before bed in order to help her sleep through the night.

Her family noticed that she was having difficulty remembering things and was getting lost in the neighborhood. They thought that they would help the situation by taking all of Wilma's alcohol out of the home. So they did. The next night her daughter received a frantic call from one of the neighbors, who said that Wilma was jumping up and down on her back patio, totally unclothed, and screaming that she had to get the worms off of her. The family promptly took Wilma to the emergency room where she was given medications to help her calm down. Fortunately, she was in good health and received immediate attention; otherwise, she may have died.

Wilma was the victim of severe alcohol withdrawal known as delirium tremens. Apparently Wilma was hiding the fact that she had been drinking several glasses of wine per day for the past couple of years, a fact that her family did not know when they took all of her alcohol away.

Sometimes, when a relative is using alcohol, family members are embarrassed to tell the appropriate people. Believe it or not, inappropriate use of alcohol in the elderly is a common problem. It is also a serious issue when older people drink. They are more susceptible to the risks of alcohol. Such use can cause severe medical problems not just problematic behaviors. Therefore it is essential that a full medical evaluation be conducted in order to avoid a life-threatening situation. It is also equally important to have open and honest discussions if you suspect that a family member is using alcohol.

COMMON MEDICAL CAUSES OF DELIRIUM

I cannot emphasis often enough that delirious states not only cause serious behavioral problems but also high-risk medical situations. In fact, delirium is often caused by medical illnesses. For example, someone who may have mild Alzheimer's disease can have a urinary tract infection, which in combination can produce a delirious state. Thus, in order to properly treat this delirium the source of the infection needs to be found and treated with antibiotics. Older persons with out-of-control diabetes can also experience a delirious state, which can be remedied with sugar controlling medications. There are even cases of thyroid disease which can cause a delirious state. Usually, these persons can be helped simply with medications, but a few cases may require surgery. These are common causes of delirium, which can be readily treated and thereby stop behavioral problems in their tracks. More importantly, if these conditions are left untreated, older persons can suffer severe medical consequences. So, in essence, the observed behavioral problems may be early warning signs of an impending medical crisis.

Other treatable causes of delirium include infections of various body organs, such as the lungs or brain, which can be treated with antibiotics. Patients who have chronic lung disease can become delirious when their oxygen level falls. Correction of this oxygen level can produce dramatically positive changes in the person's behavior. Disturbances of water or electrolyte levels in the body are other common causes of delirium that can be treated by balancing those levels with the appropriate supplements. Dehydration and excessive water drinking are two such examples of these imbalances with dehydration being by far the more common of the two. These various conditions require prompt medical attention.

We have already talked about postoperative delirium earlier in this chapter. This is a very common cause of delirium in a hospitalized patient. The elderly are particularly susceptible and may remain delirious for days or weeks after surgery. Seizures are another cause of a delirious state and may be related to other brain diseases such as abscesses, strokes or tumors. Anti-seizure medications are useful but a full evaluation is required to determine the cause for the seizure.

Another common cause for delirium in the elderly is trauma to the head. An elderly person's brain is particularly fragile. They can suffer significant damage to the brain with what seems to be a rather mild injury. It is not uncommon to see an elderly person display confused, unusual and even aggressive behaviors after they have received an injury to the head as simple as bumping it on a door. Even jarring movements can cause trauma to the brain. Often it is difficult to identify an injury because the individual may not remember that it happened or might believe that it was so minor it is not worth mentioning. Sometimes the injury is so minor a family member cannot easily see it. As always, be observant for any recent accident or injury.

There are also cases in which the patient's behavior becomes disturbed days or weeks after the injury. Therefore, it is important for a family member or significant other to question the patient carefully about any recent accidents, no matter how minor they were. As you have heard repeatedly, be observant. Check for any signs of injury, even in areas other than the head. Look for anything that may be broken in the home indicating a sign of an accident such as a fall. This investigation is very important when you see an abrupt change in the person's mental functioning, particularly a recent state of confusion.

Brain injury may cause symptoms such as double vision, acutely impaired vision, hearing deficits, impaired taste or smell and loss of sensation or movement of certain parts of the body. Ask your loved one about these signs. Prompt medical intervention may not only prevent problematic behaviors, but also, may help to reverse some of the above symptoms. The most important concern is the assessment of the brain damage and prompt treatment in order to avoid catastrophic medical problems and even death. There is also the potential for a person in a delirious state to injure themselves as a result of their confusion. Therefore delirium must be evaluated and treated promptly to avoid any further complications.

With this background on delirium and its common causes you have the foundation to help your family member obtain prompt treatment. Using the above information you will need to focus your powers of observation and note any abrupt changes in your relative's mental state. As noted above, people who have some level of dementia are at a much higher risk to develop a delirium.

THE EARLY IDENTIFICATION OF DELIRIUM

It is important to monitor an elderly person with dementia on a frequent basis in order to prevent or treat a developing delirious state. Family members can take turns visiting the individual at risk in order to share the task so that no one person is overburdened. Obviously, this needs to be done in a sensitive manner, and can be often combined with routine activities such as grandchildren visits, family gatherings and special outings. I do not mean to insult any families who are already carrying out such activities as part of their normal relationship with their loved one. I just want to encourage you to have a level of observation above and beyond these normal activities, particularly if your family member is in a high-risk category.

Families who have limited interactions with such a high-risk person need to develop some type of structure so that their loved one can be seen as consistently and frequently as possible. Remember, high-risk persons include those who have identified medical problems or those who are taking multiple medications, as well as those individuals who have some degree of dementia. If a person who already has some level of dementia abruptly becomes more confused or displays new behavioral problems, then that person should be evaluated for delirium. Do not automatically assume that the individual's dementia is the cause for these new symptoms. You could be overlooking a high-risk medical problem.

If you suspect that a family member is developing a delirious state, your observation needs to be more frequent and thorough. You need to look for signs such as confusion, disorientation, an inability to carry out normal activities, difficulties in communication and any changes in the person's level of alertness. Keep a record of what you see and exchange notes with other family members, friends, or associates of your relative. The timing of your observation is important. Since delirium can develop over the period of hours or days, this observational period will be brief and intense. If there is a suspicion that such a state is developing, medical attention is required immediately. Do not wait for an appointment. Take the individual promptly to the nearest emergency room. Prompt treatment may prevent any further deterioration as well as any serious behavioral and medical consequences.

There may be early signs of a delirium causing illness that can be detected even before the general signs of delirium appear, as described in the previous paragraph.

These symptoms are related to the original illness that may cause a delirious state.

Alex was a 74-year-old man who had been a smoker throughout much of his life. When he turned 70, he was diagnosed as having chronic lung disease. Over the last two years his family noticed that he would have some difficulty breathing but neither Alex nor his family felt there was an acute problem. One day, when he was babysitting his grandchildren, his daughter noticed that he was having a bit more difficulty breathing. When she picked up her children later that day, he was perspiring, so she took his temperature. He had a fever of 103.5. She waited for her husband to come over and take care of the children, while she took her father to the emergency room. In the waiting area Alex became confused and agitated. He believed that the people in the emergency room were out to kill him. Fortunately, he was in a place where within seconds the staff responded by providing oxygen and a mild sedative. Within a few minutes Alex was calm and coherent. Later it was found that he had a fairly severe pneumonia, which was remedied with the use of antibiotics.

Just think what might have happened if the daughter had not been observant and her father became delirious and agitated in his home around her or her children. She was able to note that these physical symptoms were not normal for her father and promptly took him for an immediate medical intervention. Her quick response was based on the observation of early clinical signs related to her father's illness. Let us take a look at other early signs associated with some of the common medical causes of delirium outlined above.

Early signs of infections that may precipitate dementia often include an elevated temperature, sweats, flushes and specific symptoms related to the infected area of the body.

In pulmonary infections one may see cough, production of sputum, shortness of breath, chest pain and increased pulse rate. In urinary tract infections one could see frequent urination, a frequent urge to urinate with little urine in the bladder, difficulty urinating as well as burning when urinating. Blood in the urine can also be seen in severe cases. One can have infections of the skin that can be easily seen unless the older individual is trying to hide the condition. Do not hesitate to ask about this possibility. I have even seen slightly demented patients become extremely delirious when they have had sinus infections or even a bad cold.

High-risk patients, such as those who already have mild dementia or those taking multiple medications, need to be carefully questioned about any new symptoms they may be experiencing. Some older people tend to deny their illnesses for a variety of reasons. Sometimes they feel it is a sign of old age to be sick and therefore they just accept it. At other times they may feel that revealing any type of illness would put a burden on their family. However, in the case of Alex the early signs led to an immediate intervention and prevented more serious behavioral problems.

Signs of dehydration can include dry flaky skin, dry mouth, decreased urination, constipation, decreased weight and a darker than normal urine. Sometimes certain body salts, or electrolytes, can become unbalanced. A variety of symptoms can occur under those conditions, such as decreased energy, sleepiness, confusion, thirst, high pulse rate, dizziness, anxiety, tremor, weakness and agitation. There are so many causes of metabolic imbalances that all of them could not possibly be covered here. However these conditions, if left untreated, could lead to seizures, coma, cardiac arrhythmias and even death. It is also important to remember that agitated behavioral states caused by these conditions may lead to severe injury and death.

Persons with diabetes may show signs of fatigue, weight loss, excessive thirst and frequent urination. If patients with diabetes cannot keep a normal sugar level in their blood, they are predisposed to complications such as electrolyte imbalances, poor wound healing and severe infections. Another complication of diabetes occurs when an individual takes too much insulin or another diabetic medication. This is sometimes seen in patients with some degree of dementia who mistakenly take the wrong amount of medication due to their memory problems. If they take too much medication, their blood sugar level drops and they can become quite anxious, panicky and agitated. If they are taking too little medication, high levels of blood sugar will result that can cause confusion and agitation. It is important to talk with the family member who has diabetes to see if any of these symptoms have appeared, so that an early intervention can take place. This could prevent a number of complications, both medical and behavioral.

Thyroid disease can cause a variety of behavioral disturbances. There are two main types. One is called hyperthyroidism, which occurs when the thyroid hormone level is abnormally high. Before abnormal behaviors occur, we usually see symptoms such as sweats, heat intolerance, weight loss, increased appetite, shortness of breath, decreased sleep, heart palpitations, tremor, muscle weakness, chest pain and frequent urination. In severe stages of this illness a psychotic and agitated state can develop.

The other common thyroid illness is called hypothyroidism, a state in which an abnormally low level of thyroid hormone is produced in the body. Symptoms include fatigue, constipation, weight gain, cold intolerance, decreased appetite and decreased heart rate. Severe forms of this illness can produce suicidal depression, agitation and psychosis.

Almost all of these symptoms related to thyroid disease can be easily seen with a modest amount of observational skills. For example, in hypothyroidism you may see your family member dressing warmly in a heated room. On the other hand, in hyperthyroid states you could see a person with a minimal amount of clothing sitting in a cold room. Sweats, tremor and weight loss can be easily observed. If you noticed some of these symptoms, you can then question your relative about some of the other signs listed in these two paragraphs.

The one positive aspect of delirium is that it almost always can be treated. Each one of the common causes of delirium that we have just discussed can usually be remedied with straightforward interventions, mostly medical, less often surgical. The downside of delirium is that, if it is not recognized early and goes untreated, it can result in severe medical as well as psychiatric consequences. You will repeatedly see this advice in other areas of this book. Please seek prompt medical attention for your loved one, even if you are unsure as to whether you are observing a questionable early onset of a potential medical problem, such as delirium. It is far better to be safe than sorry.

PREVENTING DELIRIUM

Before we end this discussion of delirium, I would like to take some time to talk about the prevention of one of its most common causes, the side effects of a medication or multiple medications. What can you do to prevent a delirious state as a result of these side effects? First, it is important to know what medication your family member is taking. Once you have established a trusting relationship, you should be able to inventory the area where your relative keeps their medication. Throw out old or expired medications, whether they be prescription or over-the-counter. Discuss with your relative the reason why you are doing this and include some conversation about the current medications they are taking. Make sure they are taking their medications correctly. Ask how they are taking these drugs, for example, the amount and time of day. Then compare this with the instructions on the bottle.

Do not hesitate to talk to your relative's physician to confirm that they are taking only the medications prescribed. You would be surprised to learn how often an older person continues to take a medication that has been discontinued by their doctor. It is also common for elderly individuals to forget or refuse to fill their prescriptions. Financial problems and the high cost of drugs are often reasons for this behavior.

There have been numerous studies showing that large numbers of young, coherent patients do not take medications according to the physician's instructions. This problem is even more complicated in the elderly, and even more so, in the elderly patient with cognitive difficulties. Before we talk further about medications, there is one recent issue that has been problematic for families. That is the recent change in confidentiality laws.

It used to be easy to discuss an elderly relative's case with their physician with no worry about the repercussions of confidentiality laws, because it was being done, usually, in the best interest of the patient. While these new laws were written in the interest of protecting the patient's privacy, which clearly is an important necessity, these laws have been interpreted in such a way that it has been more difficult to exchange information among interested and caring family members. More forms need to be signed. All of this has led to a new level of bureaucracy, which makes the act of sharing information frustrating for concerned family members. Therefore, it is important initially to have your relative sign releases of information so that key family members can exchange important data about medication and other clinical issues, resulting in better care for your loved one. If you are having difficulties with this new bureaucratic process, you may need to talk to an attorney for assistance. Contacting one of the organizations in the back of this book can also be quite helpful. Once there is an established communication process between you and your relative's health-care providers, you can help your loved one take their medication appropriately and thereby minimize the chance of side effects, behavioral problems and delirium.

In addition to taking an inventory of the medications and discussing the proper use of medications, check out their side effects. There are numerous sources available. Pharmacists commonly distribute side effect profiles with the medications they dispense. Physicians also give their own handouts along with the medications that they prescribe. Ask for these documents. Libraries are full of books that provide all types of information regarding medications both prescribed and over-the-counter. You may have heard of the Physician's Desk Reference, which is a book that health professionals use. This reference contains many complicated medical terms, which might be confusing for a layperson. Most libraries, however, have a number of books that provide information regarding medications in simple terms.

Another good source of information is the patient's pharmacist. Not only do they provide written information regarding medications, they are available to consult with family members in order to answer questions regarding medications and their side effects. In addition, most pharmacies have the capability of providing computerized medication profiles for each patient. This is useful for determining what medications your loved one is taking as well as how they should be taking them. You can then crosscheck this profile with the medications that your family member says they are taking, as well as, how they are taking the prescribed medication. Pharmacists are also helpful providing information regarding over-the-counter medications and how they might interact with other medications and foods.

Another important point concerns the recent trend of the use of natural or organic "medications". I have seen many cases recently of elderly patients who were given herbal remedies or some other type of natural ingredients in order to help them with certain medical or psychiatric illnesses. A number of these patients had significant deterioration of their mental state as a side effect of these so-called benign medications. Stopping these natural medications proved helpful in restoring the patient to their normal state. It is important to coordinate the use of any such remedy with a physician so that any side effects or drug interactions can be minimized or eliminated. I often use the example of the Foxglove plant, which is a source for digitalis. This is a beautiful flowering plant that is often seen in summer beds. It is natural as natural can be but when ingested can cause cardiac problems, delirium and even death. Natural does not necessarily mean safe. So check these remedies out.

Once you have used the resources above, you should have good knowledge about the medications your loved one is taking as well as the potential side effects. Elderly persons can have side effects at much lower doses than the regular adult dosage. Do not assume that, because you may have taken a medication at a certain dose without any problem, it is safe for an older person to take that medication at that same dose. The elderly are more sensitive to medications in general, requiring only a small amount to obtain the desired result. Consequently, side effects can also occur at these low doses, particularly in elderly who have some degree of dementia.

Martha was a 69 year-old woman who was brought into the emergency room by police after she became combative with her family. She was wielding a knife and threatening her daughter. In the emergency room Martha was given a minor tranquilizer, which helped her to calm down. Once it wore off, she became combative again, requiring additional dosages. The family reported that she had never shown such behavior in the past. Fortunately, they were able to provide the emergency room physician with a list of medications that she was currently taking. They reported that she had been on these medications for the last five years or so without any problems. They also noted that she had become a bit more forgetful over the past year or so, but they merely attributed it to growing old. After about 20 hours in the emergency room Martha was back to normal. Later, Martha said that, over the last few days, she kept forgetting to take her medication. She would take it later in the day, believing that she had not taken it earlier. The emergency room physician, after careful questioning, was able to calculate that Martha had at least five or six episodes during the day when she believed that she had forgotten to take her medication and then took an additional dose. It appeared that she actually had been taking five or six times the normal amounts. Thus, she accidentally overdosed on these medications, and this led to her combative and delirious state. On the bright side, the medications had a short half-life and were able to leave her system rather quickly.

Patients with even mild cognitive impairment cannot always be trusted to take their medications appropriately. As in the above example, it is not unusual for an impaired elderly person to believe that they had forgotten to take a medication dose, when in reality, they did take the medication. This can result in overdoses that can lead to a variety of medical problems, as well as delirium.

There are techniques that may prevent a person from inappropriately taking their medication. These tips are useful even for those people who only have minimal memory impairments. Drugstores sell plastic containers with compartments that are labeled for each day of the week. The patient can then tell that they have taken all of their pills for that day. This makes it less likely that they would take more than prescribed. I would suggest that a family member or caregiver, and not the patient, fill these containers.

What if a patient is so confused that they cannot even remember the day of the week? If a person has significant memory impairment, then a caregiver must monitor the amount of medications taken. Even in the early stages of memory loss, it would be prudent to monitor a person's medication habits. The caregiver should inform the elderly person that you are doing this out of concern for his safety. If a person has questionable memory impairment, he or she may be defensive regarding this intervention. Therefore,

I advise family members to focus on the fact that this monitoring is a preventive technique, and it does not mean that the person is demented. However, if the patient has significant memory problems, I find that it is helpful to be open and honest with them about their impairment. Many times this opens the door to a broader discussion regarding any other needs they may have as a result of their poor memory. The bottom line to be communicated is that you care about them and their safety.

In order to monitor medications appropriately you need to know what they are taking, and how they are taking them. You cannot always trust the information your loved one is giving you, because it may not be accurate due to their cognitive limitations. You will need to set up a type of observational process. Do not worry; you can organize family members and friends to help. First, it is a good idea to go to the doctor's office with your relative. The physician can tell you exactly what medications they prescribed and how they should be taken. You can work along with the physician in arranging a schedule of taking the medications that is simple enough to be monitored.

Many medications can be given either once or twice a day, allowing family members, or other concerned parties, to actually observe the patient take the medication at the beginning or end of the day. This makes it convenient for family members to divide up the task. For example, a family member could stop on the way to or from work to perform this task. Similarly, one person could be responsible for monitoring the daytime dose and another for monitoring the evening dose.

Make sure that there are no other medications available that they can accidentally take when you are not there. Clean out any medication storage areas so that they are left with only the medications they should be taking.

Store any additional drugs in an area that is inaccessible to the impaired person. It is also important to actually observe them swallow the pills and thereby getting it into their system. Some cognitively impaired individuals will sometimes put a pill in their mouth and forget to swallow, only to later spit it out.

Once you have established a way of assuring that your loved ones are taking the medications properly, you will still need to monitor for any potential side effects. It is not uncommon to have medication side effects occur prior to a delirious state. If you see any sort of physical or behavioral abnormality, check it out with the resources we talked about above or consult a pharmacist or physician. In such situations it is always better to be safe than sorry.

Treatment of a medication induced delirious state that causes behavioral problems may require some type of sedating medication and other medications to counteract additional side effects. However, it is always advisable for the physician to minimize the addition of any medications, if possible, so that these additional drugs do not further complicate the patient's condition. Please understand that sometimes the physician must do nothing but observe the patient. The most important thing for you to remember is that these interventions need to take place promptly in a safe environment such as in emergency room, the physician's office or hospital.

In summary, in order to avoid medication-related delirium and potential behavioral problems you need to know what medications your loved one is taking and the potential side effects of those medications. In addition, you need to know how they are taking their medications. If you observe side effects or changes in their mental state have them evaluated immediately. Prompt assessment in the early stages of delirium is essential. As Shakespeare said, "Delays have dangerous ends."

CHAPTER SIX

The Treatable Dementias

As I stated in the introduction, this book is not just about Alzheimer's. There are many other dementia syndromes that cause behavioral problems, which can be medically treated and even cured. This chapter will outline a number of these medical conditions and provide a brief discussion concerning their treatment and prevention.

It is unfortunate that we, as a society, tend to automatically believe that an elderly individual, who is confused and mentally impaired, has a dementia process like Alzheimer's disease, which is not expected to improve. On the contrary, there are many types of dementia that have distinct causes. Moreover, there are specific interventions that can eliminate their symptoms to some degree. Some of these illnesses have treatments that can completely reverse the dementia.

Imagine you had an elderly relative who was showing signs of memory loss, confusion, or some other deficit in brain functioning that you wrote off as an untreatable dementia. Maybe you thought they had Alzheimer's, or you thought this was just part of getting old. But what if they had one of these illnesses that could be totally cured? The only way you would know is to have them medically evaluated and properly treated. With this type of intervention, you could be instrumental in giving them back their old life. The bottom line is that every individual showing signs of dementia deserves a thorough assessment to determine if they have such a treatable illness.

When people talk about disorders that produce dementia, it's like talking about medical illnesses that cause fever. You can find elevated temperatures in many medical syndromes, but you do not prescribe medications just to reduce the fever. Dementia, like fever, can be a sign of a condition that may be curable and, indeed, may require treatment to prevent severe complications, just as was the case with delirium in the previous chapter. It is not unusual for the elderly to display a slow and progressive mental deterioration and subsequent behavioral problems as a result of a medical illness. Remember, dementia is a slow process as opposed to delirium, which occurs over a short time span. The following cases show some of the common causes of the treatable dementias.

VASCULAR DEMENTIA

Ben was an eighty-year-old man who, according to his family, became senile over the last 15 years. His family watched him decline but never intervened because they thought that this was just part of growing old. At Ben's funeral I spoke to his sister, and she told me that, other than his senility, his last 15 years were rather positive. He would often go boating and fishing, or hang around the fire house where he worked for most of his life. She later spoke about these senile episodes, which were always very brief. During those times he would become confused for a few minutes or even only seconds. Following the episodes, he would usually complain that his leg or arm would feel weak and sore. On a couple of these occasions he noticed that he would have trouble with his vision, but this symptom like the others would quickly pass. Then he would be fine for several weeks. Because Ben always quickly improved, no one ever felt that anything needed to be done. By the way, Ben passed away due to a massive stroke.

Those episodes may have been transient ischemic attacks, a condition in which the blood supply is temporarily cut off to certain areas of the brain. The blood flow restarts, and the symptoms quickly resolve. This condition however is a sign that a person's blood flow is deteriorating and an evaluation is needed. Ben's senility may have also been related to the deteriorating blood vessels and could have been prevented to some extent, if the appropriate action had been taken. Ironically, if he would have had some type of behavioral problem that required an assessment, his underlying condition may have been identified and treated.

The point of the case is that, even in our advanced culture, many people still believe that becoming demented is part of becoming old. I personally have seen or heard of hundreds of such cases as Ben's. Many of these individuals come into my office when it is already too late. Even though this chapter is written to outline those conditions that can be treated in order to control behavioral problems, it is even more important to point out that we should not take the diagnosis of dementia for granted; as an illness that cannot be treated. There is no doubt that Alzheimer's is the leading cause of dementia, and treatment options are limited. On the other hand, there are numerous medical conditions, such as the vascular type discussed here, which can produce a similar picture of dementia. Yet with simple medical interventions, these medical conditions may be prevented, reversed and even cured.

Vascular dementia can be treated in order to minimize future problems. People with this dementia usually have hypertension, which can be controlled with medication. They can also be obese, which obviously may be controlled with diet. There are other risk factors that can be treated such as elevated sugar or cholesterol in the blood. Smoking is also a common risk factor that can and should be eliminated.

Surgical procedures are available in order to prevent certain types of strokes and dementia. There are less common abnormalities of the brain's blood vessels such as aneurysms and malformations, which, in certain cases, can be surgically corrected if identified in time. Even though these conditions are not commonly known to produce a dementia, there are cases in which dementia is surprisingly the initial symptom particularly if the blood vessel abnormalities are small and numerous. Because of the many causes of vascular dementia as well as numerous treatment possibilities, it is important to get a comprehensive assessment in order to identify and address all the possible factors that can prevent future episodes of circulatory problems.

There is also a relationship between vascular dementia and atrial fibrillation. Atrial fibrillation is a cardiac arrhythmia that can cause serious medical complications. This disorder can be treated with medications that thin the blood as well as a medical procedure called cardioversion.

Sometimes minor strokes can occur with barely noticeable symptoms. If you notice your family member displaying any of the following signs have him or her see a physician. You may see a facial expression in which one side of the face does not seem to move. A test to make sure that the facial muscles are working properly is to have a person grin and raise his eyebrows. If a person's facial expression is asymmetrical, meaning that each side of the face cannot move the same way, then there may be a neurologic problem that needs to be evaluated. If a person is using both arms to complete a task and one side becomes tired much more quickly than the other, have him extend both arms to the front, parallel to the ground, to see if he can keep both arms up for the same amount of time. If one drops before the other get an evaluation. Likewise, if the person complains that one of their legs tires out earlier than the other, have him lie down on their back and elevate both legs a few inches above the surface. If one side tires and falls earlier than the other an assessment is needed. As you probably noticed, I often say that if there is any doubt, get an assessment. Nothing could be truer than in the case of a probable stroke. Not only can you prevent potential behavioral problems down the road, but more importantly you can prevent a more damaging stroke in the future.

BRAIN ANOMALIES CAUSING DEMENTIA

A brain tumor is another condition that can cause signs similar to a stroke. It accounts for approximately 4% of dementia patients. Usually a growing tumor produces symptoms that increase over a long period of time, unlike the abrupt changes in a stroke. Headache, dizziness and problems with sensation or muscle movement are common initial symptoms of a brain tumor. There are occasions, however, when the tumor grows in an area of the brain where it does not cause many outward signs. Then all of a sudden it can grow into a blood vessel causing the vessel to rupture and bleed into the brain. At that point it can produce a picture similar to a person who has just suffered a stroke. Tumors in certain areas of the brain can cause a patient to have an unstable mood as well as dementia, which may lead to behavioral difficulties. Early identification of a brain tumor can require medical or surgical interventions, which can relieve the symptoms as well as prevent future brain damage.

Hydrocephalus is another affliction of the brain that can cause dementia in patients. In this condition the fluid areas of the brain expand and can put pressure on the solid areas causing physical as well as behavioral problems. This cause of dementia is often associated with a gait disturbance, which one of my patients described as "looking like a drunk person walking." Another common related symptom is urinary incontinence. Medical and surgical interventions are helpful, and at times can produce miraculous results.

Dramatic examples of a chronic dementia process are the prizefighters who, in the later stage of their careers or even after retirement, show signs of mental deterioration due to the repeated head trauma they suffered. These individuals may have had a number of concussions during their career but their initial symptoms usually resolve within a day or so. These repeated insults to the brain, however, will cause an increasing amount of damage over time that can often lead to an early cognitive decline. The only intervention in such cases is prevention, which would mean elimination of such sports. Once these repeated injuries have occurred it is usually too late for a significant recovery.

In the previous chapter on delirium I discussed several medical problems that can cause an acute mental deterioration. They included medication reactions, thyroid disease, diabetes, head trauma, alcoholism and infections. When these conditions develop slowly, they can cause a chronic dementia process. The symptoms associated with these medical conditions evolve over weeks, months and even years. Because the signs of these illnesses occur gradually, it sometimes makes them all the more difficult to recognize. I refer you to the chapter on delirium so that you can review the associated symptoms for these illnesses. The rest of this chapter will outline some of the other more common reversible or treatable dementias, which often can cause behavioral problems.

LUNG DISEASES CAUSING DEMENTIA

Anoxia, or lack of oxygen to the brain, can often cause behavioral problems related to a confused state. This syndrome is often seen in patients who have chronic pulmonary disease. When they have difficulty breathing, it is likely that they are not getting enough oxygen into their body and more importantly into their brain. These individuals often become anxious, fearful, confused, and combative. They also have associated panic attacks because they cannot catch their breath, and they feel like they are dying.

Gwen was an 81-year-old woman who had a 12-year history of emphysema. Her family often noticed that she seemed to be short of breath. She was not able to do much because of her pulmonary condition. Her husband took over almost every household duty as he was still in very good health. Over the last several months he noted that she would start to hit him when he tried to help her get dressed. This was upsetting to him because she was never a woman who would become aggressive in any manner. She would never even raise her voice. He came to my office asking for some medication to calm her down so that she could be like her old self. I asked him if she became more short of breath than usual when he helped her get dressed. He admitted that it had become harder for her to stand up and go through the movements of getting dressed. This little bit of exercise caused her to have a great deal of difficulty breathing. I asked him to take his wife to a pulmonary specialist who, after some testing, prescribed a portable oxygen device for Gwen. With use of this device, before and during physical activity, she was able to breathe much better and had no further combative episodes.

A good physician will determine the exact cause of a behavioral problem rather than just sedate the patient. If an attempt was made to tranquilize Gwen with medications, this could have complicated her breathing even further to the point where she would be at risk of dying. The moral of the story is to be patient when a physician does not automatically prescribe a medication to eliminate the problem behavior. Treatment of the underlying cause may eliminate the problem behavior and can be lifesaving.

Patients who have problems with anoxia often have been given a diagnosis such as chronic pulmonary obstructive disease, asthma, or emphysema. These persons may have behavioral problems when there is an overlying illness such as an infection in addition to their pulmonary problems. Persons with such illnesses are often at high risk of developing numerous infections and can have repeated episodes of confused and combative behavior. Medications such as antibiotics can be prescribed in order to combat these infections. Supplemental oxygen and other breathing devices can help these individuals maintain a high level of oxygen in the brain. These interventions can be quite helpful in reducing or eliminating disturbed behaviors.

From a preventive point of view smoking and exposure to allergens or toxic substances such as dust, fumes and asbestos should be avoided. Unfortunately, elderly persons often live in older dwellings where these elements are more common. These homes, including the duct system, will need a thorough cleaning to remove the offending substances. Patients who have severe heart problems may also have congestive heart failure or fluid in the lungs, which needs to be treated to prevent additional pulmonary problems.

AIDS RELATED DEMENTIA

Dementia related to AIDS is becoming an increasing problem. At one time this condition occurred primarily in the younger population. With the substantial advances in antiviral medications over the last several years, people with HIV infection are living longer. We are beginning to see a number of elderly persons who have AIDS-related confusion and behavioral problems.

While there is still some controversy regarding the treatment of this dementia, most practitioners still feel that treatment with specific antiviral agents may reduce brain inflammation, otherwise known as encephalitis, thereby reducing confusion and related improper behaviors. There is, however, a degeneration of certain areas of the brain that does not appear to be reversed by these medications. Sometimes certain tranquilizers and mood stabilizers can help control some of the disturbed behaviors seen in this condition.

NUTRITIONAL ISSUES AND DEMENTIA

There are a number of nutritional deficiencies that can cause dementia and related conduct problems. A lack of vitamin B-12, thiamine, or niacin is associated with symptoms such as a rash, diarrhea, or anemia. Patients who have a significant anemia can look pale. Persons with these deficiencies can also have decreased sensation and strength in their feet and legs. They may complain of a feeling of tingling or 'pins and needles' in those areas. Dietary supplements specifically prescribed by a physician can be quite helpful in treating these illnesses and the associated behavioral difficulties.

The lack of nutrition is often caused by improper dietary habits. Some older folks can be very picky eaters. Sometimes they will only eat a few types of food and consequently do not have a balanced diet. If you notice a family member showing early signs of dementia, it would be helpful to determine their diet. I often ask family members to construct a diary in order to document exactly what the patient is eating. More importantly, given that some elderly people who are suffering from dementia cannot remember what they eat, family members and friends may need to actually observe their nutritional intake. I realize that this is often a time-consuming task, but I tell family members that it is more important to document at least two main meals per day rather than worry about what type of snacks the patient may be eating. Usually, if an older person is eating two balanced meals a day, they should be taking in the standard nutritional requirements unless there is some type of medical illness that is preventing their absorption of these nutrients.

It is also important to note the amount of fluids that are being ingested. In the chapter on delirium we covered the signs of dehydration that can lead to medical problems as well as conduct disturbances. Thus, by documenting an older person's food intake in a daily diary you will be able to learn both the solid and liquid intake, as both are important for proper nutrition. Make sure that you note both the type of food and fluids as well as their amounts.

Elizabeth was a 94-year-old woman who was in good physical health up until the last few months prior to her hospitalization. Over the past few years she had only minor signs of dementia. In the last few months, however, her dementia seemed to worsen progressively to the point where she became delusional and panicky. She would call her children at all hours of the night believing that someone was trying to break into her room. Yet, it was a fall and a sprained ankle that brought her into the hospital. During her initial physical examination it was discovered that she had a low potassium level in her blood, which may have explained some of her anxiety. There were additional laboratory studies that showed a lack of proper nutrition. The family did not know how this could have happened. The two daughters who did the food shopping for the mother claimed that the food in the mother's refrigerator and cabinets was always being used. They were constantly replenishing her supplies. While the mother was in the hospital, they went back to her home and inspected the trash bags in the house as well as the trashcans outside. They noticed numerous cans and containers of food that were open but hardly eaten. It seems as though their mother would barely taste the food and then throw it away.

It is important to be thorough in your observation of a loved one's dietary habits. Do not make assumptions as the family did in the above example. Once, a medical student conducted an emergency room evaluation of an elderly person's mental state and came to the conclusion that the individual was clearly demented and unable to handle his affairs. That medical student was ready to recommend that the family seek the services of a lawyer in order to have the patient deemed legally incompetent. While the patient was being further evaluated in the emergency room, she was given IV fluids as well as some food to eat. A few hours later the medical student reevaluated the patient's mental state and found that she showed no cognitive impairment whatsoever. The bottom line is, whether you are a medical student, health care professional or layperson, try to obtain all possible information so that the right intervention can be made. Careful and consistent observation is the key.

OTHER TREATABLE CAUSES OF DEMENTIA

Less common treatable causes of dementia include chronic infections, autoimmune illnesses, adrenal gland malfunction and late stage kidney and liver failure. All these illnesses can cause a dementia, which is often accompanied by behavioral disturbances.

Other than signs of dementia, headache can be the only symptom in chronic brain infections. Sometimes these infections can become acute producing additional symptoms such as increased confusion. It is at that time that these chronic infections are often discovered. Syphilis, which was once widespread, is now a rare example of such a chronic brain infection. These infections can be treated with the appropriate antibiotic or antiviral agent; although the outcomes are better the earlier the intervention occurs.

Late stage kidney and liver failure are treatable but only to a limited extent. Behavioral problems are related to the metabolic abnormalities caused by the failure of these organs. In general, interventions are geared toward ameliorating the symptoms of the illness by correcting the abnormalities with diet and medications. Renal dialysis and transplants may be helpful in certain limited cases.

Autoimmune disorders are illnesses where a person's immune system attacks certain tissues of the body. One type of autoimmune disorder affects the blood vessels of the brain, causing them to deteriorate, resulting in symptoms similar to a stroke. Sometimes this is an acute process, but other times it can be quite chronic and hard to detect. I would suggest that you review the sections related to stroke and brain tumor so that you can identify any early symptoms. There are medications available that can help to control these illnesses.

One type of medication used in autoimmune disorders is a category of drugs known as steroids. These drugs are often used to treat many other types of illnesses such as asthma, skin disorders, and arthritis. However they can also cause a dementia, delirium or psychosis with concomitant behavioral problems. In fact, patients who have a certain type of an adrenal gland disorder produce excessive steroids that can cause the same problems. Sometimes it is difficult to determine whether the mental symptoms are the result of the autoimmune disorder or the medication used to treat the illness. Adrenal gland problems can be remedied using both medications and surgery.

Remember, these dementia-producing disorders discussed above can be treated, and conduct disturbances can be brought under control. The key is to recognize the early symptoms of these illnesses so that prompt intervention can be provided, increasing the chance of a positive outcome.

CHAPTER SEVEN
Depression

Depression is a common malady of the elderly, and the related incidence of suicide in this age group is particularly high. To some extent this is not unexpected, given that older individuals are often dealing with some type of loss, whether it is a loss of job, family member, friend, financial security or good health. While depression is common in the elderly, it is not inevitable. As a family member or friend, it is important to recognize depression in your loved one, since this condition is quite treatable.

The depressed elderly person can display a number of behavioral problems such as irritability, profanity, unexplained angry outbursts, suicide attempts, self-injurious behaviors and a dementia like syndrome called pseudo-dementia, which we will discuss later.

THE SIGNS OF DEPRESSION

Although at times an elderly person may be able to hide their depression, symptoms of this illness are usually fairly straightforward and easily identifiable. A person with depression will often complain that they feel sad or down and may have tearful episodes. They will often admit that they have a difficult time sleeping. This includes problems falling asleep, staying asleep and early-morning awakening. This latter sign is seen in the individual who will awaken several hours before they intend to get up and then they are unable to get back to sleep. Depressed individuals will also complain of a poor appetite or, less commonly, overeating. Low energy, lack of interest or motivation and fatigue are often seen as part of the syndrome. Depressed persons will also complain of feeling helpless or hopeless, believing their future is dim. They often are unable to concentrate and may have difficulty functioning particularly in the area of making decisions. They may withdraw and skip work or fail to attend normal social activities. There may be a decrease in sexual interest and functioning. Yes, this can be a problem even for the elderly.

There are other symptoms that are not commonly thought of as signs of depression, yet they are seen as part of the illness. Persons with depression can appear sarcastic, demanding, constantly complaining and whining. Depressed individuals, particularly elderly depressed patients, may have numerous medical complaints. Sometimes it is difficult to identify depression in these people because they tend to focus on their physical problems, and their depression appears to be related to the fact that they are upset due to their medical condition. In these individuals the medical evaluation often shows no specific physical cause for their complaints. A more complicated situation occurs when a depressed person with a legitimate physical problem has symptoms that are exaggerated or unusual. The most common example is the patient who has disabling pain, which is not consistent with what appears to be a minor ailment.

Depression is often associated with a significant loss or a major change in the person's life. As we have already discussed, elderly people are more prone to suffer losses. Retirement or a similar change in lifestyle can be a major issue for someone who is depressed. Therefore it is not surprising that depression is often seen in the elderly. Some studies show that anywhere between 25 to 50% of the elderly have some form of depression.

There have been a number of studies that claim that depression is often under-diagnosed in the elderly population. This likely occurs because the elderly may only have medical complaints, and the classic symptoms of depression are minimal. Another explanation for this under-recognition is our cultural belief that it is normal for the elderly to be depressed. Thus, depressed elderly patients may not seek help for their depression because they, as well as many members of society, believe that this is a normal burden that they have to bear when they get old. This can be a real tragedy since there are numerous interventions available that can greatly improve a patient's mood.

Barbara was an 81-year-old woman who was brought into my office because her family felt that she was becoming demented. They noted that she stopped doing many of her normal activities and appeared to be in a daze. They first noted that this was a problem about three years earlier but failed to get any help because they thought this was a normal process of aging. After I evaluated her cognitive skills, it was clear that she was still able to function quite well mentally. During the history taking process, I was able to determine that about three years ago her pet cat had to be put to sleep. The patient never really complained much about this loss, and therefore, the family felt that it was not that important. We tried a number of non-medication interventions initially focused on providing daily meaningful activity for Barbara. Given that Barbara had a three-year history of decline, I decided after a few weeks of no improvement to prescribe a trial of an antidepressant. By the end of the month she became much more alert and resumed most of her daily activities.

I hope the message is clear. Just because depression is common in the elderly, it does not mean that depression cannot be successfully treated. Indeed there are numerous interventions, which I will describe later.

AGITATED DEPRESSION

The uncommon signs of depression noted above seem to be more commonly seen in the elderly. There was an old term, agitated depression, which was useful for describing an elderly person who appeared to be angry and irritable on the outside, but after a careful evaluation was clearly sad on the inside. These individuals might even be profane or demeaning to others around them. They saw the world as one negative place. The commonly used term to describe them was the proverbial crotchety old man or woman. Because they would tend to drive people away and see everything in a negative light, their depression was not easily recognized and treatment rarely occurred. Nevertheless, it is important to have these individuals evaluated for possible depression, as these uncommon symptoms can be eliminated or minimized.

Jack, the father of one of my colleagues, was a crotchety old man according to his family. He was always critical of his sons and daughters. They could never do anything right. He would complain that they did not visit him often enough, and that they would pay more attention to strangers than him. No matter what his sons and daughters did for him, he would always point out what they did not achieve. He was also critical of doctors and would refer to them as quacks. It was not surprising that he refused to go for help. The family claimed that he started to act this way after the death of his wife 10 years earlier. Even though he fit the mold for a person who was suffering from an agitated depression, I knew at the outset that he would not go to see a psychiatrist. After all, he claimed nothing was wrong with him. The problem was that his family could not get him the help he needed because of his uncooperativeness. Need I say that they were also turned away by his negative attitude toward them? It took several meetings with the family members to develop a plan that would bring him in to see his physician, where he would ultimately be given an antidepressant. Several weeks after the start of his medication trial, his complaining lessened somewhat, and he was able to notice an improvement in the way he felt about the world. The outcome was not perfect, but at least he was more acceptable to his family and friends.

Typically, the average person would want to have nothing to do with someone like Jack. After all, why would anyone want to take the abuse? It is ironic that a person like Jack actually needs people to intervene for him so that he can be evaluated and properly treated. Yet, if Jack drives away the people that he needs he may not get the help he requires. When dealing with someone like Jack, even though it is difficult, you should not take his criticisms and demeanor personally. Try to see his behavior as symptoms of an illness that can be helped. This is particularly true if the person's irritability and obnoxious behavior are not in keeping with the personality they had when they were younger.

Unfortunately, there are persons who, by nature, have always been mean-spirited, and this may not change when they get older. In fact, their personality may actually worsen. It may be worthwhile, however, to have even these people evaluated so that one can be sure there is not a treatable illness present. There is a possibility that these mean-spirited people have suffered a lifelong history of depression. With the proper treatment, these individuals could develop into pleasant and somewhat happy people. If, however, they just have mean personalities, it will be unlikely that they benefit from traditional antidepressant therapy. I will talk more about personality disorders in Chapter Eight.

SOMATIC DEPRESSION

Abby was a 72-year-old woman who had many medical complaints, which interfered with her job as a clerk in a candy store. She was referred to me by her family physician, after he had performed numerous evaluations. All of the tests were negative, and he had nothing more to offer her. Her family was concerned because they would often find her in a tearful mood at family gatherings. She was adamant about the fact that she was not depressed but just worried about her job. Initially Abby was quite upset that her doctor referred her to a psychiatrist, since she felt that she was not crazy. I reassured her that she was not crazy, but at the same time I tried to focus on the fact that she seemed to be suffering from pain in a variety of areas of her body. Pain, as I explained to her, was a very real symptom that needed to be taken seriously. She could easily talk about her pain and how it prevented her from doing her job. Abby had been out on sick leave for the last three months, due to perceived physical problems. After further discussion, she admitted that her place of employment had been the main source of stress in her life. She was actually glad that she did not have to go to work. Ultimately, she was able to accept the fact that perhaps her work was making her feel depressed. After a few therapy sessions, she was able to go back to work for a different employer as a volunteer on a limited basis. Her pain did not fully resolve, but she was happy with the fact that she could now work through the pain and do something productive in her life. Ironically, after a few months her family doctor informed me that she was working almost forty hours per week and loving it. She never did require the use of medications.

Elderly depressed individuals commonly present with medical complaints, most often pain. It may be that it is more socially acceptable for them to have medical problems, rather than admit they are depressed. Sometimes, they even refuse to accept that they may be depressed, since they believe any person would be upset if they had all of these medical issues.

A major challenge in such individuals is convincing them to seek some form of psychiatric help. They are much more eager to put themselves through numerous medical tests costing thousands of dollars than seek mental health care. Some of these patients have a difficult time accepting psychiatric medications such as antidepressants or tranquilizers from the family physician because they assume that their physician is labeling them as crazy.

There is no single, foolproof way to convince these people to get help. It is often useful to obtain some information regarding the patient's medical and social background so that it can be determined if they have had a bad experience with psychiatry. Some of these individuals may have had a negative past experience with mental-health professionals or with family members or friends who had some type of psychiatric problem. Once you have this information you can then develop an educational plan or strategy to convince the patient to obtain an evaluation. Often they need to be told that having an emotional problem does not define them as crazy. More importantly, they should be informed that many of these psychiatric disorders could be easily treated.

Another way to bring a patient in for proper care is to initially focus on the person's physical complaint and gradually tie it in with a discussion of how their symptoms affect them emotionally. This roundabout dialogue can make them accept mental health care more readily, because they will find it easier to seek treatment for their physical problem. Once they establish a strong relationship with their physician, they will be more likely to accept a fully explained mental health referral.

Certain movies, articles and talk shows have painted a negative image of psychiatric patients. If this causes the older individual to have a bias against receiving mental health care, they need to be educated fully about the positive aspects of psychiatric treatment. It is often helpful, if possible, to introduce your loved one to someone who has been helped by a mental health professional. Then, a plan can be developed to make a psychiatric consultation more appealing based on a more thorough understanding of mental illness.

THE UNCOOPERATIVE DEPRESSED PERSON

George was an 81-year-old man who had been treated by his family doctor over a 40-year period for high blood pressure. Over the last year or so, he had been having angry outbursts particularly at family gatherings. At his recent birthday dinner he became upset because he could not remember the name of his friend who organized his 50th birthday party. He hit his fist on the table in anger and accidentally hit the edge of his plate causing it to fall on the floor. His sister was quite upset with him and told him that she was going to go with him the next time he saw his family doctor. During that visit she discovered that George had been given a diagnosis of Alzheimer's and had been on one of the anti-dementia medications. When the doctor heard about George's angry outbursts, he suggested that George might need to see a psychiatrist for medications that might help him control these episodes. George was so upset with this recommendation that he left the office abruptly. Since his younger sister drove George that day, she told him to wait in the hallway for a few minutes so that she could talk to the doctor. George's doctor was able to learn from the sister that George had a favorite aunt, who apparently became psychotic and had to be put away in a state hospital. From time to time, George would say that he would never see a psychiatrist because all they do is put people away. When the sister drove George home, she talked to him about modern-day psychiatry with the help of some pamphlets that his doctor had given her. He wasn't immediately sold on the idea but was willing to go back to his family physician in order to discuss it further. Ultimately, George agreed to see a psychiatrist who was able to develop a plan to handle his anger without the use of psychiatric medications.

As you can see, it is quite important for family members to discover the reasons why their loved one refuses to get the help they need. Previous negative experience with psychiatry or a lack of understanding of what a psychiatrist really does are the two most common reasons for a person's reluctance to seek psychiatric help. It may also be helpful to reread chapter two for additional tips as to how you can get your family member in for an evaluation.

THE EVALUATION FOR DEPRESSION

As I stated at the beginning of this chapter, there are numerous interventions to treat an older person with depression. Let me describe the elements of a comprehensive evaluation that will lead to a plan to treat a depressed individual. This way you will have some background so that you can carry out your part of this helpful intervention. Once again, I do not mean to put the burden on one individual alone, as this section applies to all those who care about the depressed person. Try to divide the various tasks among concerned family members.

The first component of the evaluation is a comprehensive history of the patient's depression. It is important to know when the first signs of depression occurred and under what circumstances. Did anything change in the life of your loved one? Try to note any changes in the way your relative functioned or behaved. Remember the symptoms of depression outlined at the beginning of this chapter. Do not be afraid to thoroughly but gently discuss these signs with your loved one. Depressed individuals often do not like to talk about their illness and may try to hide any problems.

Next it is important to determine if any other family member has been depressed. This is important because depression seems to run in families. It is also helpful to know what that family member received in terms of medication or therapy and whether it helped. I have found that medications that have been helpful for other family members are likely to be helpful for the currently depressed individual. This is also true for non- medication interventions.

It is also helpful to know if the depressed individual had ever received treatment for depression in the past. Obviously, if they responded to a certain intervention in the past they may respond to that same intervention now. The converse is also true, as you may not want to use approaches that have failed in the past.

Edna was a 70-year-old woman who was brought in by her family for an evaluation after the family was upset with her previous physician. She had been severely depressed for the last year since her husband had died. The family reported she had had been depressed numerous times in the past. They became very concerned that Edna was not improving and found out that her physician recently prescribed a medication that had not worked for her in the past. They felt that her doctor should have known this fact. I asked the family to obtain medical records from Edna's previous physicians with her permission. With the help of these records, we were able to determine that the patient had been on a certain antidepressant in the past that had been quite successful. Surprisingly, no particular reason was documented as to why this medication had ever been discontinued. After two or three weeks on this medication Edna was back to her old self.

It is extremely helpful for a family to know what medications their loved one is taking, as well as what medications they had taken in the past and whether or not they were helpful. It is also useful to know what side effects or allergic reactions the patient may have had in the past due to specific medications. The best way to obtain all this information is to collect all of the patient's medical records and keep them in a folder in a secure place. Once you do this, you can update the folder with any new information. This will take a little bit of time initially, but when you have this file together in one place, you can easily make copies for various physicians or caregivers. This will not only save a great deal of time in the future, but it will provide a readily available source of information, which can help a physician develop a timely treatment plan. With the new confidentiality laws, you may need to have your family member give you the authorization to do this. Any physician's office can assist you in this procedure.

It is also important to have information available regarding the patient's current and past medical problems including any non-psychiatric medications that they are taking. One of the common causes of depression in the elderly is medication.

David was a 67-year-old man who was depressed and not enjoying his retirement. He assured me that he was not upset by the fact that he was no longer working, because he always looked forward to the years when he would be able to do all the things that he could not do while working at his busy job. Sailing, fishing and volunteering at the Smithsonian Institute had been his passions. For some reason, over the last several months, he had no motivation or energy to pursue these endeavors. After taking a careful history I found out that his depression coincided with the start of a medication for his high blood pressure. I talked to his family physician who agreed to change the type of medication for his hypertension. In less than three weeks David told me that he was feeling better than he ever had in his life.

There are numerous medications given for a variety of illnesses that can have psychiatric repercussions, such as depression, as a side effect. For example, I stated in the previous chapter how steroids, which are used to treat a number of medical problems, could cause not only a depression but also a psychosis. Physicians, as well as pharmacists, can provide information regarding these potential medication problems. A physician should also be informed if a person has any mental or physical changes soon after the start of a new medication. Family members may notice these changes even before the patient does.

Another area of information that is very helpful in evaluating the depressed patient is any new developments or transitions in the patient's life that may be related to the start of the depression. This may include the loss of a job or loved one. Medical illnesses, family conflicts, or financial problems are additional causes of depression in the elderly. Sometimes the cause of the depression is not immediately apparent. A problem that had occurred several weeks, months, or even years earlier could lead to depression later in life. It may be that the individual was able to cope with the initial cause, but, as they grew older, their mental defenses weakened and they became outwardly depressed. Elderly persons may also be susceptible to minor stressors in their life, which could lead to a depressive episode. An elderly woman who I treated several years ago came to the conclusion that losing her purse a few months earlier caused her to become depressed because she felt this was the beginning of a cognitive decline, even though she had no signs of dementia whatsoever. A series of brief therapy sessions helped her put this incident into perspective and noticeably lessened her depression.

It can be helpful to gather family members together and brainstorm about what factors may have led to a depressive episode in their loved one. These psychological factors can be treated with verbal therapy, thus eliminating the need for psychiatric medications, which have their own side effects.

The final phase of the evaluation process is to determine whether the patient is a danger to themselves or others. You will need to be fairly straightforward by asking your loved one whether they are considering harming themselves or other people. This includes a discussion about how they would do it and under what circumstances. Remember, suicide occurs at the greatest frequency in the elderly. The chapter on Dangerous Patients will cover this process in detail. That chapter will also include a discussion advising you how to get immediate help.

TREATING DEPRESSION

Once the physician has information regarding the possible causes for a depressive episode, the second phase of treatment comes into play. This is the development of a treatment plan. First, you have to identify the specific symptoms of depression such as crying spells, lack of motivation, decreased energy etc. that are occurring in your loved one. It is often helpful to describe these symptoms in measurable terms, so that progress can be monitored.

Nick was a 70-year-old man who had been depressed over the last few years since the death of his wife. He had numerous symptoms including crying episodes, a lack of energy, decreased sleep, decreased appetite, weight loss, temper tantrums and occasional thoughts that he would be better off dead. His family physician gave him an antidepressant that seemed to work. His sleep, appetite and energy all improved. Numerous family members accompanied him to his next doctor's appointment three months later. They did this because they were unsure as to whether the medication was actually working. They felt he still had some crying episodes as well as periods of irritability. The various family members were in some disagreement as to whether the patient had actually benefited from the medication. Nick's doctor called me for a consult, as he did not know who to believe. I told him to have the family members measure each of Nick's symptoms as best they could. For example, they needed to write down how often Nick would cry, how much he would eat per day, and how often he would have temper tantrums. Once they were able to measure each one of his symptoms, they could then monitor his progress, or lack thereof, and treatment could be adjusted accordingly. The family members agreed to carry out this process. After some medication adjustment, they were able to see the exact progress that had been made by monitoring those measurable symptoms. We will talk more about this in a later chapter on developing a treatment plan.

Once a person's symptoms are measured, the next step is to agree on measurable goals. This is usually relatively easy. For example, if a depressed person is only able to sleep four hours a night, then a measurable goal would be to have the person sleep seven hours a night. Each significant symptom of depression should have an associated goal. Using this approach progress can be easily measured.

GENERAL INTERVENTIONS FOR DEPRESSION

The final phase of developing a plan is to choose the appropriate intervention. Just because a patient is depressed, this does not mean that that individual needs an antidepressant. In fact, sometimes it is helpful to discontinue a certain medication. Various forms of verbal therapy and behavioral interventions can be quite effective in the elderly population. Numerous therapies that are available cannot be covered here, since it would take another book to do so. Yet, there are general guidelines that are helpful in developing an intervention for the depressed elderly person.

FINDING A REASON TO LIVE

I once heard a story of a group of Jewish refugees who were escaping the Nazis. They were walking over a mountain and they carried with them the sick, the old, and the children. A number of the old people fell by the wayside, stating that they were a burden, and that everyone should go on without them, leaving them to die. In response, the younger people said that the mothers needed respite, and they asked the older folk to take their babies and carry them as far as they could. Once the elderly took the babies close to their bosom, they started walking, and all of them made it over the mountain. They had a reason to live.

Give a person a reason to live and you take the first step in improving a person's life, whether they be depressed or demented. Everyone needs meaning in life, and this should be the first consideration of any intervention for a depressed person. Family members are often helpful in providing information about what has been important in the patient's life. It is obviously important to ask the patient directly, but in a caring manner, what purpose do they feel they have in their life. Answers can vary widely from working in a productive job to caring for a spouse. As people age, so may their purpose in life. It is not uncommon for someone, who has lost his or her purpose in life, to become depressed. The death of a family member or retirement from the job may take away an individual's reason for living, particularly if this was a major focus of their life prior to that event. This can often lead to a major depressive state. A new focus for living needs to be developed during this phase of treatment.

Karen was a 90-year-old woman who became progressively depressed over the last decade after all of her friends had passed away one by one. Though she was still physically and mentally in good health, she was feeling quite alone. Her family had moved away years ago, and their visits decreased over time. Her neighbor noticed that she was staying indoors almost constantly. This was unusual for Karen, who had been very sociable up until the last year or so. The neighbor asked her daughter who was a therapist to stop by Karen's house and have a chat with her. She found out that Karen had always been a person who helped other people. This gave her life meaning. Now that most of these people had died, she felt that her life was useless. She thought about applying for a volunteer job, but believed no one would hire someone who is ninety years old. The neighbor's daughter introduced her to the director of a local assisted-living home for Alzheimer's patients. They eagerly accepted Karen as a volunteer, as she proved to be a role model of an elderly person who functioned at a high level. The residents of the home welcomed her because she was so sociable. The staff felt that Karen, by virtue of her high functioning, motivated the residents to become more independent. It was truly a win-win situation.

Karen never did require antidepressant medication as she now had a new purpose in life. Yet, when you really look at the situation, Karen had the same ambition. She always wanted to care for others and was merely given a new direction.

In order to develop a new mission in life, as a treatment intervention for the depressed individual, you will not only need to look at the person's interest but also their skill level. You do not want to give them a goal that they cannot achieve. In Karen's case it was quite obvious that she had care-giving skills. Sometimes it is a challenge to find the skills that are remaining in certain elderly individuals. Knowledge of previous work experience, social activities and relationships can help determine the depressed person's aptitude for a new goal in life. When I make a suggestion regarding new tasks that can be accomplished, I still caution the individual not to be upset if the situation fails because everyone is different. My message is clear. Keep trying, because something will usually work. The philosopher Confucius said it even more eloquently. "Our greatest glory is not in never falling but in rising every time we fall."

There is no doubt that, as we get older, our options in life become more limited. Friends and family members pass away. Fewer jobs are available. Even our health restricts what we can do. A depressed elderly person may, however, see these limited options as no options. Therefore, we must educate these individuals. There are, indeed, choices that are possible even at an advanced age. It is often helpful to have depressed people read about other productive older persons, or more importantly, put them in a situation where they are near these people. This approach, however, may not always be helpful for the depressed elderly patient who sees his entire life as a failure, for some individuals would only view the comparison as proof that they were incompetent. Even certain behavioral interventions can have negative effects and should be exercised with caution, as another approach may be needed. Carefully talk about these options with your loved one, so that it is more likely that they see this intervention as a positive approach. One should also be careful that the older person does not interpret the suggestion to find a new purpose in life as a way to get rid of the individual. A caring and thorough discussion is essential in these types of interventions.

Mike was a depressed individual. He was in treatment with a therapist, when his family suggested that he get a volunteer job working in an accountant's office. After all, Mike had been a financial adviser in the past, according to his family. Mike, however, became upset with his family members for suggesting this because he felt that he was being cast away to spend his days with a bunch of strangers. What the family did not realize is that Mike always wanted to spend his retirement taking his grandchildren to various activities. He always felt that he had worked too hard in his earlier years and did not spend adequate time with his own children. Once these issues were brought into the open, the intervention was changed to family oriented activities such as babysitting the grandchildren. Mike now got what he wanted. Being with his grandchildren was his main reason to live. Needless to say, his depression quickly lifted.

In summary, the initial therapeutic intervention for the elderly with emotional problems, particularly the depressed individual, should be to help the patient define a purpose in his or her life based on a careful understanding of what the person actually wants and can achieve. I will talk more about other therapeutic interventions in the chapter on treatment planning.

Once the focus of the patient's future is adequately defined, the next step will be to determine any obstacles to the patient's happiness. For example, if an elderly person wanted to spend the rest of his life fishing, that person may not necessarily find happiness if there are other serious conflicts in his life. The family needs to identify these conflicts or obstacles and try to find solutions to them. Family, financial and medical problems are the major areas of conflict for the elderly. Sometimes the solutions are relatively straightforward, and assistance can be provided in each of these areas. There are times when these problems are more complicated. Do not hesitate to ask for help from friends, clergy or professionals. Removing or minimizing these obstacles in a depressed person's life and defining the meaning for their life can be the real antidepressant.

ANTIDEPRESSANT MEDICATIONS

After various verbal or behavioral interventions have been tried, and the patient is still depressed, treatment with medications may be helpful. There are also those patients who are so severely depressed that medication may need to be used at the outset. This is particularly true for patients who may be acutely suicidal or so depressed that they are placing themselves in jeopardy because they are not taking care of themselves. Depressed persons, at times, will not eat because of their disturbed mood. They may become dehydrated or develop a chemical imbalance, which would place them in medical jeopardy. Sometimes depressed individuals do not care about their safety and may drive recklessly or do something else impulsive that may place them in danger. Treatment with antidepressants should be strongly considered in these cases along with careful monitoring.

There are several categories of antidepressants that are used in the treatment of despondent patients. A physician cannot predict, with 100% certainty, which antidepressant will work in a specific individual. Therefore, if one medication fails, other trials should be attempted. The doctor will usually prescribe an antidepressant that will treat certain symptoms of the patient's depression. For example, a sedating type of antidepressant will often be prescribed for nighttime use for the patient who is having a difficult time sleeping. Obviously, that medication is usually given just prior to bedtime. Sedating antidepressants can also be used for patients who are both anxious and depressed. These types of antidepressants, used with careful dosing, can calm a depressed and nervous patient. Care must be taken in their use, as they should not cause daytime sedation that would put the person at risk for accidents.

Patients who have little energy or no motivation may be given activating antidepressants, which tend to revitalize the patient, making them more energetic and animated. They are typically given in the morning to avoid late day stimulation that could interfere with their sleep.

I always give a few words of caution to the patient, as well as the family members, when starting antidepressants. First, it may take up to four to six weeks before you see any improvement. It is important to take the medication consistently as prescribed for the full trial period. Second, a minority of persons do not respond to the first medication trial. However, they will likely respond to subsequent medication attempts.

Finally, medications at times can cause significant side effects, and patients, as well as family members, must be observant so that they can be promptly identified and treated. A depressed person has a hard time dealing with any stress, let alone the side effects from the medication that is supposed to help, not harm them. If any side effects are noticed, the physician must be contacted promptly. Sometimes, adjusting the dose of the medication or its timing will improve the situation. For example, if the patient complains of sedation during the day, the drug can be taken at night. Conversely, if the medication prevents the patient from sleeping, it should be taken first thing in the morning. Lowering the amount of medication can reduce other side effects. If the basic adjustments do not work, then a different medication is an option.

Be observant during this period, as your family member starts medication. Make sure that you have identified specific signs of the patient's depression so that you could determine whether or not he or she is responding to the medication. In addition, look for any possible side effects by talking with your relative about any changes that they have noted physically or mentally. Ask about symptoms such as dizziness, constipation, shakiness, a lack of concentration, agitation etc. It is important to periodically have these discussions because some side effects may lead to disturbing consequences. For example, dizziness may increase the risk of a fall, which could lead to severe injury.

Earlier in this chapter, there was a discussion about medications that can cause depression. Older individuals tend to be on multiple medications. Therefore, the more medications one takes, the more likely one might be taking a drug that can actually cause a depression. Often a physician may discontinue a particular medication, rather than starting an antidepressant. It is then important to monitor that individual to see if the symptoms of depression are eliminated. Sometimes, it is even necessary to eliminate more than one medication to achieve a successful outcome.

The duration of time it takes to see an improvement is related to how long the offending drug remains in the system. Remember, it is important to be patient because it is better to eliminate the cause of the depression, rather than add additional medications. There are rare times when the offending medication cannot be discontinued because the patient needs it and there is no reasonable substitute. The careful use of an antidepressant in such a situation may be required.

THE NORMAL GRIEF PROCESS

Before I conclude our discussion on depression, there are two important syndromes that need to be distinguished from the depressed state that has been our focus. First, there is a condition called the grief reaction. This is a state similar to depression that occurs following the death of a loved one. Following such a loss, the surviving person can have symptoms of decreased appetite, weight loss, feelings of weakness, difficulty falling asleep and staying asleep, guilt, and, of course, sadness. As you can see, these symptoms are also seen in a depressed person. However, in a normal grief reaction, a person will initially experience a state of shock or emotional numbness. We have often heard of a person who says that, when they first heard about the death of their loved one, they could not cry or feel emotion. They may also have feelings of denial or disbelief that the person is actually dead. This usually occurs if the death happened suddenly. Later, however, they may have thoughts of the dead person and may often dream about that individual. There may even be times when these individuals believe that they hear the deceased person's voice or feel that person's presence.

The normal grief process usually lasts about six months to one year. In a minority of cases the grief reaction may persist for a longer period of time or turn into a chronic state of grief where some symptoms remain at a lower level of intensity for a number of years.

Here are some tips to help you differentiate a normal grief reaction from a depressed state. A grief stricken person normally improves as time passes. Usually, within a few months, they are eating and sleeping normally and return to the normal level of functioning without the use of antidepressants or intensive psychotherapy. The depressed individual will typically require treatment before an improvement is seen. Guilt experienced in a normal grief reaction centers on the relationship to the deceased. For example, they may feel that they could have done more for the deceased person when he or she was alive, or there was something they wanted to tell them. On the contrary, depressed persons will blame themselves for being overall worthless or bad. A depressed individual is more likely to have feelings of worthlessness, as well as an inability to function. Suicidal ideation is rare in the normal grief reaction but common in the severely depressed individual. It should be noted that persons who have a history of depressive episodes might develop a full-blown depression instead of the normal grief reaction.

It has been shown that a few counseling sessions for the bereaved can be quite helpful. Just talking about their feelings regarding the deceased individual can help them come to terms with the loss. Sometimes the survivors need to be told that angry or mixed feelings regarding the deceased are quite normal.

Self-help groups, focusing on the loss of a loved one, can also be helpful for the surviving family members. These groups offer mutual companionship as well as emotional support. Members of these groups can be in various phases of the grief process and may be able to assist the other members who are in the earlier stages of bereavement. Physicians or social workers can supply information about these groups, including contact numbers.

Another important intervention is the continued discussion of the deceased by close family members. This usually starts when the family gets together soon after the funeral service. This initial mutual support is quite helpful, particularly for those individuals who were closest to the deceased. It is also important that this conversation continues to take place over the next several weeks or months. Thus, family members will be essentially doing informal group therapy that will help with their bereavement issues.

Continued family support during the next several months and years is important, particularly around holidays and anniversaries of the loved one's passing. Visits to the cemetery, family events such as dinners, and just plain discussion regarding the loss of the family member can be quite helpful during these times. It is important for family members to support the relative who was most affected by the loss. They can help by finding other meaningful relationships and activities for this loved one. This individual needs to understand that there are other people in his or her life who are important. Even more critical is that this person comes to the understanding with the help of family or friends, that there is still substantial reason to live a meaningful life.

Most cases of a grief state are treated without medications. However, if a person is suffering from a severe emotional bereavement, tranquilizers can be given on a short-term basis in order to stabilize the person's mood. This would help that now calmer individual to deal with their loved one's death. On rare occasions, the grief state lasts for a prolonged period, or the symptoms become worse instead of better. These individuals may require psychotherapy or treatment with antidepressants. If a person does not show an improvement in their emotional state over a few months following the death of a loved one, they may need an evaluation. If an individual is so distraught following a relative's death that they are unable to function or are a danger to himself or herself, then they should receive a prompt evaluation. People who have a history of depression are much more likely to become clinically depressed following the death of a loved one and may require psychotherapy or medication. It is important to be on the lookout for this possibility.

PSEUDODEMENTIA

The final issue that that needs to be discussed in any chapter on depression in the elderly is the concept of pseudo-dementia.

Susan was a 75-year-old woman who was brought to my office by her family because they felt that she was developing Alzheimer's disease. Over the last six months the family noted that she had become extremely forgetful and was unable to concentrate. Even the simplest of decisions were very difficult for her. One of her family members stated that just thinking would make her tired. According to all of the family members, she would lie around the house most of the day in a listless manner to the point where she was no longer taking care of herself. They would often find her during their visits looking disheveled and, at times, partially dressed and starving. Her family essentially was asking me to prescribe the anti-Alzheimer's medication that they had read about. They hoped that this would prevent her from having to be placed in a nursing home. My first impression of Susan was that of a sad and lonely individual who had lost her best friend. I asked both the patient and her family about any significant events that had occurred in the last year or two. Susan told me in a slow and sad manner that her husband had died of a heart attack about 2 1/2 years ago. The family also mentioned that her 14-year-old dog had to be put to sleep about six months ago. The patient admitted that since that time she had lost all of her energy, even the energy to think. I told the family that I would like to give Susan a trial of an antidepressant. At the same time, I asked that she go to an elderly daycare program that would provide her with some daily activity. For the first couple of weeks, she sat around at the elder care center just watching the other people. By the end of the month, she claimed that her energy suddenly returned. She was now involved in numerous activities at the daycare center. In fact, she was even talking about taking a volunteer job.

It is not unusual to see a dramatic improvement in patients who have been mistakenly diagnosed as having Alzheimer's disease but are really depressed and are treated with antidepressants. Pseudo-dementia is a condition that looks like Alzheimer's disease since the predominant symptoms are related to the patient's inability to think, concentrate, or remember. In true Alzheimer's disease, a person's deficits develop gradually and slowly worsen over months or years. In a patient with pseudo-dementia, their deficits occur over days or weeks and rarely months. Once established, their symptoms remain generally the same unless treated. These patients sometimes show brief temporary improvements in their functioning, as opposed to dementia patients who do not. Depressed patients who display cognitive deficits often do not try to answer questions, stating that they are too tired or they do not know. A demented patient may try to confabulate or make up an answer.

There has been more than one medical student who has performed what is called a "mental status" examination on a patient to determine their cognitive abilities and come to the conclusion that someone is suffering from dementia when they are actually suffering from depression. This usually occurs because this examination takes place at the end of a long psychiatric assessment. By that time, the depressed patient is just too tired to think and cannot provide the correct responses. It is better to perform this mental status examination at another time, when the patient is alert and rested. It can also be a more reliable assessment when the process is carried out in divided steps, so that the depressed person does not have to think over extended periods. A demented patient will tend to give the same answers regardless of the time of day or specific conditions. Sometimes, during these examinations, the depressed patient can be taught to provide the correct responses, but the demented patient is unlikely to do the same.

Family members should try to remember these tips when they are talking to their loved one. Therefore, speak with these individuals when they are well rested and alert. Keep your interactions from being too long and tiresome. This way you will see them at their best. If you feel your loved one, who has been diagnosed as demented, has suddenly deteriorated, have them evaluated by a physician. Pseudo-dementia related to depression, as well as other treatable illnesses already discussed, could be the cause.

Patients with pseudo-dementia can have subtle signs of depression such as loneliness, withdrawn behavior, problems sleeping or eating, guilt, and, of course, sadness. These symptoms are less likely in the pure Alzheimer's patient. In my experience, it is often difficult for the layperson to clearly separate the depressed patient from the demented patient. After all, when a person is developing a dementia, they begin to realize their inability to function and become depressed because of this. Patients with early Alzheimer's disease also become depressed because they worry about their future. The bottom line is that a demented patient often will have some degree of depression, particularly in their initial stages of deterioration. Since this is such a common combination, it is not unusual for physicians to prescribe an antidepressant at least on a trial basis, to see if it improves the patient's overall mental state. While psychotherapy may be helpful in a few patients with pseudo-dementia, the proper use of antidepressants is essential.

In summary, patients who have dementia along with some signs of depression should be evaluated early on by a physician. Please do not assume that their condition is just a natural phase of growing old. Proper treatment can lead to dramatic improvement. Depression in the elderly is a treatable condition and should not be assumed to be a natural part of old age.

CHAPTER EIGHT

Treatable Geropsychiatric Syndromes

Dementia, delirium, and depression account for the large majority of behavioral problems in the elderly. However, there are still a substantial number of psychiatric illnesses that can cause significant behavior problems in the elderly. Since many of these conditions can be readily treated, they deserve their own chapter.

It was once thought that many of the psychiatric illnesses that begin at an earlier age did not occur in the elderly population. Over the last two decades there has been more study of the elderly population. We have found that many psychiatric conditions that were once thought to occur only in the younger population can sometimes first be seen in the elderly. This may be due to the fact that, during their earlier years, these individuals were able to compensate for an underlying psychiatric problem. As they grew older, these compensatory mechanisms failed, and the first signs of a full-blown mental illness became apparent. Of course, there are also older persons who have been mentally ill all of their lives and still continue to have active psychiatric problems in their later years.

Finally, there are those elder individuals who now have combinations of psychiatric conditions such as dementia in addition to their lifelong psychiatric problems. Nevertheless, many of these psychiatric problems can be effectively treated.

SCHIZOPHRENIA

We previously talked about conditions that may have been hidden at an early age only to surface later in life. The first signs of schizophrenia are not commonly seen in the elderly. Yet, when this illness occurs in an older age group, we usually see signs of this diagnosis earlier in a person's life but not to degree where it was brought to anyone's attention. These persons may have been described as eccentric or unusually withdrawn. Their social skills may have been quite poor. Family members have often said that these individuals just appeared to be different.

Once the full-blown illness occurs, these patients can have hallucinations, such as hearing voices or seeing things that are not there. They sometimes look emotionless, or at other times have a mood that does not fit with the situation. For example, they can be laughing while talking about the death of their best friend. On occasion, their speech can be incoherent, or they talk in a nonsense fashion. Often they will have delusional thinking, which means believing in something that is clearly not true. This thinking can often have a paranoid focus. For example, they might feel that the FBI or the Mafia is out to get them. A common paranoid theme in the elderly centers around the belief that a person or persons are breaking into their home to steal things. They may believe that people can read their thoughts, or that they can read other people thoughts. They sometimes think that other people can transmit thoughts into their brains. The most problematic symptom is what we call "bizarre behavior". For example, patients may undress in public for no apparent reason. Other paranoid individuals may abruptly run away, if they believe that someone is trying to come after them. For a person to be given a diagnosis of schizophrenia, they must have at least two of these symptoms I have mentioned for at least six months.

There are several types of schizophrenia. In paranoid schizophrenia, people will have delusions of being watched or that there are people out to get them. They also tend to hear voices that are confirming their paranoid ideas. For example, an 80-year-old man, who had an elderly form of schizophrenia, told me that he heard voices plotting to poison him. A disorganized type of schizophrenia is hard to distinguish from dementia because these persons have both disorganized and confused speech and behavior. When they are given anti-psychotic medications, their dementia like symptoms can be reduced. Schizophrenia of the catatonic type is seen in patients who seem to have no ability to move or have excessive activity without any purpose such as pacing in circles. Patients can have a mixture of the symptoms noted above. That condition is called an undifferentiated type of schizophrenia.

MEDICATIONS FOR SCHIZOPHRENIA

The primary treatment for patients who have schizophrenia at any age is anti-psychotic medications. Within minutes or hours these drugs can produce a calming effect, but it may take days or weeks to produce significant improvement in the symptoms of schizophrenia.

Unfortunately, these medications do not cure the illness but provide some relief from the symptoms. There is a sizable number of patients who do not readily respond to these medications, and sometimes these individuals will require multiple drug trials before seeing some improvement. There are some patients who receive no benefit from any of the anti-psychotic drugs. Another significant problem is that these medicines may cause a variety of side effects including tremor, severe muscle rigidity, sedation, abnormal muscle movements, and a life-threatening though rare illness called "neuroleptic malignant syndrome".

If one of your family members needs an anti-psychotic medication, their physician should initially follow them closely. Weekly or even daily doctor visits in the beginning are not unusual. This process is important in order to assure that no serious side effects are left untreated, particularly given the fact that side effects tend to occur more often in the elderly individual. If a person shows side effects of one medication, it does not necessarily mean they will have side effects from another. The impaired individual, as well as the family, needs to be patient because an adequate trial of these medications may last for four to six weeks or longer. If the first drug fails, then anti-psychotic medicine from another class will be used. Sometimes the physician will use a sedating anti-psychotic drug in order to help the patient sleep by prescribing it for bedtime use. Let the doctor know if your family member is having a difficult time sleeping.

Once the patient obtains significant improvement from the anti-psychotic medication, then the physician will usually lower the dose of that medication to the lowest possible level, in order to minimize the possibility of side effects. During this time, all family members need to be very observant of any changes in the patient's behavior or physical status. Anything unusual should be reported to the patient's doctor in a timely manner.

When the patient is not taking the medication specifically as prescribed by the physician, this is called noncompliance. Noncompliance is a major reason for the failure of the medication to produce symptomatic improvement. It is also the number one cause for the schizophrenic symptoms to reoccur. This is particularly important for patients with schizophrenia who have a difficult time concentrating and cannot remember to take their medications properly. Elderly people, who have a combination of dementia and schizophrenia, are at an even higher risk of taking their medications inappropriately due to problems with concentration or memory. Therefore, close monitoring of medication intake in these individuals is an essential part of treatment.

PSYCHOSOCIAL THERAPY

Along with the use of medication, the elderly patient, just like the younger patient, can benefit from psychosocial treatments.

Matilda was a 67-year-old woman, who according to her family, was always a loner. She never married, lived by herself, and worked as a proofreader for a local newspaper throughout much of her adult life. When she retired at age 65, she spent most of her time watching soap operas and talk shows. She rarely went outside of her home, and, when she did so, it was with the strong encouragement of her family. Over the past year she started to call the local police station in order to report men who were in her bedroom in the middle of the night. She never saw these men but would always hear their voices as if they were behind her. In the last few weeks she started to hear these voices periodically throughout the day, and her calls were becoming a nuisance to the local police. After taking the medication for a few weeks, the voices disappeared. However, she continued to worry that these men would come back and from time to time would call the police. After a few sessions with the patient and her family, we were able to design a series of activities, including a day program for the elderly that would keep this patient busy throughout the week. She rarely bothered the police after these other activities were established.

Psychosocial treatment involves training a person to develop appropriate social skills and behaviors with the use of positive reinforcement such as praise, privileges, or gifts. I will expound on this approach in later chapters. Family therapy, as noted in the above example, is often used as a psychosocial treatment. The elderly can also benefit from activity, occupational, group and individual therapies, particularly if there is a strong educational and social component.

DELUSIONAL DISORDER

A somewhat more common illness in the elderly is called the "delusional disorder". A person who has this syndrome does not have the other signs of schizophrenia noted above, such as hallucinations or disorganized thoughts. Their delusions are based on situations that could be real. For example, they might feel that their spouses are cheating on them, or that they are being followed. This is different from the bizarre delusions of the schizophrenic patient. An example of a bizarre delusion would be the belief that a person was a Martian sent to here to conquer the world. The schizophrenic's delusion is usually so outlandish that it could not possibly be true.

Fred was a 70-year-old man who, for the last several years, complained to his wife about the neighbors on each side of his house. He believed that they were out to harass him in order to get him to move. He would tell his wife that they would adjust their rainspouts so that the rainwater would erode his property and ruin his garden. If something happened to his property such as a tree falling or a bush dying, he would automatically blame his neighbors for poisoning their roots. Fred was not only articulate, but also sincere to the point where he convinced most people that these events were actually happening. However, if one investigated the incidents it became clear that they were just not true. Fred's wife brought him in for an evaluation because she could not stand the constant complaining about the neighbors. Unfortunately, Fred did not believe that he needed medication because he was convinced that the neighbors were the ones who had problems, not him. After a few sessions, Fred was willing to try anti-psychotic medication because we were able to convince him that it would prevent him from becoming so upset about his neighbors. We did not focus on the issue that he was delusional. His mood did improve after a few weeks, and though he still had the delusions, they did not seem to bother him as much. His complaining decreased, and his wife's mood improved.

There are a number of delusional themes seen in this disorder. One type is the grandiose delusion, where people believe that they are involved in a relationship with a famous person, such as a movie star or government official. They may write letters or send these people gifts. Another delusional theme focuses on the fact that the person has special talents or a special relationship with a private or government agency such as the FBI. One other common delusional category focuses on jealousy. An example of this is when a spouse believes that their partner is unfaithful. They will interpret indirect clues, such as a spouse being away too long shopping, and will accuse their partner of meeting with their lover.

A persecutory theme is often seen in elderly individuals. These persons believe that they are being spied on, followed, harassed, drugged, cheated, or are being exposed to some type of poison or irradiation. Unfortunately, they may act out on these delusions by suing the person they believe is the perpetrator, or they may call the police on them. On rare occasions, they might actually try to harm these individuals because they believe that these people are attempting to hurt them.

Perhaps the most common theme in the elderly person with such a disorder is the delusion that the individual has some type of illness. This is called a "somatic delusion". They may believe that they have some type of infection, cancer, or some other type of medical illness, in spite of the fact that the physical evaluation has shown no evidence of illness. They will argue that the medical tests were wrong, and they go from doctor to doctor in an attempt to validate their condition. These delusions are different from those beliefs a hypochondriac would have because a person with a delusional disorder adamantly believes that they have a specific medical condition with no evidence of any physical symptoms. A person with hypochondriasis usually feels that there is something generally wrong based on a misinterpretation of some physical symptoms. Sometimes it is difficult to make a distinction between these two conditions.

Patients with somatic delusions can be quite costly to the healthcare system. They will seek numerous medical tests to confirm something that is just not there. Once a physician tells them that there is nothing medically wrong with them, they may stop seeing that doctor and will go to another. It is important for family members to point out to the patient's doctor that the relative has been seeing numerous physicians. It is also helpful for these family members to accompany the patient to their primary care doctor, although at times the delusional individual will resist this. If this occurs, then the individuals who are most trusted by the patient should explain to their relative that they understand that there is a problem, and that they want to work with them until that problem is resolved. It is often helpful for family members to focus on the relative's emotional response, rather than to argue about the validity of their beliefs. The bottom line is that we want them to feel better.

Once the patient has received a comprehensive evaluation, and nothing is found, then it should be recommended that the patient see someone who can help them with this frustrating situation. The truth is this person actually does have a problem. A tactful primary care physician can often convince the patient to seek psychiatric counseling. Sometimes family physicians who have had extra training in psychiatry, may attempt to counsel the patient and provide them with therapy and medications that may not only help with their frustrations but also their delusions. It is also helpful for doctors, with the help of family members, to convince the patient that certain medical tests have their own risk.

TREATMENT OF DELUSIONAL DISORDER

Treating a person with delusional disorder is oftentimes difficult. The bottom line is that they do not believe they have a problem. They are extremely committed to believing their delusion, as if it were 100% reality. So, if a family member says there is something wrong with their belief, they will usually become defensive and angry in their response. In addition, many persons with this disorder do not respond to anti-psychotic medications. Because of this complication, I would like to spend more time going over the treatment of these individuals.

Jerry was a 67-year-old man who came to my office with his family members literally holding his elbows in order to bring him into the room. They told me, "They had it with him." Jerry accused his sister Sarah of stealing from him. He would call his relatives at all hours of the night complaining about his sister. Then he would go on for an extended period of time talking about why she would do this. The final straw was when Jerry refused to let Sarah come into his house. It was Sarah who cared for Jerry on a daily basis after a stroke left him paralyzed on the right side of his body. The family was not only upset about the phone calls, but also about the fact that now they had to find someone to provide for his care.

Initially, Jerry refused to talk to me, and the family members had to provide all the information. I then told Jerry that, if he chose not to talk, he would need to come back for another session to meet with me alone. During the latter half of the session, he did begin to talk with me because he did not want to meet with a psychiatrist alone, since he was not crazy. Ironically, during the last few minutes of his visit, Jerry asked his family to leave the room so that he could talk to me privately and give me his side of the story. He gave me a number of examples that, at least for him, proved that his sister was stealing. For example, Sarah would wash his clothing, and he would then find that his best shirt was missing. I told him that he did not need to prove anything to me. Instead, I told him to make a list of all of the items that he thought were stolen, and if we replaced them, he would agree to let his sister back into the home. When he came back to the second session with his list, I told him we would work on a plan with his family to restore these items. It took a few more sessions with the family and Jerry to agree that everything had been put back into place. This process was a real struggle for all concerned. While Jerry stopped the phone calls, he still insisted that his sister must have been stealing the items, even though a number of the items were found misplaced in his house. Those that were not found by the family were replaced.

A secondary issue that arose from the sessions was the fact that Sarah became overwhelmed by this caretaker role. She reported that she did not have time to take care of all his needs and look for any lost articles. We had to develop a second plan to provide Sarah with some relief from her care taking tasks. The alternative for the family was to pay a health-care professional to come in and provide the services for a rather expensive price. To avoid this choice, the family was more amenable to work with Sarah in order to relieve her of some of her duties, as well as find or replace any missing items. The family made a more cost-effective decision allowing Sarah to continue to play the major role as Jerry's caretaker. By the way, Jerry refused to take any psychiatric medications because, if he did so, everyone would think he was crazy.

As you can see, there was no perfect resolution for Jerry's case. Both sides had to reach a compromise in order to achieve some success. This is true for most cases of a delusional syndrome. The first step in dealing with a person with a delusional disorder is to avoid any arguments. These individuals are so committed to their delusion that they cannot see reality. Arguments will only lead to defensiveness, as well as hurt feelings for both sides. The best initial approach is to state to the patient that you believe they have a valid issue that needs to be investigated. Using this approach, you, along with the patient, can examine the data that lead to their belief. Try not to prove that their belief is wrong but examine the facts surrounding their delusion. Do not be judgmental but try to be as objective as possible. When open-mindedly discussing the facts with a delusional person, they may begin to consider some alternative ways of interpreting these facts.

Should the neutral approach fail after repeated attempts, then it is wise to try to reach some type of compromise with the individual. This begins with the acceptance that the patient will not change their delusion, but now they have to live with it within the conformity of society's rules. During this phase, you will need to determine who is being affected negatively by the person's delusion. In Jerry's case it was pretty clear that he was being negatively affected by his belief that his sister was stealing from him. In this type of situation it is important to ask the patient what will make this situation right. Obviously, if the individual is making demands that are unrealistic, you will need to work on some type of compromise. If Jerry wanted to have his sister charged with theft, I am sure that the family would have considered that option to be unreasonable.

At times you will have to draw the line concerning their delusional behavior, and that can be difficult. In such cases it is helpful to bring the significant family members together, along with the patient's friends, and provide a unified front in order to convince the patient that they need to be more reasonable. This should be done in a compassionate and caring way. Sometimes this is difficult because these friends and relatives may have been insulted or harassed by the delusional person. Remember, this delusional person is suffering from an illness. So, try not to take it personally. We all have feelings, and we should not feel guilty if these people upset us. I often recommend to family members, as well as friends, that they discuss their feelings with each other. Finally, it is helpful to gently confront the patient with your wishes on more than one occasion so that the individual receives a consistent message. A consistent and unified approach is often effective.

But what if this approach fails? At this point family members and friends should convey to the individual what the consequences will be, if they do not cooperate in order to resolve the problem. This family discussion should not be angry or threatening but merely an objective portrayal of what the situation will be like if nothing changes. If the individual continues to remain uncooperative during this phase, I would recommend professional intervention.

Once the delusional person becomes cooperative, it is important to outline the specific details of any compromise. Try to make the compromise a win-win situation. At the same time, you need to remember the definition of compromise, which is a process where you give up something in order to get something. Some of Jerry's family members were not happy when they had to purchase new clothing items for him. Nor were they happy when they had to conduct searches throughout his house. On the other hand, they were able to keep his sister in the home providing the daily care that he required, relieving them of this task. As I will discuss more comprehensively in a later chapter it is important to provide specific measurable details of any compromise, so that no one on either side will be able to question it at some time in the future. It can be quite helpful to put the compromise agreement in a written form.

Sometimes the compromise needs to be changed depending upon the circumstances. Some persons with delusions can be very manipulative. They will look for loopholes in compromise. A gentleman who I had seen in consultation thought that his house was being poisoned by gas, which he believed was being pumped in by his neighbor. He would often register his complaints with the local authorities. As is usual for this type of case, it was his family that brought him in for a psychiatric evaluation. After three sessions, a compromise was worked out where he would not call the police or fire department. This deal worked for a few weeks, but then the patient started to call the governor's office because he thought it was not covered by the contract that we had developed. Obviously, the compromise was changed to produce a new agreed-upon outcome. The message here is to anticipate any possible loopholes and seal them before the contract is finalized. Be as specific as possible about what is expected from both sides and, if needed, put it in writing.

Delusional patients may also believe that they have special relationships with famous individuals. They may try to contact them or stalk them. Sometimes they will break the law in order to accomplish this. It is important to point out the consequences of their actions to these individuals. In many instances, this will stop the inappropriate behavior, but there are certain occasions in which the delusional individual believes that he or she is not breaking the law because they truly believe that people just don't understand that special relationship. In order to avoid legal charges, family members may need to limit the patient's access to these famous persons. Examples of this would be taking away a patient's car or disconnecting their phone service. Before taking such extreme measures, it is wise to consult not only a physician, but also a lawyer.

At times the judgment of delusional patients is so impaired that they may place themselves in dangerous situations. Paranoid individuals may strike out first, believing that they are actually protecting themselves. Patients with somatic delusions may become so depressed, because no illness can be found, that they consider suicide. In such situations it is important for family members to seek help for their loved one immediately. Because of the importance of this issue, a later chapter in the book will provide a comprehensive discussion of dangerous behaviors.

ANXIETY DISORDER

Anxiety disorders are commonly seen in the elderly. These disorders are usually seen following a loss or a change in the person's life. The person who has recently retired or has experienced the death of a loved one surely has some reason to be anxious due to the significant change in their life. This is particularly true if the person has been dependent on their spouse in order to help them function in their life.

Irene was a 78-year-old woman whose husband, Charles, took care of her every need, since she was disabled with arthritis. He would shop for groceries, cook, and handle all of the bills. When her husband died, she said that she literally fell apart. The family doctor gave her some tranquilizers to help with her anxiety, but she started to develop an addiction to these medications. Her family became upset because either she was very anxious, or sedated by the medications. With the help of her family, we were able to develop a plan to handle many of her physical needs, which alleviated much of her anxiety. At the same time, we were able to taper off the addicting medications and replace them with ones that had fewer side effects. As time passed, and with some family therapy, Irene was able to trust that her family would take care of her and ultimately discontinued all psychiatric medications with continued success.

A brief period of counseling and family support is usually all that is needed to calm an anxious older person. Tranquilizers should only be used for a brief period of time, and only if the anxiety is so severe that it is disabling to the individual. Long-term use of these medications in some instances can be more harmful than the condition they were intended to treat. So, please, do not be upset if your family member is not initially given medication for their anxiety when they see their family doctor.

Family members and friends can provide the support and counseling needed, often without the help of a professional. Gentle reassurance by a relative or friend can be quite helpful to the anxious person. It is also important to find out specifically what is making the person anxious. In Irene's case she thought that she simply could not handle what her husband had done for her over the years. Once the problem was resolved, she was no longer anxious. Older people with this disorder often worry about the simplest of problems. They can be upset if they cannot go out and get their groceries or drive the car to visit friends. With the support of family and friends to help them take care of these activities, their anxiety can be dramatically reduced.

There are cases, however, when the simple problems are resolved but the person remains quite anxious for no apparent reason.

Hilda had a heart attack at age 75 and came into my office a year later complaining of extreme anxiety. Her family members were caring individuals who were able to help her with all of her needs. Hilda made it a point to explain to me how helpful her family has been over the last year. In spite of their support, she still thought that she was on the verge of dying. Her cardiologist reassured her that she had recovered almost completely from that heart attack, and she should not be afraid. Her son, who was also a physician, tried to explain to her that she should go on with her life and not worry about another heart attack. Hilda still remained very anxious. During the initial session she said she had been healthy her entire life. She said that she never had a broken bone or required any stitches. Her heart attack was devastating. At the same time she told me that, in spite of that event, she had recovered physically and had been performing all of the functions that she had done prior to her heart attack. I saw Hilda for a few more sessions, and we talked about her confronting death for the first time in her life, since her mother had died of a heart attack when Hilda was only fourteen. She said she felt helpless back then and was always worried that someone else in her family would die from an early heart attack. A year ago, her worries intensified to the point where all she could think about was the possibility that she might die. It took some time before she truly understood that everyone must face death. More importantly, she also came to the understanding that she needed to face the rest of her life within the context that she, like all of us, will die eventually. Once she came to terms with this inevitability her anxiety decreased substantially.

Older folks with an anxiety disorder commonly have the theme of death as their focus. In contrast, younger individuals, particularly teenagers, almost never think about death. It happens to someone else. As we grow older and our friends and family members pass away, we realize that we are now part of that age group and must deal with our mortality. This, as one would expect, is a complicated issue, and counseling should be individualized, based on the patient's past experiences with death. Important questions to answer are as follows. What deaths did the person experience in the past and how did they handle it? Did the person have a near death experience such as a serious accident or illness? How did they handle it? Similar questions are useful in order to determine the patient's understanding of death.

Knowledge of a person's individual beliefs regarding religion and death are also important in helping the patient deal with his mortality. As we come to terms with our mortality we become less anxious and can live a fuller life. For ages, dealing with our ultimate demise has been the subject of discussion and anxiety, especially among older individuals. As the writer, Ram Dass, stated in eloquent terms, "Death is the wake-up call, the unavoidable mandate, that makes enlightenment possible, and helps our souls to grow." This is what Plato, when asked on his deathbed for one final word of advice, responded to one of his pupils, "Practice dying."

Family members or friends who have experienced death in the past can be a helpful support for the person whose anxiety is based on this mortality issue. Talking with the anxious individual about his understanding of death can be helpful in reducing anxiety. It is also important to point out to this person that the family members, friends, and other concerned individuals are there to help with their feelings and concerns. The fact that this person is not alone is often times quite reassuring. We all must deal with our mortality and even famous people are not exempt from their destiny. Even actress Bette Davis realized that "old age ain't for sissies."

In summary, when dealing with a person who has an anxiety disorder, identify the reason for the anxiety, eliminate the cause, if possible, and provide support and reassurance. If this simple approach fails, then consult a health-care provider who is skillful in counseling.

PANIC ATTACKS

Another complication of anxiety is called a "panic attack". The symptoms of a panic attack include heart palpitations, an increased heart rate, sweating, shaking, a feeling of shortness of breath or smothering, a choking sensation, and chest pain or tightness. Other symptoms include nausea, abdominal distress, feeling dizzy or lightheaded, numbness or tingling of the hands or feet, chills, hot flushes, and most importantly, a fear of dying or losing control.

One of the main concerns for the elderly is that a panic attack simulates a heart attack. This is particularly a problem for the individual who had a heart attack and is worrying about having another. Many elderly patients brought to the emergency room with symptoms of a heart attack are found to have a panic disorder. It is necessary to conduct a thorough evaluation in order to make sure that the individual does not have any cardiac problems before making a diagnosis of a panic disorder. Even if the patient has been diagnosed as having panic attacks in the past, it would still be wise to evaluate that person to make sure they do not have a heart problem. Some persons feel they are able to differentiate between a panic attack and a heart attack, but unless a thorough evaluation is conducted, one cannot be sure.

In some instances, a trigger for the panic attack can be identified. There are a number of medications that may cause a panic attack as a side effect. A physician consultation may be very helpful in identifying the offending drug. Caffeine is a commonly used chemical in many food products that has been associated with panic attacks. Medical conditions such as low blood sugar or thyroid problems can also precipitate a panic attack. There are actually numerous medications, as well as medical problems, that are associated with panic attacks. It is important particularly for an elderly person to obtain a thorough physical evaluation in order to make sure they do not have an underlying medical condition as a cause for the panic. If no physical causes are found, then the diagnosis of panic disorder is made and specific treatment can be provided.

There are numerous non-addictive medications that can be used in the treatment of a panic disorder. A physician can outline the positive benefit as well as potential side effects of these medications and choose the one that best fits the patient's needs. Tranquilizers can be used in order to help in the acute phase of a panic attack but should be limited to short-term use because of their addictive nature. Antidepressants are often used with reasonable success in this disorder. Unfortunately, a trial of one medication may not work and the person may need to try a drug from a completely different category. Friends and family members can be helpful during this time of medication trials by providing support and reassurance to their loved one.

There are also various styles of therapy that can be used in treating a person with a panic disorder. These therapies can focus on helping the patient relax or identifying triggers in the person's environment that lead to panic attacks. People closest to the patient can be helpful in identifying these triggers. Educating a person about panic attacks is often helpful in reducing the frequency and intensity of these attacks in the future. Therapy is particularly helpful for the patient who is nervous about having another panic attack. Breathing into a paper bag for several seconds can sometimes shorten a panic attack.

There has been controversy about whether medications or therapy are best suited for the treatment of the panic attack. My suggestion would be if one approach does not work after a fair trial, then try the other approach. It is generally accepted that a combination of therapy and medication is most useful for persons with a severe panic disorder.

AGORAPHOBIA

Another mental health problem in the elderly is "agoraphobia". This is a condition where a person avoids certain situations in which they feel anxious and helpless. Sometimes they will avoid busy streets, crowded stores or closed-in spaces. In extreme cases these individuals do not want to leave their house. Elderly persons are particularly susceptible to this condition, because as they get older and become more fragile, they do not feel that they can handle outside situations. They become fearful and anxious and want to leave as soon as possible. Panic attacks commonly occur when an individual is exposed to these situations.

Agoraphobia can be quite problematic for family members or friends of the patient. It is not unusual for the person with this disorder to expect their loved ones to accompany them when going into fearful situations. In fact, they may insist that every time they leave the house, they can only do so in the company of a friend or relative. After a while, this may cause some conflict among the various individuals. As a result, it is not unusual for the friend or family member to bring the patient in for an evaluation because of their frustration with this behavior.

Beatrice was a 77-year-old woman who had extensive arthritis. She had fallen on a couple of occasions and developed severe anxiety about going out into public places where she felt she might injure herself. Finally, she would not leave her house unless she had the assistance of one of her children. Over time, they were becoming frustrated because of her excessive dependence on them and brought her in to see me. After obtaining some clinical history, I found out that she had been plagued with her arthritis over the last 10 years. When she saw her family doctor, she tended to downplay her symptoms because she felt he did not want to hear about an old woman's aches and pains. Because of that, her doctor only prescribed aspirin. I also found out that her older sister, who also suffered from arthritis, fell and broke her hip five years ago while waiting for a bus. Thus, Beatrice became very panicky when she had to go outside, fearing that the same thing would happen to her. The first intervention was to have Beatrice evaluated by a specialist in arthritis, a rheumatologist. She prescribed a medication that alleviated much of Beatrice's pain. Then, Beatrice and I talked about her fears of becoming like her sister, who was bedridden following her broken hip. Once Beatrice was able to understand that her staying at home was almost like being bedridden, she was willing to take the risk of going outside. She actually realized that her real fear was being isolated in her home like her sister. Her family also provided her with a cell phone with their numbers programmed in so she could reach them easily if she had an accident while out in the community. The combination of all these interventions helped Beatrice function at the level she had several years earlier.

When you think about it agoraphobia is a pretty easy disorder to develop in the elderly, particularly as they become more fragile. Neurologic disorders, arthritis, cardiac problems, and other medical conditions can cause a person to worry excessively about how they will function in the community. These individuals are also at risk due to the malevolent people in the community who will take advantage of them. It is not surprising that older persons are reluctant to leave their home and then develop symptoms of agoraphobia.

Sherman was an 82-year-old man who lived for over 60 years in what was at one time a fashionable neighborhood. Unfortunately, over the decades the neighborhood became rundown, but Sherman refused to leave. It was now an area where drug addicts congregated. Sherman always liked sitting on his porch watching the activities of the neighborhood. He was now afraid to leave his house or even sit outside because he had received a threatening note accusing him of spying and calling the police. Together with his family, we explained to him that it was unsafe for him to live in his neighborhood. With some encouragement we were able to convince him to visit a senior citizen housing project. With more encouragement, we were able to convince him to move to that senior housing.

Sherman, like many older individuals, had legitimate reason to fear going into the community. It would be difficult to diagnose these people with a true agoraphobia, since their anxiety is justified. Sherman's case is not uncommon because many older individuals do not want to leave their home where they have been living for many years. It is helpful for family members to encourage these individuals to visit other possible placements and show them the advantages of moving. I will admit that this is often easier said than done.

There are three general ways to help a person with agoraphobia. The first way is to treat the panic or anxiety with medication or therapy, or combination of both so that the person is not so upset when they go into fearful situations. The second intervention is to remove the risk factor, which is upsetting the patient. In the case of Beatrice, we were able to remove much of her arthritis pain so that she would not worry so much about falling. In Sherman's case, we were able to remove him from a risky environment. There is usually a readily identifiable risk factor that concerns the patient, and sometimes it can be corrected with a modest amount of effort.

The situation becomes more complicated when there are multiple risk factors. Obviously, correcting these factors will take much more effort and time. Professional counseling or seeking help through a support group is, at times, necessary to resolve some of these more complicated problems. These services may also be needed for the third intervention that is required to treat agoraphobia, which is called "in-vivo exposure technique". In this process, the patient is exposed on an increasing basis to the feared stimulus or situation, while at the same time trying to remain calm through some relaxation method, such as slow deep breathing. There are various relaxation tapes, available in bookstores, which can help with this latter procedure. For example, you might need to start with your relative imagining being in the particular stressful situation and then trying to relax. Let's say an older man becomes panicky when he is in a crowded situation. If he is anxious just by thinking about going into a crowded situation, then he will need to learn to relax while thinking about that situation first. Once that is accomplished, he can then go to a crowded situation but stay there for a short length of time. If he can relax during that process, then he can start spending an increasing amount of time in the crowded situation before leaving. That person will need to learn to relax for shorter periods of exposure to the fearful situation before being exposed to longer periods. As the process goes on, you can slowly increase the amount of time that the individual can handle. A successful outcome occurs when the patient no longer worries about spending any time in the problematic situation. Most mental-health professionals can provide the expert consultation needed to carry out this treatment technique.

OBSESSIVE COMPULSIVE DISORDER

Obsessive-compulsive disorder is another type of mental disorder in the elderly. An obsession is a repetitive and intrusive thought, feeling, or sensation. A compulsion is a repetitive behavior, such as checking or counting. Obsessive-compulsive disorder usually begins at an early age but becomes particularly problematic as a person grows older. We all have heard of the cultural stereotype that older persons are set in their ways. A person who has had obsessive-compulsive disorder over many decades is

difficult to treat because certain elderly individuals tend
not to like change.

Margaret was a 71-year-old woman who was formerly a
registered nurse. She washed her hands approximately 20
to 30 times per day. She lived with her husband and did not
have many visitors. Nevertheless, she was fearful of germs
and continued to wash her hands numerous times per day
to the point where her aging skin was starting to break
down. In fact, by the time I saw her she was hardly able
to use her hands to eat or dress because of this condition.
She had seen numerous therapists in the past, as well as
psychiatrists who prescribed multiple medication trials.
As she started to get older, her hands just could not take the
excessive washings. In collaboration with a dermatologist
we were able to get her to substitute the use of hand creams
for the hand-washing episodes. This helped to soothe and
heal her hands. In fact, we were able to have her substitute
the cream use for her hand washing. It was still a struggle
trying to get her to reduce the hand washing because she
had done it all of her life. This treatment intervention
was only somewhat successful, for even with continued
treatment; her hand condition still flares up from time to
time because of this repetitive behavior.

There are numerous medications that can be helpful
for a person with obsessive-compulsive disorder. Some of
these choices include the newer antidepressants that can be
quite effective in controlling these repetitive behaviors. In
serious cases of obsessive-compulsive disorder, however,
psychotherapy is required. Sometimes family therapy
is needed because the relatives are frustrated with the
patient's behaviors. While family members can make
some suggestions in order to help the patient avoid the
repetitive behaviors, it is not helpful to argue. It is also not
helpful to force the individual to change. You must realize

that the person with a compulsion has an uncontrollable urge to complete the activity. This is an illness, and they are not doing it to deliberately harm or harass anyone.

PERSEVERATION

Another symptom similar to a compulsive behavior is called perseveration. Perseveration is a repeated act due to a neurologic disorder. One might see this symptom in dementia, brain damage, or as a result of a medical illness that is affecting the brain. Medication for obsessive-compulsive behavior is not usually effective for this type of condition. Traditional psychotherapy is often not helpful. Sometimes one can find a medical cause, and if that medical illness can be treated, the perseveration may decrease.

Perseveration is like a short circuit in the brain where the brain has a difficult time moving on to another circuit and, consequently, another behavior. This causes the person to repeat the same behavior over and over again. Some examples would include wiping a counter repeatedly or pacing from room to room. Like in obsessive-compulsive disorder, it is not helpful to argue with the person or get upset with them. This could actually cause other problems. Sometimes these repetitive behaviors can be stopped if you give the person something similar to do that is simple and more productive. For example, if someone is pacing aimlessly then you can gently take the person by the arm, go for a short walk and eventually hand him or her a mop with which to clean. Sometimes a simple distraction can help. If a person is constantly moaning, try singing or whistling a song to get their attention and stop their behavior. The key is to substitute a similar but more productive behavior. It is important that the person perform something useful or helpful so that they can feel needed.

HYPOCHONDRIASIS

Another common diagnosis seen in elderly is "hypochondriasis". An individual with this disorder is preoccupied with the fear of having a serious disease based on a misinterpretation of the person's symptoms. People with this illness are upset because they believe something is seriously wrong with them to the point where it causes impairment in their functioning. Even though their physical symptoms may be minimal and doctors reassure them that there's nothing seriously wrong, they cannot believe it.

Dora was referred to me by her primary care doctor because she felt she had a brain tumor. She had received a thorough neurologic evaluation, but there was no evidence that anything was wrong with her brain. She had also been seen by a number of specialists, but there was no confirmation of her brain tumor. Instead, they diagnosed arthritis in her neck that may be causing some spasms resulting in a headache. The more they tried to convince her that she did not have brain tumor, the more she believed that they were wrong. Just prior to seeing me, she was referred to a pain clinic in order to help treat the headache. She did not cooperate with the staff at the pain clinic because she felt that they were going to hide the pain, which would prove that she had a tumor. After a great deal of encouragement, she was able to come in to see me for an evaluation. I pointed out to her that I was not going to perform another neurologic evaluation but would try to help with her frustration about the fact that no one would believe that she had a brain tumor.

While she was initially hesitant, she was ultimately able to tell me about all of the problems that this fear of a brain tumor had caused her. For example, she stated that she would never bend over, fearing that the tumor would rupture and kill her. She also stopped any strenuous activities fearing that the tumor would burst. I was never able to convince her that she did not have brain tumor. Instead, I told her that I would recommend an evaluation every six months, which seemed to calm her to some extent. Obviously the evaluations were kept at a basic level and did not require many expensive tests. I also asked her to gradually increase her activities to see if her pain also increased. With repeated encouragement and family monitoring we were able convince her do a few more tasks each week. Within a few months she was able to resume most of her previous activities.

Essentially, I helped her believe that we were keeping an eye on her condition so that it would never get to the point where it was untreatable or dangerous. Since she had seen so many other doctors before me, I knew it was fruitless to try to convince her that nothing was wrong. If I did so, she would probably have continued her doctor shopping. As a result, we minimized her unnecessary tests, and she was able to develop a supportive relationship with me that helped calm her fears. Family members and friends can take this same approach.

Hypochondriacal patients are usually reluctant to seek therapy. Family members can be very frustrated because the person's lack of functioning places more of a burden on them. As in the delusional disorder, it is useless to argue with the individual. It is better to provide them with the support that they need in order to handle their anxiety about their disorder. At the same time, family members should encourage the patient to take small steps in order to increase their activity.

Sometimes hypochondriasis is secondary to some other mental illness that can be treated. Persons with depression or anxiety disorder can also have exaggerated physical fears. If one can successfully treat the depression or anxiety, the physical fears may disappear.

BIPOLAR DISORDER

Bipolar disorder is another mental illness that is seen in the elderly. Typically, the older person has already been given a diagnosis of bipolar disorder at an earlier age. It is relatively rare that this diagnosis is made for the first time in the elderly. A person with this illness in the acute stage has a decreased need for sleep and is often quite distractible. They speak at a fast pace and oftentimes cannot stop talking. They think very highly of themselves. Frequently, they complain of thoughts racing through their mind. These individuals will have an increase in activity such as staying up all night and cleaning their house. They also can be very agitated or irritable to the point where family and friends do not want to be around them. They can have episodes of impulsive behavior such as gambling, buying sprees and foolish investments.

The elderly person with bipolar disorder will more often show symptoms such as distractibility, impulsiveness, decreased sleep, and irritability. These are symptoms of what is known as a manic episode. Sometimes these episodes alternate with periods of depression.

Relatives and friends are usually already aware of the fact that the affected individual has a bipolar disorder.

Treatment with medications such as mood stabilizers is almost always needed to help the person with this illness. A psychiatrist should be consulted. Because the irritable and impulsive behaviors can cause serious conflict among the person's relatives, family therapy is often helpful in order to reduce any animosity. Noncompliance with treatment is also seen as a part of this disorder. This is another issue that requires family involvement.

SUBSTANCE ABUSE IN THE ELDERLY

Alcohol and drug abuse commonly occur in the elderly. About 7% of men and 2% of women over 65 years of age are heavy drinkers. This means that they drink almost every day and are intoxicated a few times a month. Older persons, like younger individuals, try to hide the fact that they are abusing alcohol. Family members need to be observant for the warning signs of this abuse. The smell of alcohol is the most obvious sign. Sometimes, perfumes, mouthwash, or breath mints are used to hide this odor. Slurred speech, incoordination, unsteady walking, and impairment in memory or attention are often seen during an intoxicated state. Other signs include sleepy or lethargic behavior, impaired judgment, or inappropriate social functioning. Common findings in the elderly who moderately abuse alcohol are periods of confusion that come and go for no apparent reason.

Raymond, a 74-year-old man, was brought to my office by his family because they felt he was showing signs of dementia. The family noticed that he was more confused on weekends when they came to visit. Raymond only admitted that he had a glass of wine at night to help him sleep. After I noticed Raymond's heavy use of after-shave lotion and hand tremors, I asked the family to search his house in order to find anything that might be affecting his thinking. After they went through his entire house they could find nothing. The family as a whole started to monitor Raymond's behavior more closely. A week later Raymond's younger brother took out the trash during a visit. In one trash can he found numerous empty beer bottles; in the other trash can he found about 40 unopened bottles. Later, Raymond admitted that one of his best friends would buy him a case of beer every Friday, which he would try to drink over the next few days.

Many people who abuse alcohol start at an early age. It is not rare that drinking can begin in an elderly individual. After retirement, a person can have less structure in their lives, and they may turn to alcohol to fill the void. An older person can use alcohol to treat anxiety, depression or a grief reaction. Raymond started his drinking after he joined a social club. When he was no longer able to attend because of his arthritis, his friends brought the beer to him.

Alcohol abuse in the elderly can have many detrimental effects. Older persons are frequently on several medications. Combining alcohol and medications can cause severe side effects. For example, there are a number of medications that have sedation as a side effect. Certain over-the-counter cold medications, as well as anti-anxiety agents, combined with alcohol can produce severe sedation, which can result in falls or other more serious accidents. This can lead to injuries in frail older persons, causing broken hips or blood clots in the brain. Even when an older person is drinking a limited amount of alcohol, one can still have severe side effects in combination with certain medications. It is important for family members and friends to educate their loved ones about this consequence.

Some older folks do not understand that they cannot drink the same amount of alcohol as they could when they were younger. Alcohol has a more profound effect on our body as we age. It can cause an acute delirium or a chronic dementia, as well as problems with depression, anxiety, sexual functioning, and sleep. Alcohol is also associated with numerous medical problems including liver and stomach problems.

ALCOHOL WITHDRAWAL

The abrupt discontinuation of alcohol can have life-threatening side effects. Signs of alcohol withdrawal include anxiety, tremor, and restlessness. An individual in withdrawal can also complain of a stomach ache, nausea, vomiting, hallucinations, sweating, a racing heart, and facial flushing. This withdrawal is commonly known as "delirium tremens" or "DT's." The possibility that this could occur in an older individual is twice that of a younger person. In some cases, a person in withdrawal can have a seizure, which can lead to serious injury. Delirium tremens in the elderly can be a deadly condition.

Confusion is often the first sign in an elderly person who is coming off of alcohol. If you feel that someone is having an acute withdrawal from alcohol, that person should be taken to an emergency room immediately. It is important that they be observed for an extended period of time, because alcohol withdrawal in the elderly can start later than in a younger person and may take a longer time to resolve. In addition, the elderly individual in withdrawal has a higher risk of severe complications. As you may recall from the chapter on delirium, any abrupt change in the person's mental state requires an immediate evaluation.

Once you find that a family member has problems with alcohol, there are a number of interventions that can be made. The first is education. There are numerous books available that discuss alcohol abuse and its consequences. It is more helpful, however, to speak to your loved one in person. Literature is also available through Alcoholics Anonymous, an organization available in almost any community. You can find them in your local phone book. I usually advise family members to do the reading, and then try to educate their loved one in a deliberate and caring way. If the person has only recently started abusing alcohol, they need to be told that older individuals have a difficult time handling that substance. The effects of alcohol during intoxication are more pronounced and potentially more dangerous. They need to be told about the alcohol and drug interactions that we have discussed previously. Finally, they need to be educated about the effects that alcohol has on other bodily organs such as the liver, which can cause severe medical problems in the elderly.

I do not mean to sound as though alcohol should be prohibited in the elderly. Nevertheless, it is important to stress that alcohol does carry a higher risk of problems in the elderly and should be used cautiously.

If the person does not cooperate with their family's advice and educational efforts, then outside help should be sought. You should also seek outside expertise for patients who have a long history of alcoholism and are now in their later years. Alcoholics Anonymous is a voluntary organization of persons with alcohol-related disorders. There is a nationwide network of these groups. They conduct regular supportive group therapy sessions for persons with alcohol problems.

Al-Anon is an organization similar to Alcoholics Anonymous. They are support groups made up of family members who have a difficult time dealing with a relative with an alcohol problem. They provide, not only group support, but also educational interventions for family members. Their focus is not only on the alcoholic, but also on the family member, so that they can help them continue living a productive life.

Sometimes an older person refuses to seek help. The previously mentioned organizations are helpful in providing techniques in order to bring the alcohol abuser in for treatment. For example, there are family interventions that are facilitated by AA members, in order to confront the patient with his illness in a caring manner and encourage him to get help. In my experience, the downside of these organizations is the fact that they have relatively few groups geared toward the elderly who abuse alcohol.

Other treatment techniques include behavior therapy that can be conducted by an expert in this area, usually a psychologist or drug treatment counselor. They will work with alcohol abusers and, at times, family members to develop a plan to encourage the patient to stop the alcohol use by eliminating the triggers to the persons drinking. Local psychological associations and alcoholism treatment groups can be a referral source for these experts.

Lastly, a number of older people use alcohol to treat a mental disorder. Persons may use alcohol as a sedative in order to calm their anxiety. Other individuals may use alcohol in order to numb their feelings, particularly if they are depressed or have suffered a loss of a loved one. Older persons, who use alcohol in order to decrease their irritability, may actually become angrier when they drink. However, because of the alcohol influence on their brain they perceive themselves as being calm and reasonable.

Family members must observe how alcohol is affecting their loved one. They must be aware of any changes in the patient's life such as a loved one's passing. Talking directly with the troubled individual is often helpful, when done in a gentle manner, in order to find out if there is any cause for their drinking. Care should be taken that one does not focus just on the alcohol use for fear that an argument will develop. It would be a mistake to only talk about how the person's alcohol use is affecting people around him or her. Make sure that the individual is truly aware that you are concerned about him or her.

Lenora was a 68-year-old woman who came into my office accompanied by her family because they were concerned about her excessive alcohol use. According to Lenora, her family was the problem because they were always on her back about her drinking and never seemed to care about her. She claimed that the only time they ever paid attention to her was when she had an accident at her workplace as a result of her drinking. This resulted in a family intervention in order to get her into treatment. She felt they resented this. In this case, Lenora was right. As the story unfolded, the family could only focus on how Lenora's drinking impacted them. They were so frustrated with her alcohol abuse that they could not get off that topic. When I talked with the family separate from Lenora, I was able to help them understand that they were in a vicious cycle. I reassured them that it was certainly upsetting to see a family member cause so much frustration. Yet, at the same time I was able to point out to them that their approach of venting their anger toward their mother was not productive. It only left both parties more frustrated. After the family was able to let out their anger, which took some time, they were able to work on a plan to help their mother. The plan included making a compromise list of goals that both Lenora and her family members needed to achieve, in order to maintain harmony and decrease her drinking. For example, Lenora expected to see her grandchildren twice a week. In exchange, her relatives expected to visit her four times a week to check if there were any alcoholic beverages around and she promised not to complain about this oversight. As a result of this compromise, her drinking substantially decreased.

Families can be especially helpful in the treatment of alcohol abuse. They can provide support and education, and play an integral part in the treatment plan to reduce their relative's substance abuse. If the first few simple interventions fail, do not hesitate to consult an expert in alcohol abuse by contacting one of the organizations mentioned above.

MEDICATION ABUSE

One of the most misunderstood problems in the elderly is their own version of drug abuse. The elderly do not typically abuse illegal substances such as heroine or cocaine. Instead, they misuse over-the-counter and prescription drugs. I believe that this is a more widespread problem than previously thought. Over the years, I have seen far too many elderly individuals who mix their medications without the guidance of a physician. They may also use medications from their friends or relatives in order to treat their illnesses on their own. Also, they may combine prescription medications with over-the-counter medications, which can cause a serious reaction. Some elderly persons will go from doctor to doctor in order to get the medications that they want. Thus, an older person can obtain numerous medications that they do not need and can accidentally take.

Elderly people do not typically use medications in order to get high. Many misuse medications in order to treat some type of perceived illness or symptom.

Georgia was a 71-year-old woman who came into the emergency room when I was a resident on call. She was in a delirious state. The family noticed that she could not recognize them and was talking gibberish. After a careful physical examination and history, we were able to determine that Georgia had been using over-the-counter cold medications in order to help her sleep. One of the family members went back to her home and found a receipt for an antihistamine that she had purchased about a week ago. They also found a bottle of that medication, which was a third empty, indicating that she had used approximately 10 pills over that seven-day period. At first, the family thought that she had taken a deliberate overdose in order to kill herself. Georgia quickly responded to the supportive treatment provided in the emergency room, and her mental state cleared within several hours. Once Georgia was able to provide a coherent history, she told me that she had been having a problem getting to sleep. A friend of hers recommended that she take this antihistamine, because that friend found it useful when she had insomnia. After the first few days, Georgia doubled the dose because she was not sleeping the eight hours that she expected. She could not remember what happened the day that she was admitted into the emergency room. Fortunately, Georgia did not suffer any serious medical consequences in the long run. She did consult her family physician for the proper treatment of her insomnia.

The misuse of medications seems to be a cultural phenomenon in certain elderly individuals. Doctor visits and prescription medications can be quite expensive, even if the patient has medical insurance. Transportation to a doctor's office can be costly and at times difficult to arrange. So, it is not hard to understand how the elderly come to the conclusion that just trying a medication from a friend would not be that bad. After all, the medication worked for them.

Believe it or not, some elderly individuals treat themselves with medications so that do they do not have to admit to their family physician that they have a certain problem. A friend of mine asked me to talk to his mother because she had been trying to treat her depression with a nasal decongestant. In the past, she realized that when she used this medication for a cold it gave her more energy. She did not want her family doctor to know that she was depressed because she thought it would be embarrassing for him to know that she was crazy. After I provided this lady with information regarding depression in the elderly, she was willing to try an antidepressant that ultimately helped her.

It is not unusual for elderly individuals to be ashamed if they have some type of emotional problem. Older persons with anxiety, dementia, or depression often are afraid to admit this to their physician for fear that they will be considered crazy. So, they may try an over-the-counter remedy or a medication from a friend.

Some older folks are embarrassed to admit to problems with sexual dysfunction or personal hygiene such as a fungal infection under the breast or other illnesses that will reflect poorly on the individual, at least in the individual's mind. Sometimes older persons will use homemade remedies passed down from generation to generation to treat certain conditions. Herbal medications are now seen as a panacea for numerous maladies. They are not without side effects and, at times, serious side effects. Just because herbal remedies are natural, does not mean that they are safe.

Another person's medication, over-the-counter drugs and herbal remedies can all interact with each other to cause significant medical, as well as, psychiatric problems. This might be good time to review the chapters on delirium and dementia. These two categories of mental illness are often related to drug interactions. If you see you relative's mental state abruptly change with symptoms that include confusion, hallucinations, emotional instability, or cognitive decline, you should promptly have that person evaluated by a physician.

It is important for at least one family member to be aware of what medications that person is taking. Try to do this when your older family member is in a stable and talkative condition. This is much more difficult to do when this individual is in a crisis or a confused state. In fact, information obtained during that time may be far from accurate.

Do not always assume that what is in the medicine cabinet is all that is available to the individual. An older person may be embarrassed to display what he or she is taking. For example, if they are taking a medication from a friend that is to help with their sexual desire, they are most likely not going to leave it in the medicine cabinet for anyone to see. They are probably going to hide it. Therefore, someone in the family needs to have a frank discussion with the elder family member regarding the exact amount and type of medications they are taking. That person would also need to explain what exactly is meant by a medication. Some elderly persons consider a medication to be a drug that is prescribed by a physician. They feel over-the-counter medications and herbal remedies do not count. In this discussion, over-the-counter medication and herbal remedies do count and are important to know.

It is a good idea for that responsible family member to communicate this list of medications to the person's family physician. Handing over the list in a written form is the most helpful way to ensure that there are no errors. In fact, it is even more efficient to have a number of copies of this list for the various health-care providers. It is also important to update this list periodically, particularly after the family member has visited a physician or other health care provider. Keep this list, as well as other important health documents, in a folder that is easily accessible to the patient and other family members. This folder should hold items such as health insurance forms, legal papers, such as power of attorney, and names and numbers of individuals to be contacted in case of emergency. Store a number of copies of these important documents in the folder so that you can readily hand them out to healthcare providers who need them. Keeping these documents in one place will save you time and hassle in the future.

If it is possible, put all of this information on your personal computer. This way you can easily store, change, and print out these lists whenever you need them. Always keep a paper copy as a back up in case you run into computer problems.

As I said in earlier chapters, it is important to establish relationships with older family members. If you have a good connection with them, then they can be open and honest about anything that might embarrass them. A frank, yet sensitive conversation regarding issues that might be troubling them can prevent trouble down the road. Offer to go with them to meet with their family physician or health care provider, so that you can help them discuss their issues and provide additional information. If your family member feels it is awkward for you to accompany them, then help them get their story together ahead of time. The ideal way to do this is to write down the patient's concerns or problems, a brief summary of their medical history, and a comprehensive list of their medications including doses and the time of the day that they take the medications. They can take this written document to their health care provider so that a proper evaluation and diagnosis can be obtained.

As you jointly put together the above documents, you can help educate your family member regarding the proper use of medication, so that elderly drug abuse will be minimized, reducing potentially serious side effects. Do not hesitate to firmly, but diplomatically, tell your elderly family member to only take the medications that had been prescribed or recommended by their family doctor. Also, you should tell them that they should not go from doctor to doctor asking for different medications. If a referral to a consultant is needed, such as a cardiologist or neurologist, the family physician can coordinate that referral, so that there is one person, the family practitioner, who is tracking all of the medications and therapeutic interventions. This will substantially reduce the possibility of medication interactions and potentially dangerous side effects. I would also recommend that one pharmacy track all the prescription medications that the patient is taking. Pharmacists have computer programs that can monitor the medications that person is taking. These programs can warn the pharmacist of any potential side effects or drug interactions. As you can see, communication with healthcare providers, as well as communication amongst family members, is important in helping the older individual maintain their health and well being. Make this a top priority as you help your loved one get the proper care.

CHAPTER NINE
Personality Problems

Personality disorders are commonly overlooked as a cause of behavioral problems in the elderly. This may be due to a lack of research regarding personality traits in the elderly. There is also the possibility that we do not want to place negative labels on older people. In simple terms, a person's personality is made up of a pattern of character traits that help them interact with their environment, as well as their inner spirit.

It appears that an individual's personality develops as a combination of genetic predisposition, as well as environmental factors. Personality development begins on day one. Ask any mother who has more than one child. She will be able to tell you what type of personality each child had as an infant. Those traits continue to develop and mature as one grows older. With proper upbringing, we hope that the negative traits have been reduced and the positive traits have been accentuated by adulthood. What you are left with is called your personality. Simply, it is what you are.

If a person displays unfavorable traits, then we would likely place some type of negative label upon them. That would be called a personality disorder. For example, if an individual had traits of stealing or cheating, we may call them an antisocial person. If they were so organized that they filed their garbage, they may have an obsessive-compulsive personality disorder. Sometimes it is difficult to determine whether a person has a type of personality or a personality disorder. We all have a type of personality. A personality type becomes a disorder when it interferes with our functioning or our ability to relate to other people. Individuals with an antisocial personality disorder, for example, damage their relationship with other people when they cheat or steal from them. Because "normal people" do not like these behaviors, they make laws that will punish the person with an antisocial personality disorder.

It is difficult to treat many individuals with a personality disorder. They tend to believe that there is nothing wrong with them. In fact, they often blame others as the cause of their problem. It is only when they admit that they actually have a problem that they can receive help through therapy. They must believe that it is they who need to change.

We tend to talk about personality disorders as only occurring in the adult years. As a rule, psychiatrists consider it inappropriate to give a personality disorder diagnosis to someone who is under the age of 18. We also rarely give this diagnosis to an older person. It is clear that more research is needed in order to determine why we tend to defer making a diagnosis of a personality disorder in the elderly. It may be simply that we need to see an elderly person as having a specific illness that can be treated. If an elderly person is mean and nasty, it must be that there is something wrong with them that hopefully can be treated. In other words, they must have an illness. There are no mean old people. Right?

Ivy was an 81-year-old woman who was admitted to a psychiatric hospital because she had been physically aggressive with her caretakers at a nursing home. She would strike out, curse, and use racial slurs towards the staff at that facility. Ivy lived by herself all of her life with the exception of the last 2 1/2 years, when she was in the nursing home. While she was there, she had always been a problem for the nursing staff. The Director of Nursing referred to her as a mean old woman. After three months in this psychiatric hospital, which is a relatively long time in this modern era, she had been given numerous medication trials to no avail. Her behavior was essentially unchanged. One day Ivy's oldest daughter, who lived in another state, visited and talked with the staff. She described her mother as a person who had always had problems dealing with people. Ivy would always curse and threaten other persons who would not agree with her. If she were frustrated, she would slap a person who was not cooperating with her. In fact, during Ivy's younger years she had been arrested on a number of occasions for assault and battery. Her daughter even admitted that Ivy had been abusive to her and her siblings. The nursing home staff did not have this information about her life, since her family had nothing to do with the placement in the nursing home. The staff believed that Ivy had a mental illness since nothing else would explain her behavior. That is why they sent her to the psychiatric hospital. The hospital staff realized that putting Ivy on psychiatric medications was the wrong approach. Instead, they developed a behavioral management plan, which was to some extent helpful in reducing her negative behaviors. I will talk more about this later.

If there are mean young people, why can there not be mean old people? It is important to differentiate a personality disorder from a treatable mental illness in the elderly. The main reason is that personality disorders are usually not effectively treated by medications, and from our previous discussions, you know that medication use in the elderly has the potential for severe side effects.

As a person ages, it is not uncommon to see an individual with a certain personality type, develop a personality disorder. There are some younger persons who are able to hide their personality disorder. However, as they get older, their brain is not as sharp, and these personality traits are out in the open and can become exaggerated.

Rita was a 73-year-old woman who was brought to my office by her family after she had been arrested for shoplifting. She walked out of the store with several packs of batteries. Rita justified stealing the batteries because she stated that the manufacturer did not make them as long lasting as they used to, and they wear out too soon. Therefore, she thought the manufacturer was cheating her, and she was justified in stealing the batteries. Her family stated that she had never stolen anything before. In her younger years, she found two wallets that she never returned. She also admitted that she had cheated on taxes on a couple of occasions, when she was younger but it only saved her a few dollars. Rita stated that she did not agree with what the government was doing with her money, and therefore, she was justified in keeping some of it. She also admitted it was not the first time in the past year that she was stealing items from the store. In fact, she was stealing on almost a weekly basis. Rita thought that no one would arrest an elderly woman.

Certain older individuals display this behavior and even rationalize it with similar thinking. This was even the theme on some popular television comedy shows. Some people, when they get older, do not have the capacity to make proper judgments and consequently behave inappropriately. If they do not have the capacity to make proper judgments, these people may be found to be incompetent and, therefore, not responsible for their actions. This is usually seen in patients who are significantly demented or psychotic. Yet, there are a substantial number of older folks who reveal negative personality traits that they have kept hidden all of their younger lives, as their ability to think deteriorates.

THE ANTISOCIAL PERSON

There are several common types of personality disorders that can produce behavioral problems in the elderly. The first class, which we have already discussed to some extent, is the antisocial personality disorder. In the extreme form these are the criminals of our society. They lie, cheat, and steal. Persons with antisocial personality disorder can be very charming but only if it suits their purposes. They will use their charm to manipulate others. Their philosophy is "if I can get away with it, and it benefits me, I am going to do it." It does not matter if their behavior negatively affects other people's feelings or rights.

The individual with an antisocial personality disorder has a history of repeatedly performing acts that are against the law or societal norms. They are often impulsive, irritable, and aggressive, as seen in the above example of Ivy. Because of their aggression, they can have complete disregard for the safety of others, as well as themselves. They are often called deceitful, dishonest, and irresponsible. They almost always have a lack of remorse as they use excuses for having hurt, mistreated, or deceived others. Essentially, these people have no conscience. The only thing that they perceive is wrong is that they might get caught. H.L. Mencken described the antisocial person's philosophy perfectly when he said, "Conscience is the inner voice that warns us that someone may be looking."

The clever person with antisocial personality disorder can get away with a number of behaviors without experiencing the proper consequences. As long as they do not get caught, they feel that they are doing nothing wrong. They also tend to rationalize, as Rita did in the above example, that they are innocent, because there is a special reason that excuses their behavior. An elderly person with an antisocial disorder often uses their age as an excuse for their behavior. For example, they might say that they walked out of the store with an item because they forgot to pay for it. Some of these people even believe that, because they are so old, no one will have them arrested because no one is going to put an older person in jail. In reality, this statement is sometimes true.

If an older person is caught in a criminal act, they may not be charged with the offense, because many people in our society feel sorry for these individuals. There is also the stereotype that these older individuals may not know what they are doing, and therefore, they should not be arrested. When an older individual who was arrested, goes before the court, a judge often orders a psychiatric evaluation to determine if the older person knew what they were doing was right or wrong. As you can see, society does tend to keep the elderly individual who was arrested out of jail. Yet, there have been older persons who performed criminal acts, were arrested and suffered legal consequences. Each case is judged on an individual basis and older folks need to know this.

An older person with an antisocial personality disorder is often an embarrassment to the family. They often first come to attention when the person who catches the elderly individual in a criminal act notifies a family member. Usually, the situation can be handled with a calm discussion and an offer to make restitution. If this type of situation occurs, I would suggest that the family member who has the greatest negotiating skills be called in to lead the discussion. In order to avoid legal involvement, you might have to provide assurances that this type of incident would not happen again. For example, if the incident occurred in a store, you may need to tell the owner that your family member will no longer come into that store. Usually, the proprietor of the business just wants the situation to go away and not be repeated. However, if the storeowner has had a series of thefts, he or she may want to set an example. Hopefully, your family member will not be that example.

In order to prevent your family member from committing an antisocial act, you will need to be aware of certain warning signs that may occur early in the process. First, do they have a history of being involved in illegal activities? Have they been manipulative or demanding in the past? Do they try to bend the rules, or in other words, have they tried to get away with actions that society would judge as wrong. Have they been aggressive or abusive?

If they have displayed any such antisocial behaviors, be observant for any change in their mental state. As we discussed previously, persons who were able to hide their antisocial acts in the past may not be able to do so as they get older and are no longer as cognitively sharp as they were. They are now much more likely to be caught in the act. Some older persons get caught because they simply do not care. This may be a sign of an underlying depression.

The first intervention you must take is to set firm limits with this antisocial individual. Tell them that you care about them and are concerned that their behavior may get them into trouble. You will need to educate them that older people can indeed be arrested and suffer significant consequences. Even if they tried to plead not guilty by reason of insanity because of their old age, dementia, or some other type of mental illness, they may be placed in a psychiatric hospital for an indeterminate amount of time. You will need to repeatedly educate them about the effect their behavior is having on others, particularly other members of their family.

Medications are rarely useful for individuals with an antisocial personality disorder. Sometimes even older individuals can change to some extent in psychotherapy. I have seen older persons who have committed antisocial acts referred to a therapist instead of being sent to jail. However, they will only truly alter their behavior when they are internally motivated to change. External reasons, such as legal consequences or family pressure, will motivate a person to initially seek help, but long-term adjustments of a personality disorder will only occur if the person truly believes that they need to change.

Sometimes it is helpful for the family members to get together and decide on a punishment or consequence for the antisocial behavior. For example, an older woman, who had a long history of speeding without getting caught by the police, received four citations over the last year for going at least ten miles an hour over the limit. Her family decided that a safe consequence was to take away the independent use of her car for three months. During the next three months, the patient could only drive when another family member was in the car.

As older individuals become more dependent on family members to function, consequences are usually simple and straightforward. If a person needs to be transported by a family member to shop, then their stealing will need to stop, or the family member will no longer take them out. It is important, if at all possible, to explain what the consequence will be before the person acts in an inappropriate manner. It is better to prevent the antisocial behavior than to punish it after it occurs.

THE HISTRIONIC PERSON

Another character problem that can be seen in the elderly is called the "histrionic personality disorder". These are persons with showy, emotional, and colorful traits that may prove embarrassing to family members.

Lenore was a 79-year-old woman who was always known by her family as the drama queen. During her younger years, she would act as if she were ready to die, if the slightest thing did not go her way. Even in her later years she would exaggerate her emotions, if her family did not agree with her. She would rarely act this way in public. This changed over the last year. She would routinely make scenes in the community when things did not go her way. For example, she would yell at perfect strangers if they bumped into her. Throughout her entire life Lenore did not like to wait. On one recent occasion, when she was waiting in the express line at the grocery store, she screamed at the customer in front of her, "You either can't read the express sign or you don't know how to count your groceries." Needless to say this incident proved to be embarrassing, not only for Lenore, but also for her daughter, who was standing by her side.

As some people age, the front part of their brain does not work as well as it did in their younger years. This part of the brain called the "frontal lobe" controls our judgment. If this area of the brain starts to decline, our social behaviors can become inappropriate. While Lenore was able to get away with the fact that she was the drama queen within her family, her melodramatic behavior in the community was unacceptable and embarrassing. Even her family members agreed that it was not like her to act this way in public.

An individual with a histrionic personality disorder is often called dramatic, extroverted, or colorful. They may also be described as excitable and emotional. Some of these individuals may dress in a provocative manner. These people like to be the center of attention. At times, they may be inappropriately sexually provocative or seductive. They may be flirtatious but are rarely sexually aggressive. A common theme is that they like to make everything sound more important than the situation really is. Loud, tearful episodes and temper tantrums are not uncommon.

Most histrionic and antisocial individuals tend to mellow as they get older. However, some older persons with a declining mental capacity can show a recurrence of these traits. Their histrionic behaviors may become more public and occur much more frequently. In fact, their behaviors may be even more exaggerated than when they were younger. This can be quite embarrassing for their family members. There is also the added problem that histrionic sexual behavior in an older person is even more socially unacceptable.

It is fairly easy to see the warning signs of the histrionic personality disorder. This is because the symptoms are so dramatic and attention getting. A common finding in older persons with this disorder is somatization. This means these elderly individuals are melodramatic in describing their physical problems, no matter how minor the ailment. Even insignificant medical problems can produce exaggerated emotional responses in these people. They will act as if a simple splinter will bring on death.

There are a few points to keep in mind when dealing with the elderly who have a histrionic personality disorder. Remember, they want attention. You can actually use this to help them. Their problem is that they are doing the wrong things to obtain attention. Your job is to teach them to get your attention or others' attention in a more appropriate manner.

Edith was a 76-year-old woman who was brought into my office by her family because they were tired of her dramatic crying jags. They thought that she was depressed. Her daughters described numerous episodes when Edith would literally wail when her needs were not being met, or when she believed her daughters were not taking her needs seriously. At other times, they noticed she would be smiling and quite happy. Recently, Edith fell and bruised her elbow. She screamed for her daughters to take her to the emergency room. In the hospital she was moaning so loudly that she had to be placed in a separate room away from the other patients. After a thorough evaluation, the emergency room doctor stated that she did not break any bones but only had a superficial bruise. As soon as he reported his findings to Edith and her family, Edith abruptly stopped her crying and quickly became calm. The daughters also described a number of episodes where Edith was extremely dramatic when they were around, but when they left and observed her without her knowing, she was quite calm and functional as if nothing ever happened. Except for these well-defined episodes Edith did not have any standard symptoms of a depression. I met with her daughters for several sessions, and we developed a plan to reward Edith with attention when she displayed appropriate behaviors, such as asking for help in a calm and direct manner. If Edith became demanding and emotional, the daughters told her that they would come back to talk with her when she calmed down. Over the next several weeks Edith's attention-getting behaviors decreased substantially.

Older persons who have behavior problems often respond to this type of behavioral modification approach. Individual therapy is the treatment of choice for an individual with a histrionic personality disorder, but studies to show that this is effective in the elderly are lacking. A plan involving a system of rewards and consequences is a sound approach in dealing with the elderly histrionic person. An important point to remember is that you and other family members need to be consistent in this approach. If someone gives positive reinforcement for inappropriate histrionic behavior, this can undermine the entire plan. For example, if one of Edith's daughters gave her some attention when she was whining and demanding, this would have given the message that inappropriate actions would still be rewarded. In order for Edith to change the opposite message needs to be drilled into her consciousness over and over again without exception. This is sometimes hard for certain family members because the dramatic person can be quite convincing, and they may feel sorry for the individual.

One of the complications in dealing with the histrionic person is the fact that they are like the proverbial boy who cried, "wolf." Sooner or later, something bad may actually happen, and the overly dramatic response may be ignored. Thus, these individuals make it difficult to determine whether or not they really have a problem. If you feel there is a possibility that they have some type of serious disorder, then you must give them the benefit of the doubt and take them to see a physician for an evaluation.

There are times when the histrionic person is so clever in their acting abilities that family members will need to seek professional help in order to resolve what appears to be a psychiatric disorder. Medications are not usually helpful in treating people with this condition unless there truly are some secondary symptoms such as depression, anxiety or psychosis.

In summary, therapy is the first line of treatment if the person is sincerely motivated to change. Behavior modification is the alternative intervention if the individual refuses to accept that they have a problem.

THE PARANOID PERSON

Paranoid personality disorder is another condition that can affect the elderly, often causing severe behavioral issues. These individuals suspect that others may be trying to exploit or harm them. They may lose their trust in long-standing friends, associates, or family members. It is not uncommon, for example, for a person with early dementia to blame a friend or family member for stealing an item that they have unknowingly misplaced. They may become suspicious without any justification regarding the faithfulness of their spouse or lover. At times, they may believe that people are trying to undermine their reputation. Consequently, they can bear grudges toward others when there is little proof to support their belief. Some of these paranoid individuals will read hidden negative meanings in remarks that people make about them. Essentially they interpret others' words in a suspicious manner.

Fritz was a 75-year-old man who believed that his neighbor did not like him and was out to harass him. He said that when his neighbor said good morning to him, he did so with a wink in his eye. He believed that his winking really meant that the neighbor wanted something bad to happen to him. Fritz became upset when one of the neighbor's tree branches fell on his lawn. He was not sure, but he thought it was a possibility that his neighbor had tree trimmers partially cut branches that were overhanging his property so that they would fall on his lawn and harass him. Fritz would spend many hours during the day looking out of his window behind closed curtains to see if his neighbor was trying to do something to his property. One day his neighbor was working on the rain gutters of his home. Fritz felt that he was trying to redirect his water in order to flood his property, and thereby, further harass him. At that point Fritz started calling numerous county officials in order to complain. This started a long feud, which embarrassed the family, because numerous outsiders were now aware of their father's paranoia. This problem became even more complicated when Fritz decided that his family was now against him, because they would not support him in his fight against his neighbor.

A person with a paranoid personality disorder is often quite difficult to treat, because they have a basic problem with trust. They believe that nothing is wrong with them. If a person does not agree with them, they believe that the person is against them. They will not be able to trust that person, even if that person is trying to get them help. It is not surprising that they rarely seek treatment themselves.

Individuals with this disorder are best treated by psychotherapy. The trick is to get them to come in for treatment. There is usually one family member whom the patient trusts the most. That person should talk to the paranoid person in a non-threatening and matter-of-fact way. Try to be as diplomatic as possible. It is counterproductive to argue with a person who has paranoid beliefs. If at all possible, try to avoid taking sides. It is not helpful to be condescending, as the paranoid person will feel that you are only trying to humor him or her. This will only cause more resentment. The most important goal, initially, is to maintain their trust.

A paranoid person truly believes that someone is out to harm or harass them. This makes them hostile, irritable or angry. They may even become quite anxious, if they are waiting for something to happen to them. Often, they are tense, unable to relax, and hypervigilant. Sometimes it is better to focus on these negative feelings rather than the patient's erroneous beliefs. They do not want anyone to challenge their beliefs, but they are usually willing to receive help for their disturbed feelings. The trusted family member could use these negative feelings as a way to motivate the paranoid person to seek treatment. Fritz's daughter in the above example brought him into my office because she told him that I could help him with the anxiety and stress caused by his neighbor.

Even a therapist has to be careful how to treat such paranoid individuals. If the paranoid person no longer trusts his therapist, it is likely that he or she will stop coming for treatment. A trained psychotherapist and caring family members are the most effective combination to help the paranoid individual.

There are a number of other helpful hints for family members who have to deal with a paranoid relative. Make it clear that you are concerned about the feelings of the individual. Rather than challenging their beliefs, help them to understand how they can deal with their situation in the most productive way. For example, I instructed Fritz's family members to consistently explain to him that it was less upsetting to handle the situation on his own than to confront his neighbor or call the police. The next time a branch fell from Fritz's neighbor's tree onto his property, his son helped him cut the branch up and dispose of it as soon as possible. He explained to his father that it was easier to handle the situation this way, rather then spend an enormous amount of time calling county officials or police. The son was also able to convince his father that if Fritz argued with his neighbor and then became upset, his neighbor wins. Fritz finally figured out that the best way to handle his neighbor was not to let the neighbor get him angry. Even though Fritz still maintained his paranoid beliefs, he was acting in a way that was more socially acceptable and less embarrassing to his family.

Sometimes a paranoid individual may act out in potentially dangerous ways. There was a recent example about a paranoid seventy-year-old man who shot his friend because he thought that his friend was sleeping with his wife. He apparently told his daughters a few months earlier that he suspected that this was going on. In addition, he mentioned that he would have to get rid of his friend, if he found this affair was true. No one took him seriously until it was too late.

If a paranoid family member makes any type of threat, whether direct or implied, the family should seek professional help as soon as possible. It is often helpful for someone in authority to explain the serious consequences of such threats. In addition, the professional will explain the options that are available, in order to prevent any dangerous behavior.

Medications can, at times, help with the negative feelings that a paranoid individual has as a result of their beliefs. Sometimes a trial of anti-psychotic medication can be helpful, particularly if the diagnosis of paranoid schizophrenia is in question. Anti-anxiety agents, as well as tranquilizers, in small dosages and for brief periods of time can help decrease anxiety, agitation, or other problematic behaviors that are the result of paranoia.

THE OBSESSIVE-COMPULSIVE PERSON

Older persons with a history of obsessive-compulsive personality disorder may develop significant problems as they age. Even individuals with obsessive-compulsive features and not a personality disorder can have a difficult time adjusting to the problems of aging. These people have a history of being extremely orderly and preoccupied with details. They are perfectionists, and everything they do must be "just so". These individuals are very productive and overly devoted to work. They are quite conscientious and responsible. Often they are stubborn or rigid in their beliefs. Obsessive-compulsive persons believe that they need to fully control their lives.

It is not surprising that an obsessive-compulsive individual can become quite upset when their body and mind start to deteriorate. They now have to come to terms with the fact that they are no longer in total control of their life. This process is an emotionally difficult one and may lead to a severe depression. They may become less productive due to mental and physical problems. Because they valued this productivity all of their life they are saddened by their new limitations.

All of us have to deal with the problems of aging, whether they be arthritis, memory deficits, or some other type of medical or mental problem. An obsessive-compulsive person, who has been in control of their life, has a difficult time dealing with these changes. For these individuals, life is no longer perfect. Therefore, obsessive-compulsive persons have a much higher rate of depression and anxiety in their later years.

It is difficult, if not impossible, to treat these obsessive-compulsive traits when they have existed for decades. It is not usually helpful to try to change the patient's personality. Instead, therapy in these individuals will focus on supportive themes, in order to help them adjust to these changes. The same approach works best for family members in dealing with the relative with an obsessive-compulsive personality. Be supportive and caring. Help them develop new and more realistic goals that will allow them to perceive themselves as still productive.

Milton was a 71-year-old successful businessman who had retired two years earlier due to arthritis. His mind was still as sharp as it was when he was 20 years old. His plan for retirement was to visit each state in the US. He had extensive and detailed travel plans for the several years after his retirement. Unfortunately, his arthritic pain limited his traveling. Milton was heartbroken when he had to remain near his home for treatment of his medical condition. His depression became so severe that he would only leave home in order to go to his physician's office. He stopped visiting his friends and even failed to attend a number of routine family functions. His family doctor prescribed three different trials of antidepressants, but they provided only a limited amount of improvement.

I spent about 20 sessions over the next several months reeducating Milton in terms of setting realistic goals for his life. We also talked about how his life was so perfect and efficient before he became ill. However, Milton was able to recall a number of significant obstacles in his life that he had overcome in order to keep his life perfect. His daughter died when he was 42. He nursed his wife through extensive cancer treatments when he was in his early sixties. Ultimately, he was able to see his arthritis as just another obstacle that he could overcome in order to keep his life in perfect control. At that point, he was able to accept limited goals so that he could still see himself as a productive 71-year-old man. At the end of the therapy, Milton was able to work three half days per week as a consultant at a nearby business school. Once again, he enjoyed seeing his friends and relatives. Finally, he was able to write a travel book about planning day trips.

Even older persons can benefit from counseling. As you can see, many of my interventions during this therapy process could have been easily performed by knowledgeable adults. However, sometimes professional counseling is needed because the family members are so upset by their relative's behavior that they are unable to be objective and calm enough to be helpful. I will talk extensively in a later chapter about how family members can provide advice or counseling to their troubled loved one whether they suffer from an obsessive-compulsive disorder or some other type of mental illness that is causing a behavioral problem.

THE DEPENDENT PERSON

Dependent personality disorder is another commonly seen problem in the elderly. It is found much more often in women than men. Persons with this disorder may have had a serious medical problem in their earlier years. As the name says, they depend on other people to do things for them. You might say that they are the opposite of the person with the obsessive-compulsive personality. They do not want to make decisions nor do they want to be in control. They are happy when others take charge and tell them what to do. If they do have to make a decision, they will only do so with an excessive amount of advice and support from others. These individuals avoid positions of leadership or responsibility. They would rather be submissive.

Persons with dependent personality disorder do not like to be left alone. They like to have others nearby on whom they can depend. In fact, they usually seek out people who like to be in control. They will develop a strong bond with such an individual to the point where they feel that they cannot live without that person. Because they do not want to lose this person, they have difficulty expressing any kind of disagreement for fear that they may drive him or her away. They may take extreme measures in order to keep the relationship in place. If the relationship ends, they feel depressed, uncomfortable, and helpless. At that point, they feel the need to develop an immediate relationship with another individual. They are constantly fearful that they may be left alone and have to take care of themselves.

It is easy to see elderly individuals develop dependent personality traits as they start to have medical or mental problems. In most instances, it is quite acceptable for older persons to depend, to a reasonable extent, on others. The individual with a dependent personality disorder goes to extremes. Sometimes it is difficult to determine when the person crosses the line and becomes an individual with a dependent personality disorder. One way to make this determination is to look back at the person's life to see if they had these traits when they were younger. It is also helpful to consult with an objective person, or even a professional, to make this judgment.

Victoria was a 74-year-old woman who was brought into my office by her daughter, after she had made some suicidal statements. She recently had a mild stroke and was afraid to be left alone. It is important to note that all of her stroke symptoms had fully resolved. After the stroke occurred, she went to live with her daughter for about two weeks and refused to return to her home. Victoria had been living alone for the two years, following the death of her husband. It was now four weeks after the stroke, and Victoria did not want her daughter to go to work for fear that she would have another stroke while she was gone. She pleaded hysterically every morning when her daughter was about to leave for her office. Victoria even threatened suicide if her daughter left her. The situation deteriorated to the point that it was causing marital problems between Victoria's daughter and her son-in-law. After evaluating the situation, I prescribed short-term anti-anxiety medications for Victoria. It was clear that she was having panic attacks when her daughter was leaving the house. I was also able to discover that Victoria had a long-standing history of dependent personality traits. She had been married for 47 years, and her husband had done everything for her. He took care of the finances, did all the shopping, and made all the meals. Her daughter said that all of her female friends were extremely jealous of her marriage. It was clear that I was not going to change her lifelong dependent traits. Instead, I helped the family members set up a realistic support system to make Victoria feel safe and secure. At the same time, we had to teach Victoria that she did not need someone physically by her side to keep her protected. Her daughter now carried a beeper to reassure Victoria that she would always be available to help her. Victoria went back to live in her home. She was visited either by her daughter or one of her two sons on a daily basis. Her daughter also arranged for her to be visited several times a week by various church members.

In general, the treatment of a dependent person revolves around the development of a reasonable support system. I have been involved in cases where family members are so frustrated by these individuals that they basically stopped seeing them. The rationale they use for this type of intervention is that they are trying to teach the dependent person a lesson. This approach often backfires. For example, on one occasion when the dependent person was left alone, that individual began calling 911 at all hours of the day. Some dependent people will also call family members in the middle of the night.

Individuals with this disorder need reassurance and support. At the same time, you must set limits if they make unrealistic demands. As you can see in the case of Victoria, you can create a support system by dividing the tasks amongst various family members and friends. This spreads out the work so that no one person will feel overwhelmed. Later I will talk about how one can monitor an individual using the newer technologies. Beepers, cell phones, and cameras can keep track of a dependent individual and, more importantly, provide them the reassurance that they are being carefully watched.

Anti-anxiety medications, used on a limited, as needed basis, can prevent panic attacks or severe anxiety when the dependent person feels that they are about to be left alone or abandoned. Behavior therapy, family therapy, and support groups have all been used to help decrease dependent personality traits. Such professional intervention can achieve a fairly successful outcome, even in a severe case of this disorder.

THE ORGANIC PERSON

Another personality disorder that is commonly seen in the elderly is called a personality change due to a general medical condition. Another term for the same condition is the "organic personality disorder". This condition is typically caused by some type of brain damage, which leads to a personality change. Brain tumors, strokes, and injury to the brain itself can lead to this disorder.

The individual with the organic personality disorder often wants an immediate gratification or reward. For example, if they are hungry, they demand to eat immediately. If they are tired, they may lay down in a public place to sleep. They can be quite impulsive and may make inappropriate sexual advances or steal something they feel they must have. They cannot wait to have their needs met.

Their emotions can change rapidly. One second they can be cheerful, and the next second they can be irritable and angry. A number of these individuals can be apathetic or have an "I don't care" attitude.

These individuals can have cognitive disturbances and appear to be demented. They can have problems with memory, concentration and speech. In fact, it is not unusual for dementia and an organic personality disorder to overlap in their presentation.

If one of your family members has these symptoms, it is imperative that they have a full medical evaluation to determine the location and cause of the brain damage. Sometimes these personality changes are only the first phase of a full-blown dementia. In other cases, the organic personality disorder may be caused by a medical problem that is treatable. Some causes require prompt intervention, because if they are left untreated, they can cause more serious medical complications and even death. An example of this is the person who has a subdural hematoma, which is a consolidation of blood that presses on the brain tissue. Sometimes, the early signs of this condition are similar to the organic personality. If untreated, this hematoma, which can often be surgically removed, could be lethal.

These individuals require close supervision by family members. Their impulsive and inappropriate behaviors can get them into trouble and, at times, legal difficulties. They must be protected from making bad or impulsive decisions. For example, some of these individuals may sell or give away all of their property for no apparent reason. In severe cases, these individuals may require custodial care or a supervised living situation. Before any such decision is made, please seek professional consultation, because there are often community resources to help your loved one remain in their home.

Medications can be helpful at times for a person with an organic personality disorder. Drugs called "mood stabilizers" can prevent emotional swings or moodiness. Antidepressants can reduce some of the anxiety or sadness seen in these patients. Psychiatrists or neurologists are the experts you should consult regarding these medications. They will be able to thoroughly evaluate and treat these individuals.

THE NARCISSISTIC PERSON

It is easy to recognize an individual with a narcissistic personality disorder. In fact, these individuals are usually identified during their young adulthood. These individuals believe that they are very important and superior to other people. They believe that, because of their extraordinary talents, they will have unlimited success. Narcissistic people feel special and often refer to themselves as powerful or beautiful. They feel that others should admire their skills or abilities. Persons with this disorder often feel a sense of entitlement to the point where they expect favorable treatment and believe that people should automatically agree with them. Because of their self-centered beliefs, they lack empathy, and, therefore, do not recognize or value the feelings or needs of others. We often refer to these people as arrogant, pompous, or just downright annoying.

To some extent these people act like the antisocial person. A narcissistic person, however, bends the law while the antisocial person will break the law. Even though the narcissistic person may believe that rules do not apply to them, they usually do not become involved in illegal activities, as the antisocial person is likely to do.

As you can probably guess, the narcissistic person is often not well liked by his or her peers. Their relationships are fragile and they often make others furious. Sometimes they exploit people to achieve their selfish ends, but they usually operate within the law. Obviously, once a person finds out that a narcissistic person has manipulated them, the relationship ends abruptly and unpleasantly.

A person with a narcissistic personality disorder is difficult to treat because they believe that there is nothing wrong with them, because they are so important and special. Believe it or not, the narcissistic person actually has rather poor self-esteem. Because their behaviors turn other people off, they are often rejected or have chronic interpersonal conflicts. These individuals then become depressed. Sooner or later, they seek treatment because they believe that no one likes them, and they cannot understand why. After all, why would people not like someone so special or important?

Though persons with a narcissistic personality disorder are not common, we need to discuss them here because they have difficulty with the aging process. They have trouble accepting the fact that they no longer are as strong, powerful or beautiful as they once were. These individuals may try hard to maintain a youthful appearance. Both men and women with this disorder often use plastic surgery to look young.

No matter how hard they try to keep their appearance young, strong, and powerful, old age catches up with them. This is a very difficult adjustment. As you might expect, they are often depressed as they grow older.

Abigail was a 78-year-old woman who came to my office because of depression. In her young adult years, she was a socialite and a locally famous actress. Her husband, who died 7 years earlier, provided for her adequately but not extravagantly. Over the last two years, she had a number of medical problems, which led her to move to an assisted-living facility. This adjustment was quite difficult for her, and she never developed any true friendships. In fact, she felt quite alone. She rationalized this by saying that these common people did not understand a woman of her stature. But even this rationalization did not prevent a rather severe depression. Abigail had no children, but there was a younger sister who described her as the "queen bee." The sister was not surprised that she was having difficulties mingling with regular folks. It took a number of sessions to explain to Abigail the fact that she would have to compromise her values in order to have true friendships. It was hard for her to give up her special status. It seemed to help when I explained to her that, because of her talents, she would easily be able to find the good traits in other people. I told her that, once she found these positive characteristics in her peers, she should try to focus on them in her discussions. Over the next several months, Abigail was able to gradually win over the other ladies at the assisted-living home.

If one of your relatives has this personality disorder, you probably already know it by the time they reach their elder years. It is likely that in the past you have tried to tolerate them as best as possible. The most efficient way to do this is to not take these people so seriously. Sometimes family members tend to avoid these individuals or humor them. These approaches usually do not change the behavior of the narcissistic person. As these individuals grow older and have a difficult time adjusting to their age, they will have a series of crises or depressed episodes that require some type of intervention. Then they become difficult to avoid, particularly if you are a caring relative.

While professional therapy can be helpful for these individuals, family members can encourage positive change that may relieve the depression or any other anxieties that these individuals might have. It is often helpful to engage them by agreeing that they do have unique or special characteristics. By doing so, you will develop a therapeutic bond that you can use to help them change. Tell them that, because of their special skills, they will be able to take action in a new way that will benefit them. This puts them in a rather unique position. Essentially, they have to change in order to prove that they are indeed special.

Another approach uses the theme that these narcissistic persons will need to make some type of compromise to work with the "common" people. Sometimes these individuals will never give up the belief that they are above everyone else. In order to work around this concept, you will need to explain that compromise is necessary in order to have healthy relationships with people. Even certain kings and queens were loved by their subjects when they treated them in a fair and respectable manner. You can also ask them to think what would happen if they pretended to be normal like everyone else.

Remember, narcissistic individuals are difficult to treat, and at the same time, difficult for family members to handle. Most people do not want to deal with individuals who think that they are better than they are. Therefore, if you are going to help a narcissistic family member, you will truly need to be a caring and giving individual, who is able to tolerate a lot of their obnoxious behavior. You will need to have a great deal of patience.

It is also helpful if you have friends or family members who can help you with this task of reforming the narcissistic person. If a number of individuals gently confront the narcissistic person with the fact that they are driving people away with their behavior, they ultimately may get the message that they need to stop their obnoxious actions in order to develop true friendships. If you, along with your helpers, can consistently spell out to them exactly what behaviors are turning people away, they may be able to change their negative habits. For example, it is useless to tell a narcissistic individual that they have a bad attitude. It is better to tell them that they hurt your feelings when they criticize you, and that is why you do not want to be around them. Be specific. If they criticize the way you dress, tell them it upsets you. If they brag about themselves, tell them that it turns people off and keeps them away.

Some family members have told me that it is sometimes helpful to turn the tables on these arrogant individuals. For example, they will treat their narcissistic family member the same way they have been treated. They will act arrogant, self-important or special. In the presence of the narcissistic family member, they will brag, criticize, or manipulate them. Before long, the problem family member realizes what they look like to others and may start to change. The problem with this approach is that you run the risk that you might alienate your loved one and cause so much friction that you would not be able to try any of the other methods. You may want to use this technique when all others have failed. It also requires a great deal of discussion with your loved one about the reason you are acting in this new manner.

Because people with a narcissistic personality problem cannot tolerate rejection, and they are prone to depression, antidepressants can be helpful at times. These individuals can also have erratic emotions, which can be treated with mood stabilizers. Psychiatrists can help with these interventions.

THE AVOIDANT PERSON

Another personality problem that can become worse in older individuals is the "avoidant personality disorder". In early adulthood these individuals are easily identifiable. They tend to avoid activities where they might have interpersonal contact, because they fear that they cannot live up to the approval of others. They have an intense fear that they will not be liked. Therefore, they try to avoid any relationships particularly intimate ones. They worry constantly about being criticized or rejected. Thus, they do not like to go into new situations where they might meet people who could reject them. These individuals see themselves as inadequate and are easily embarrassed.

Persons with avoidant personality traits want to be accepted by other people, but they avoid them because they cannot handle the possibility of being rejected. In simple terms, we refer to these people as shy or timid. They tend to work at jobs where they do not have to interact much with people. For example, they are happy to remain in their cubicle working on their computer on a daily basis.

As these individuals grow older, they tend to become more withdrawn and go to extremes to avoid people. They may turn into the proverbial "shut in." If these people thought they were inadequate when they were younger just think how they believe other people will react when they discover that their health, beauty, or mental functioning are deteriorating.

Individuals with this disorder can benefit from professional therapy. Anti-anxiety medications can calm the fear they have when they deal with other people or new situations.

Avoidant individuals may have some difficulty entering into some type of therapeutic relationship. This is not surprising, because they also fear that the professional may reject them. One man with this disorder once asked me why I would want to waste my time trying to help a person like him. With some encouragement by family members and friends, avoidant persons can take the risk and seek help from a professional.

Family members can help in other ways. They can encourage their loved one to take small risks, one step at a time.

Marvin was a 66-year-old man who was afraid to come into my office. His wife had died of cancer a year earlier, and Marvin essentially stayed in his home almost all of the time. He had always been a loner, but his family was happy when he married his wife, who was a simple but loving woman. Now that she was gone, he retreated into a hermit's life. It was his sister who finally came to see me. After she told me his story, I gave her some reading material concerning his condition. I also outlined a plan to help him leave home and reenter the community. First we had many family members and friends visit him on a continuous basis, in order to give him the message that everyone was concerned about him and would support him. In essence, we brought the community to him. Once he developed a comfort level with these visitors, the sister arranged for certain family members and friends to invite him over for a quiet dinner. Later, during some of these dinners, these friends and family members began inviting him to certain events, where there were not a lot of people. The last step took some time and a lot of encouragement. Then he was encouraged to go to social gatherings such as the local church group. The sister was surprised that a year later Marvin called to tell her that he met a wonderful lady at one of the church outings.

As you can see from Marvin's case it, is helpful to take a large goal such as getting Marvin back into the community, and breaking it down into small tasks, which have less chance of causing a significant amount of anxiety. Typically, avoidant individuals will have some type of anxiety when they attempt to come out of their shell. We need to tell them that some anxiety is to be expected. It is helpful to tell them that once they take the risk the anxiety will usually subside.

If an elderly person with avoidant traits still cannot take the first step to reach out to others, break up the first step into multiple smaller steps. For example, in the case of Marvin, if he was unable to accept visits by family members and friends, then phone calls or letters may have been easier for him to handle. I have even known family members to make video or audiotapes expressing their care, concern, and acceptance of the avoidant family member. Once watching these tapes in the privacy of their own home, they may feel more comfortable and reach out to have normal interactions with their friends and relatives.

Another effective intervention is for family members to work on reducing their loved one's anxiety by giving them some relaxation tapes that can be purchased in many bookstores. Sometimes you have to find the right tape for the right person. There are numerous relaxation techniques, and some people respond better to one than others.

Assertiveness training is another effective intervention for these people. Again, there are numerous tapes outlining the various techniques for this process. Unfortunately, it is difficult to get avoidant individuals to attend an assertiveness training class. I know of a family member who attended such a class and then spent time teaching the techniques to her loved one.

There are a number of behavioral therapies that can help patients develop relationships with others as well as improve their self-esteem. Most psychiatrists, psychologists, and counselors are familiar with these techniques. Though many of the above tips have been proven to help avoidant individuals, not everyone responds to these basic interventions. So, do not be afraid to ask for help from a professional.

Thus far, I have discussed some of the more common personality disorders that pose problems for the elderly population. There are a few more that are less common, but still deserve to be briefly mentioned here for purposes of recognition. They are the schizotypal, schizoid and the borderline persons.

THE SCHIZOTYPAL PERSON

The first is the "schizotypal personality disorder". Most people refer to them as eccentric, odd or peculiar. Like avoidant individuals, they tend to have few friends, but this is because people do not want to be around such weird persons. They may have strange beliefs or speak in a rather odd way. They tend to look a little psychotic or schizophrenic but are still in general touch with reality.

One should not challenge their strange beliefs nor should they judge them. This will often cause conflict that, in the long run, will be counterproductive. Family members should try to establish a trusting relationship with these individuals. The basic technique is to help these individuals blend in with the community and allow them to adjust their strange beliefs to the extent with which they feel comfortable.

A psychiatric evaluation is often required in order to fully assess these individuals and make sure that they are properly diagnosed. Psychiatrists can also prescribe anti-psychotic medication, which may be helpful in either reducing the number or intensity of their strange beliefs.

THE SCHIZOID PERSON

A similar sounding disorder is the "schizoid personality". This individual is the proverbial loner. They do not want close relationships and tend to be involved in solitary activities. They appear to be indifferent toward others. Unlike avoidant individuals, they do not want close friends. On the other hand many of these individuals tend to have good relationships with pets. They often tend to daydream, fantasize, and stay in their own world.

Individual and group therapy can be beneficial to these patients. In fact, group therapy may be the only social contact these people may have in their lives. Some of these individuals benefit from anti-psychotic or psychostimulant medications.

Family members can help the schizoid person in two basic ways. First, they can expose these individuals to normal healthy relationships that are seen in the rest of the family. The hope is that these schizoid individuals will start to model their behavior after these normal relationships. Second, it is important for certain family members to try to develop a consistent trusting relationship with the schizoid person.

It is important that a psychiatrist evaluate these individuals, in order to determine that the proper diagnosis has been made. There is the belief that a few of these people go on to develop schizophrenia, which requires professional intervention.

BORDERLINE PERSONALITY DISORDER

Borderline personality disorder is a commonly seen diagnosis in the younger population. I have seen relatively few older folks with this diagnosis. It is not clear why this is so, and much more research needs to be conducted.

A person with a borderline personality disorder has a pattern of unstable and intense interpersonal relationships. They perceive their relationships as either extremely good or extremely bad. Nevertheless, they are quite afraid of being abandoned by their friends. Often they are impulsive, particularly in areas of sexual behavior, spending, or substance abuse. They may have recurrent suicidal behavior. It is not unusual for these individuals to be involved in self-mutilation behavior. They can have intense mood swings or, at times, have feelings of emptiness. A borderline person can have intense anger and have difficulty controlling that anger. They often appear to be in a state of crisis.

Fortunately, as I have stated previously, these individuals often seem to lose their symptoms as they grow older. However, if you do have a family member who appears to show these borderline traits, it is important that they receive a psychiatric evaluation. These patients are extremely difficult for any family member to handle without outside consultation. Because of the complicated nature of the borderline personality disorder, I recommend that family members seek professional help for their loved one. The only other advice that I would offer is that family members should help the borderline person receive prompt treatment, if there is any question of safety.

Psychotherapy is the treatment of choice for these individuals, though it can be long and difficult. Hospitalization may be required at times, particularly when they become suicidal. When the borderline patient is in the community, the family should try to be supportive as possible within reason.

It has been discovered recently that medications can be quite helpful for these individuals. Anti-psychotic, antidepressant, anti-anxiety and mood stabilizing agents have all been used with some success in these patients.

MIXED PERSONALITY TYPES

One final topic about personality disorders is that many people with this diagnosis are not easy to categorize. Even though we talked about individuals who fit into certain distinct personality groups, in reality many people have a variety of character traits. For example, someone may have antisocial as well as dependent personality traits, and you may need a combination of interventions to help them. I often ask people to imagine personality disorders as circles on a page. Then, I tell them to visualize these circles partially overlapping each other. Most people's personalities operate in these areas of overlap.

Sometimes individuals can show extreme personality traits of various types. Psychiatrists actually have a label for these individuals called "personality disorder not otherwise specified". This label is for the patient who has features of more than one personality disorder, but at the same time, cannot be put in any one specific personality disorder category. So just when you thought it was easy to identify a specific personality disorder, I complicate it with reality. Do not worry. Just identify the specific traits that you see and break them down into the various personality types. Then you can use the interventions I have already mentioned for those specific traits. Remember, if you get stuck, there are professionals out there who can help you.

CHAPTER TEN
Dangerous Behaviors

In the last few chapters we talked about psychiatric conditions that produce a variety of behavioral problems. This chapter will deal with the most extreme and precarious behaviors related to psychiatric disorders. Dangerous behaviors are divided into three distinct categories. Patients can be suicidal, combative or suffer injury through accidents. If an elderly person displays behaviors in any of these three categories, prompt intervention is absolutely necessary.

SUICIDE

Suicidal behaviors are particularly problematic in the elderly. Suicide rates increase with age. While the elderly attempt suicide less often than do younger people, they are more often successful. In fact, the elderly account for 25% of the suicides, but they make up only 10% of the total population. Elderly men are particularly successful in committing suicide. They tend to use more deadly means such as using firearms or jumping from high places.

One of the reasons that suicidal behaviors are so common in the elderly is that they seem to be related to the person's deteriorating physical health. Suicidal behavior in the elderly is linked to a number of specific medical problems such as cancer, head injury, epilepsy, cardiovascular disease, dementia and AIDS. Cancer seems to be a particularly high risk factor for suicide in the elderly.

Physical illnesses such as those listed above can often produce unrelenting pain, disfigurement or some type of loss of functioning that makes the patient depressed and potentially suicidal. These illnesses can also be stressful for their family members. Sometimes, this stress can precipitate conflicts between the elderly person and their relatives. Such family conflict can also lead to depression and suicide.

It is important to recall our previous discussion regarding the various medications that can produce depression in the elderly. Some medications used to treat the aforementioned illnesses can cause their own form of depression. For example, some anticancer agents as well as steroids can contribute significantly to this problem.

Obviously, there are numerous psychiatric disorders that can lead to depression and suicide. While someone with a diagnosis of depression will have a higher risk for suicide, other psychiatric disorders can also lead to suicidal behavior. Schizophrenia, dementia or delirium can lead to the development of self-destructive behaviors. It is important to remember elderly persons who abuse alcohol or medications. These substances not only produce depression, but they can also alter the patient's judgment leading to an impulsive act. Thus, older persons who drink or abuse drugs have a higher risk of suicide. Elderly persons who have a history of impulsive behavior when they were young are also in the high-risk category.

The majority of suicides in the elderly are preventable. Family members can play an important role in this prevention. It is significant to note that suicide is the eighth major cause of death in our population. Therefore, it is not uncommon. Any concern of family embarrassment needs to be put aside when a person is displaying self-destructive behaviors. You need to understand that many family members have handled suicidal behaviors in their loved ones, and your timely intervention may save a life.

Judith was a 75-year-old woman who had just suffered severe burns over 10% of her body, primarily her facial area. She had been diagnosed with a mild form of dementia about a year earlier. Over the years she started to display some self-destructive behaviors that the family tended to ignore because they thought it was just part of her dementia. In fact, one son stated that they thought this was just part of her getting old. On two occasions over the past year they found Judith sitting in her living room with her gas stove on but unlit and her entire house filled with fumes. On another occasion, they found their mother on the floor in an intoxicated state that was quite unusual for her. They wrote the first two events off because they felt she was just being forgetful because of her dementia. When she was drunk, they felt this was due to her poor judgment because she rarely drank before and did not know her limitations. From time to time, she would make vague statements about being "ready for God" or that she had lived "a good enough life." In retrospect, the patient's family realized the various clues that they had missed and were feeling very guilty about her most recent suicide attempt. While recuperating from her burns, Judith admitted that she had planned to burn herself to death by filling the kitchen with gas fumes and then lighting a match. She never directly talked about suicide because she felt that her sons would not receive the insurance benefit if it looked like an obvious attempt to kill herself. Later, she also admitted that her depression was clearly related to her belief that the dementia would cause her to be in a nursing home within the near future. After some education and therapy, as well as antidepressant treatment, she was able to admit that her future looked much brighter than she had once thought.

It is still surprising to hear a number of family members, even in the upper class and professional categories, say that suicide is an expected event in the elderly. This is just not true. Not only can suicide be prevented in the older population, but elderly individuals with proper treatment can also live happy and full lives.

Once I got to know Judith's family members, it was clear that they were caring individuals who were concerned about their mother. They were led astray by their misconceptions. There was, however, another problem, which I have seen in a number of families. They had a communication problem because they never were able to see their mother as an individual who needed help. Their mom was an independent individual who had always taken care of them, no matter how old they were. Therefore, they never developed a communication process that focused on what their mother needed. The importance of communication between an elderly person and the rest of the family is absolutely essential when dealing with potentially dangerous behaviors in an older person. Earlier in this book we talked about the importance of observation. Observation requires effective communication.

RISK FACTORS FOR SUICIDE

If you are concerned about a family member having suicidal tendencies, then you need to know the various risk factors. The first is age. I have already said that, as one gets older, one will have a higher risk of suicide. An important predictor of suicide is a history of a prior suicide attempt. Up to 40% of individuals who ultimately commit suicide made a previous suicide attempt. More importantly, an elderly patient who made a suicide attempt late in life is at a higher risk for a future completed suicide.

Take note of the older person who has a history of impulsive behaviors such as arguments or violence. These individuals have a higher rate of suicide. Persons who are depressed, particularly those individuals whose depression does not resolve even after treatment are also at a higher risk for suicide. An older person who is unwilling to accept help or treatment is in that same high-risk category.

A person who is single, widowed or divorced is more likely to attempt suicide than the person with a partner. Older persons who are unemployed or retired, which is quite common, have a greater chance of suicide. Obviously, a person who has suffered a recent loss or separation is also considered to be a higher suicide risk.

Alcohol, as well as certain medications, can affect a person's judgment. Even if the person is not abusing these substances, they still may be at risk for suicide. Certain medications or alcohol even when properly used can cause side effects that can lead to a person misjudging a situation. This poor judgment can result in dangerous acts.

Be aware of these risk factors when considering the possibility of suicide in one of your relatives. Listen and observe. It is estimated that 80% of persons who eventually kill themselves give certain warnings that they are about to commit suicide. They may make comments such as "there is a better life after death." Some persons will give away their belongings, particularly items of value. The observant family member can recognize many of these indirect comments or actions. One of the most important issues not to be overlooked is to realistically consider that older persons are indeed at a higher risk of suicide. In our society we often deny this is a possibility. After all it would not happen in our family. Believe me, it can.

Sometimes, it is easy to discover that one of our loved ones is contemplating suicide. They tell us. In fact, almost half of the people who commit suicide give direct warnings to friends or family members. If an older person talks about how they are going to kill themselves, that is a very ominous sign. That individual should receive an immediate evaluation.

Some older folks may talk about dying for years. After a while, it is like the boy who cried wolf. Family members and friends may turn a deaf ear.

Ruby was a 79-year-old woman who was brought to my office after she recently took a serious overdose of medications. She had never made a previous suicide attempt. However, her family reported, since the death of her husband 10 years before, she occasionally asked God to take her. Any time the smallest thing in life went wrong, she would make this request. After a while, her family became annoyed with this whining. They just thought it was a way of her expressing her frustration. Her oldest daughter admitted that the family started to ignore her comments. Prior to her recent overdose, however, her demeanor changed completely. She did not talk much about death. In fact, the family started to see her as calmer and quieter.

A person who has been threatening suicide or talking about death over a long period of time and then becomes quiet and less agitated, needs to be promptly evaluated. In fact, some persons who are about to commit suicide may even show improvement in their depression. They may appear content because they have come to terms with the fact that they have decided to kill themselves. Again, be observant for any change in a depressed older person's demeanor.

As I have repeatedly stated, effective communication is important in identifying any type of psychiatric problem in an early stage. This is especially true for the potentially suicidal person. Do not be afraid to ask the person directly if they are considering killing themselves. Asking the obvious question is sometimes overlooked, as in the following story.

A man bought a parrot that was guaranteed to talk by the pet shop owner. After three days, the bird had not spoken and the man went back to the pet shop complaining he was cheated. The owner said maybe the bird was lonely and sold the man a mirror so the bird could see his reflection, as if there was another bird in the cage. Three days later the bird still did not talk, and the owner sold the man an exercise wheel for the birdcage telling the man that perhaps the bird was not getting enough exercise. Three days later the man came back to the pet shop telling the owner that the bird died, but just before that happened, the bird did talk. The owner asked," Just what exactly did the parrot say?" The man replied," F-o-o-d."

Ask the obvious question. Do not assume anything. If your relative is depressed, ask them if they have had any thoughts of hurting themselves. If you are afraid asking a direct question about suicide might cause a conflict, you should outline some of the warning signs that you have seen that caused you to be concerned. Be caring and supportive in your approach. Encourage your loved one to talk about any intent they may have to harm themselves. At the same time, explain to them that depression is a treatable disorder. Encourage them to seek help promptly. Tell them that you will be by their side to support them through the treatment process.

INTERVENTIONS FOR THE SUICIDAL PERSON

Do not take the risk of trying to resolve a suicidal situation without obtaining professional help. Assist your loved one in arranging an appointment with a psychiatrist or similar mental-health professional immediately. If this is not possible, and you are in any way concerned about a person's safety, it is important to take them to the nearest emergency room. Evaluation of suicidal individuals commonly takes place in emergency rooms. In that setting, the professional staff will develop an immediate plan of action, in order to provide a safe place for the individual to be treated.

This does not necessarily mean that every suicidal patient who comes into an emergency room will be admitted into a hospital for treatment. Sometimes, elderly persons are afraid to say that they have a problem because they fear they may be hospitalized with so-called "crazy" patients. You will need to reassure your family member ahead of time that hospitalization only occurs in a minority of cases. In the modern era of psychiatry there are many interventions that can be used instead of hospitalization. In addition, explain to them that psychiatric hospitals are designed to help suicidal patients. If they need to be admitted, it is typically for a short time, and this step can be life saving.

Victoria was brought to the emergency room under protest by a number of her family members. Soon after her 80th birthday, she seemed to be talking about death all too often. She had a number of medical problems and saw her body deteriorating at a steady pace. One evening, her oldest daughter became quite concerned when Victoria started to talk about her will. Apparently, during that discussion she stated she was ready to die. Her daughter could not convince her to go to the emergency room, so the daughter called her brothers and sisters to come and help. After Victoria understood that her family was just trying to offer help and not put her away, she went to the emergency room but was not happy about it. In the emergency room, Victoria admitted that she started to think about ending her life because she felt so miserable. The staff in the emergency room performed crisis intervention therapy. They were able to convince Victoria that there were alternatives to suicide and set up an appointment with a psychiatrist the next day. The oldest daughter offered to stay with her mother until that appointment. She kept that appointment and ultimately the therapeutic intervention proved to be successful.

Most emergency rooms have psychiatrically trained staff on site or on call, in order to evaluate and treat suicidal individuals. They know the alternatives to hospitalization that are available. If they feel that a patient requires more support and monitoring than routine outpatient treatment, such as Victoria required, they might recommend programs such as intensive outpatient treatment or a partial hospital program.

Intensive outpatient treatment is therapy that is provided multiple times during the week. Because it occurs more often than routine once a week therapy, it can provide the additional support needed to help the patient through the tough time.

A partial hospital program, otherwise known as a day treatment program, takes place on a daily basis with the usual exception of weekends. These programs provide more support than intensive outpatient treatment because the patient receives treatment for several hours per day. Psychiatrically trained staff in an emergency room have the knowledge to determine what program will best fit the patient's needs.

In order to use one of the non-hospital approaches the patient should have a strong support system. For example, elderly persons may need the family to transport them to the outpatient program. Family members may need to be available to their loved one either in person or by phone in order to provide emotional support. Likewise, it is important for the person to make a commitment to call a family member or healthcare professional immediately if they do not feel that they can remain safe.

If, after a professional evaluation, it is felt that the person cannot be safely treated in an outpatient setting, then hospitalization is needed. In this modern era of psychiatry, hospitalization rarely lasts for more than a few days. During a hospital stay, individual as well as group and family therapy are available to provide an intense treatment experience that usually resolves the suicidal situation rather quickly. Most importantly, the hospital is the best place to provide constant observation by professional staff in order to prevent any suicidal behavior.

Suicidal patients in the hospital usually come to the realization that they are suffering from a treatable mental disorder. They will be told that they will probably make a complete recovery. They will also be educated about aspects of depression. For example, when persons are severely depressed, they should not make significant life decisions. Severe depression clouds a person's judgment. Bad decisions will only lead to more stress and more depression. Most patients will not only feel significantly better when they are discharged, but also they will be linked to outpatient follow-up that will further assist them in treatment.

THE UNCOOPERATIVE SUICIDAL PERSON

What if a potentially suicidal patient refuses treatment?

Hank was a 70-year-old man who became increasingly depressed after he retired from his job a year earlier. As he told his family, his life was his job. He would repeatedly make suicidal statements in front of his family. Yet, he refused any kind of help. One day his son found his father lining up bottles of pills on the kitchen table. Hank was still refusing to get any help. Consequently, over the next several days a variety of family members watched Hank around-the-clock so that he would do no harm. Finally, when the family members reached their limit of frustration they had to physically fight with him in order to bring him into the emergency room. It was very traumatic for all concerned.

Taking a loved one to the hospital against their will is never pleasant. There are a few basic suggestions that should make it easier and safer. If at all possible get some help. The more caring family members around your loved one, the safer they will be. This will also serve to decrease the anxiety of all concerned. Do not leave the suicidal person alone, even if they are asleep. The individual caring for the suicidal person needs to be awake and alert. Suicidal persons can wake up at night and kill themselves while other family members are asleep nearby.

The same philosophy applies to the transportation process to the physician, emergency room or mental health center. The potentially suicidal person should not sit next to a car door. If possible, that person should sit between two able-bodied individuals. Remember, it is important not to leave the person alone even for second.

If you or other family members are concerned that it is going to be difficult to safely take this person to a facility, then the police need to be involved. This is particularly important if the suicidal individual is quite large and agitated. Do not take any unnecessary risk. If something goes wrong, not only could the person commit suicide, but others in the area could get hurt. Local police departments are usually trained to deal with such suicidal persons.

INVOLUNTARY COMMITMENT

Most states have specific laws governing the process of involuntarily committing someone into the hospital. Family physicians and local mental health professionals are often knowledgeable regarding these laws. Local mental-health groups, such as the Mental Health Association and the Alliance for the Mentally Ill, can be helpful in explaining these regulations to family members who have to deal with such difficult decisions. Lawyers, police and certain government officials can also be consulted regarding these laws. Try to research this information in advance, as it is often difficult to obtain during a crisis in the middle of the night.

Once the person is in a safe environment such as an emergency room, crisis center or hospital, friends and relatives can play a helpful role in providing clinical information to the professional staff. This is particularly necessary when the suicidal person is unwilling to provide information, such as is often the case in the individual who was involuntarily brought into the hospital.

When the patient is in the hospital, it is still important for family members and friends to keep in contact with the clinical staff, as well as with the patient. No one likes to be in the hospital. Your support continues to be valuable to your loved one while they are in an inpatient setting. Sometimes the hospital staff will ask you to be a part of family therapy, where you can play a role in assisting your loved one back to health. Most importantly, family members and friends are important resources to support the patient after discharge from the hospital.

Once the patient has improved and is ready to leave the hospital, the hospital staff will put together a discharge plan to continue treatment. It is important for family members and friends to understand that usually not all of the problems have been completely resolved during the hospital stay. Your loved one will continue to require certain interventions such as therapy, medications and case management services. By the way, a case manager is someone who deals with the nitty-gritty details of helping a person live in the community. They may help the patient to arrange transportation to the clinic or doctor, set up the necessary insurance papers, or ensure that the patient has the means to obtain the medications needed. Family members and case managers can be mutually helpful.

Remember, now that your loved one is out of the hospital it does not mean that everything is back to normal. You will still need to be observant and supportive. The risk of making a second suicide attempt is highest within three months of the first attempt. This is important for the individual who was admitted to the hospital following a suicide attempt.

On the other hand, I do not want family members or friends to become overcautious or overanxious. I remember seeing an older man who was released from the hospital after attempting suicide become extremely frustrated with his family, who were now always by his side and would not give him any peace. Ironically, he came to see me for therapy in order to deal with this new family problem. I know it is often difficult to try to find the proper balance between too much and too little involvement. It can be helpful to bring all the family members together and brainstorm about what would be the most reasonable approach. It is also not unusual to have family members or friends involved in the person's therapy so that they can provide the right amount of support. Consultation with your loved one's doctor is often helpful.

I would like to bring up one other topic before we end this discussion on suicide, and that is the issue of confidentiality. When someone's life is in danger confidentiality needs to take a temporary back seat. This does not mean that the whole world needs to know about your loved one's problem. Yet, you will have to provide key information to certain professionals in order to help treat your family member.

Do not try to cover up the issue of suicide. There is no doubt that it is embarrassing, not only for the patient, but also for the family to face the fact that there is someone in their midst who wants to kill himself. It is often difficult to let people outside of the family circle know about such issues. Nevertheless, the best way to handle this serious situation is to reach out for help from a person expert in the area. Remember, suicide in the elderly is, unfortunately, not an uncommon event.

In summary, pay attention to the warning signs of suicide outlined above. If you feel there is a chance that your family member is considering suicide, monitor him constantly. Have other family members or friends help you in this process. Seek professional help promptly. Lastly, support your loved one throughout this process, even after the crisis is over. If you have any doubt of the suicidal potential of your loved one, err on the side of caution and seek professional help. I believe that with proper public education we can reduce the number of suicides in the elderly population.

COMBATIVE BEHAVIOR

Combative and threatening behavior, like suicide, requires immediate assessment and intervention. These acts can result from a variety of psychiatric disorders such as delirium, psychotic states or personality disorders. They usually occur in the later stages of the illness. Therefore, the best approach is to intervene early and prevent these mental disorders from getting to a dangerous point. Fortunately, physically aggressive behavior in the mentally ill population is not as common as most people think. Yet, you still should be observant.

RISK FACTORS FOR AGGRESSION

There is no way a person, even a psychiatrist, can predict someone's behavior with 100% certainty. There are signs, however, that can give you a general sense that someone may be ready to act out in a negative manner. The most obvious is a direct threat. Patients who are angry and paranoid can be dangerous if they believe that someone is trying to hurt them. One of the most obvious predictors of violence is a past act of violence. Other predictors of potential violent behavior include excessive alcohol or drug use and a history of criminal activity. Criminals do age.

People with a history of destroying property or using weapons can potentially be violent if they have a psychiatric disorder. A person who is hearing voices telling him to kill someone may also be giving you a clue as to potential violence. Individuals with certain personality types may have difficulty controlling their impulses or anger and are more prone to violence than the average individual.

As stated above, a direct threat is an obvious warning sign for violent behavior. This becomes a more serious threat when that individual has the means to carry out his violence, as well as a specific plan. These persons require immediate intervention.

INTERVENTIONS FOR THE HOSTILE PERSON

When I was a psychiatric resident, I was once asked to see a 79-year-old woman who lived in my old neighborhood. A social worker was helping her with some financial issues and realized that she had a delusion that if she went outside someone would try to shoot her. She apparently had not left her house in over six months. When I saw her, I discovered that she had a history of paranoid schizophrenia but had never received any treatment. She was smart enough to hide most of her symptoms over the past several decades.

In addition, she was now suffering from a moderately severe form of dementia, which was also impairing her judgment. Unfortunately, her demeanor fooled me. I saw her as a frail helpless older woman lying in bed, trapped in her own home by her delusions. What I did not see or even think to ask about was the revolver under her pillow. At the end of my evaluation, I recommended to the family that they take her to the mental health clinic for treatment. A few days later the patient's son and his friend came to take her to the appointment. As they entered they found the gun. The police were called and handled this situation without further incident.

Do not assume anything. If you feel that your relative is considering any type of violent behavior, you must approach them with caution and concern. Make sure that you talk to them in safe surroundings and they do not have any concealed weapons. Remove any weapons from their home. As with the suicidal patient, ask for assistance from other family members or friends who can help monitor the individual while obtaining as much information as possible. Try not to be confrontational in your approach. Instead, show your care and concern so that you can establish an alliance with the individual. You will need to use this relationship to convince the person to voluntarily seek help. A potentially dangerous person who is refusing help poses a high-risk situation.

In a non-threatening manner, you, or someone that the person trusts, should explain that violence is not an acceptable option. At the same time, reassure the individual that you are trying to help them in the best way possible. Speak in a calm and deliberate voice. Stay outside of striking distance. If you or other family members are not comfortable with this approach or feel that your safety is in any way jeopardized, you will need to get professional help. It may be necessary to call the family physician or even the police. Mental health clinics or crisis hotlines are also useful resources during these situations.

Physically aggressive behavior should not be ignored. If an older person shows signs of losing control such as frequent verbal outbursts, severe irritability or physically striking out, an intervention is required to prevent more serious behaviors. Even if the family considers the behaviors to be minor in nature, the offending person should not get the message that their actions are acceptable. If that happens, the violent behaviors may only become worse in the future.

If you observe carefully, you may be able to find the trigger for the person's violent behavior. Older persons with mental illness may not be able to tolerate stress in their environment. They can be easily upset and try to leave an uncomfortable situation as soon as possible. They may strikeout or push people away in order to leave what they perceive as an overwhelming or threatening situation. The best intervention is to allow the person to leave as calmly and quietly as possible. To force the person to remain when they cannot handle the situation will only serve to escalate the aggression. Make sure you continue to monitor them from a reasonable distance, so that you can intervene if their behavior gets out of control.

On occasion, impaired individuals can get upset because they do not understand what is going on. This may be due to some form of dementia or a psychosis, which is confusing their perception. You may have to take additional time in order to explain fully what is going on so that they will not be anxious or angry over their confusion. If you rush them, they will only become more upset and may become violent out of frustration.

Bartholomew was a 72-year-old man who was taken to the mall by his family in order to buy a winter coat. He had early signs of a dementia, which was later found to be due to a vitamin deficiency. Because of a poor memory, he wasn't able to remember why he was in the mall. He tried to wander off on numerous occasions. The family's response was to redirect him by stating that he needed to stay with them. The family soon became frustrated with his behavior. At one point, his daughter grabbed him by the arm and tried to escort him back to the men's clothing section. This was when he slapped her.

We are all human. It is understandable that sometimes we become annoyed when dealing with relatives who have behavioral problems. Such situations take time and effort. On the other hand, we should try to be as kind and calm as possible in dealing with these individuals. This is the approach that will work more often than not.

Repeatedly redirecting Bartholomew was not helpful. Instead, it would have been better to explain to him continuously what was going on and what he needed to do next. This way he could have focused on the consistent dialogue, which more likely would have held his attention to the point where he would have been more cooperative. Physically forcing a person to change their behavior can lead to a violent confrontation. A better way to redirect Bartholomew would have been to extend a hand so that he could take it willingly and then gently lead him back to the proper area.

If an older person is starting to become upset and irritable, it is quite appropriate to ask what is bothering them. Certain stimuli in the environment can be upsetting to an older person, while a younger person does not even notice that same stimuli. Again, it is important to ask the question in a caring and concerned manner. This may be hard to do when one is frustrated with the individual. It helps when other family members share the responsibility, and the person usually in charge is allowed to take a break. Dividing up care giving amongst family members and friends is crucial for everyone's mental health. A fresh person is less apt to become frustrated. This leads to less conflict and less confrontation. Ultimately, this reduces the chance of any violent acts.

Sometimes combative behaviors can occur with little warning. This usually occurs in an acute psychiatric condition where the person's mental state deteriorates rapidly.

Ezekiel was a 74-year-old man who was found lying on the floor of his home. His daughter thought he had a heart attack, and when she tried to arouse him, he punched her in the face. He did not recognize his own daughter. When she backed off, he continued to thrash about, as if he were in a fight with some invisible creature. She promptly called 911, as well as other family members, for assistance. Once in the emergency-room, Ezekiel was found to have a severe cardiac arrhythmia, as well as other signs pointing to a toxic reaction to a common cardiac medication. His agitated state was actually a blessing in disguise. It led to a prompt medical intervention, which actually saved his life.

As you can see, one cannot always predict when an individual is going to be violent. In Ezekiel's case, there was no question that prompt intervention was mandatory. In such acute situations, you will not have the time or the luxury to go through the process that we described earlier on violent behavior. Your response must be quick and decisive. Contacting 911 is the first intervention. Calling the person's physician is a good second. Also, remember to call on family members or friends to help you and your loved one during this crisis.

While keeping your own safety in mind, it is important to try to protect the individual from inadvertently harming him or herself. Ironically, violent individuals often wind up harming themselves. If possible, remove any dangerous items or potential weapons that are available to the person. While you wait for help, try to engage the person in a calm and rational conversation. Make sure you are standing or sitting close to an exit, so that if your safety is in question, you can remove yourself from the situation as quickly as possible. An agitated person often responds well to a group of people who are giving the calm and direct message that it is best to behave in a relaxed and considerate manner. If you anticipate any difficulty with your loved one, it is not recommended that you go into a situation alone if at all possible.

Once the patient is taken to an emergency room or a hospital unit, the cause of the violent or suicidal behavior can be evaluated. There, a person can be given medication for a calming effect, and the individual will be monitored for any other unusual behaviors.

As I stated before, hospital stays in the recent years have been relatively short. This means that follow-up treatment after discharge is essential. Your family member will need your support and guidance more than ever. This might be difficult for you because they may have hurt you physically or emotionally during their crisis. Try not to take it personally. Remember, they were suffering from a mental illness that clouded their judgment. They need you. If you are not emotionally able to get beyond the incident, I would recommend you talk to family, friends or a professional.

We have been discussing fairly severe situations that might lead to an emergency-room intervention or a hospital stay. Let me reassure you that only a small minority of these cases requires such an intervention. Nevertheless, the old axiom, "better safe than sorry," is the best way to handle a potentially dangerous situation.

WANDERING

Besides homicidal or suicidal issues, there are a number of other potentially dangerous circumstances that can affect the elderly. One of the most common is wandering. This behavior not only occurs in Alzheimer's patients but also in other persons who may be confused or psychotic. These people may have a lapse of memory, and consequently, cannot remember their way home. They may become disoriented and cannot recognize their neighborhood.

Wandering often begins or increases when a person is in a new environment. They may have recently moved to a new neighborhood, for example, into their children's home. They may start to wander for the first time after they are admitted to a hospital. Sometimes the person who starts to wander in a new environment may be actually trying to find their old home. On occasion, wandering can be dangerous.

Lenore was an 87-year-old woman who left her building to take out the trash. Once she deposited her trash in the dumpster, she started back to her home. She, however, started to walk back to her old home where she had lived 15 years ago. It was about 12 miles away from her current residence. She had driven back and forth between the two locations many times in the past, using the interstate expressway. On this occasion, she began to walk onto the ramp of the expressway where she was being passed by high-speed vehicles. Luckily, a police car came by and stopped to pick her up. They brought her back home unharmed but quite shaken.

It is not uncommon to hear news reports about older people who have wandered away from a hospital, nursing home or their own personal residence. This is particularly a problem during the cold winter months when many of these confused individuals may be wandering around inadequately dressed for the weather.

Besides confusion and poor memory, there are other signs that a person may be predisposed to wandering or getting lost. If the person is repeatedly locking themselves out of their home, they are at a greater risk of wandering. Let me provide you with a few examples of some risk factors. They may notice new buildings in their old neighborhood when, in fact, nothing has changed. They may repeatedly refer to a previous residence when talking about their current home. You may note that they seem to be losing their sense of direction, even in their own home or in an environment with which they should be familiar. Constant minor episodes of getting lost are a sure sign of potential wandering problems.

When an older person first begins to wander, he or she may not realize that they have a problem. There is usually a tendency to deny the fact that this is a problem, or they may hide it from the rest of the family. It is not unusual for the individual's neighbors to be the first to discover that there is a problem with wandering. Therefore, I would suggest that family members get to know these neighbors. Observation is the key to determining that your loved one is beginning to wander. So, be alert.

INTERVENTIONS TO HELP
THE WANDERER

You can help some mildly confused persons from wandering by providing simple instructions. These instructions can be written on a card that the person can carry in their pocket, so that they can refer to it if they are lost. This should include the person's address, phone number and the phone number of the family member who can be called in case help is needed. Including a sentence to help calm the individual can be very reassuring since they may be quite upset when they are lost. An example would be a statement such as "stay calm and remain in one place." Another sentence could be "don't worry" and "ask a friendly looking person for help." Even mildly confused individuals can become more confused because they are upset about being lost. They may have to rely on another kind person for assistance.

In this era of inexpensive cell phones, the job of finding a lost person becomes somewhat easier. Give your confused family member a cell phone that is programmed to speed dial your number with a touch of one button. You can even paint that button with a brightly colored permanent ink marker. On the back of the phone you can tape the following message, " If you are lost just press the colored button and hold it down until the phone starts to dial me. Then listen for me to answer. I will come and get you." Unfortunately, because cell phones are getting smaller, you may have to write this message on a separate card. I would recommend that you practice the use of the cell phone with your loved one so that they will be comfortable with this process.

Conversely, if you lose your loved one, you have the ability to call them. Make sure that both cell phones are on. Most cell phones have the capability of being locked in the on position so that the confused person is not able to turn it off inadvertently. I have also seen this method used with an inexpensive walkie-talkie system. To take this a step further, a friend of mine has a GPS navigation system installed in his mother's car just in case she were to get lost while driving. Phones are now coming onto the market that use this same technology. You can locate the exact position of the person carrying the phone. While this technology is still expensive, over the next few years I am sure it will become cheaper to the point where others might be able to monitor their confused family members. In fact, there is a system out now that allows the tracking of an individual who is wearing a special bracelet. In the back of this book there is an appendix dedicated to the various new technologies in this area along with contacts for their manufacturers.

There are a number of more traditional, and less expensive methods that will help with the person who wanders and becomes lost. Bracelets can be purchased either in jewelry stores or drugstores that say the individual is memory impaired. It can also provide the name and the phone number of the person to be contacted if this person is found. Please do this as soon as you feel there is even a remote possibility that your loved one is at risk of becoming lost. In pharmacies, these are often referred to as Medic Alert bracelets.

Another cheap yet reliable method is the routine identification card. This can be carried in a person's wallet or purse. Unfortunately, confused people do not always carry their belongings with them. They may lose them or simply throw them away. So, for all these items, including the cell phone, it would be helpful to buy clothes that have pockets that button or zipper. You will still have to occasionally check their clothing to make sure that they are carrying the proper items. Also, they need to be able to open these pockets. You may have to practice this task with them. Velcro pockets can be useful for some people.

Although these methods seem reasonable, the confused person may resent the fact that they have to use these items. They may act insulted if they are requested to do so. This may be the first time that a family member has pointed out that they have any kind of deficiency. Therefore, it is important to have this discussion in a kind, caring and diplomatic manner. This dialog may take time and require numerous discussions.

THE PREVENTION OF WANDERING

Prevention of wandering behavior is clearly a better approach than having to find the lost person. First, there is no guaranteed method of preventing wandering and keeping the person safe. Also, interventions that help to prevent wandering may carry additional risk. For example, if you lock your loved one in their apartment to prevent them from wandering, then you run the risk that something could go wrong in their apartment, such as a fire, and they would be unable to get out. I would also point out that this could be illegal. It is helpful to have a family discussion about how an intervention is to be accomplished, so that the overall risk is minimized. Getting some advice from a professional, or one of the organizations we have previously mentioned, can also be useful. Every situation is different. What may work for one person may be a greater risk for another. Whatever you do, you will need to explain the method carefully and in detail to the confused person.

Chester was a 77-year-old man who was brought to my office a few days after he trashed his apartment. His family said that this behavior was quite unlike him. When I asked Chester why he did this, he told me that he was upset that there was a fire in his apartment because he smelled smoke. I later found out that he was making toast. Chester became very angry because he felt that he was trapped in his apartment by all of the fancy locks that his family installed. So, he took a hammer and destroyed every item that was locked in his apartment. He was so angry that he even destroyed the front door of his apartment with this hammer. When his neighbor from across the hall came home from work he saw the mess and called Chester's son. The family was surprised about this behavior since these locks had been installed years ago, as Chester had gotten lost on the number of occasions. Chester refused to have the locks put back on. It took a couple of sessions to work out the method whereby Chester was comfortable with having the locks reinstalled. The family installed a cheap buzzer alarm, which would go off when the front door opened. It would serve to remind Chester not to go out. He agreed that, if he would go out, he would call his son first. The son arranged to have his number on speed dial. In addition, Chester's family asked his neighbors to call if the alarm went off. This intervention was effective for the next several months.

Chester's family thought years ago that installing the locks would be the one time solution to resolve the problem of his wandering. Please note that confused persons rarely stay the same. They have a tendency to deteriorate over the years. Therefore, it is important to consistently talk with them about their condition and the remedies that are needed. It would have been helpful for Chester's family to discuss the use of the locks from time to time. They would have been able to explain the need for the locks and address any of his concerns. They also could have developed and communicated a plan to handle an emergency situation in the home. This may have prevented the situation cited above. An ongoing dialogue with a person who is suffering from a mental disorder is necessary to avoid or resolve any problems. This is particularly important for people who are wandering. They will need to be reminded repeatedly about the dangers of wandering. Reassuring these individuals that you are concerned about their safety will make the wandering easier to manage. If they perceive you as kind and caring, they will tend to cooperate.

There are number of ways to change an individual's living situation in order to prevent him from wandering. Locks that are difficult to operate will help keep the confused person in their home. Sometimes, installing locks in unusual areas, such as at the bottom of the door, can make it more difficult for the confused person to leave. Hardware stores also carry childproof locks, as well as childproof doorknobs. A normal adult should still be able to open the door, but the confused person is unable to understand how to operate it.

These difficult locks can also be used as a reminder for the confused person. Repeatedly instructing these individuals to stay inside when they encounter such a lock can be just as helpful as having the lock itself. Writing short notes and posting them around these locks can be helpful in reassuring individuals as to their purpose. It is also important to thoroughly explain to these persons that the locks are to help them stay safe. If these devices cause an out-of-control situation, such as in Chester's case, other interventions may be required. Make sure that you have a plan to address how the confused person can easily get out of their residence if they must leave. You should also check the legality of the method you are using.

Other interventions to help prevent a person from wandering should be based on two themes. First, the intervention should be a striking reminder for the person not to wander. Second, it should include a backup plan for the confused individual to seek help. This is necessary because, if the confused individual has a strong urge to wander, he will ignore any reminder.

One of the best examples of such an intervention was a door decorated by two grandchildren of an Alzheimer's patient. They painted a mural on the door depicting the family saying to the patient, "Grandmamma, please do not leave." It was brightly colored and, therefore, a reminder that could not be ignored. At the very top, there was a bright orange arrow pointing to a number that could be called in case the grandmother needed help. The latter was a simple back-up plan.

Be creative in designing these reminders, as you will need to get the attention of the confused individual. Bright colors, bold letters and vivid pictures will usually accomplish this. A backup plan needs to be simple, clear and easily seen. The simplest plan is merely a call to a person who is available to talk with the confused individual.

Another plan would be an alarm system, which can notify a nearby neighbor to come for assistance. Video cameras connected to a computer system are becoming less expensive. They can monitor specific exits in a person's home. Security companies that sell burglar alarm systems also have motion detectors and other sensors that can track a person's movement within a certain area. As stated above, there are global positioning system devices available that can identify the exact location of the patient.

This useful technology becomes cheaper every year. To obtain more information about these devices consult a security company in your local phone book. It is important to discuss these measures thoroughly with your relative, as a balance of safety and privacy issues needs to be considered.

The simplest interventions are still the most effective. Asking a person why they are wandering off is a reasonable approach. When a family asked their mother why she kept locking herself out of her apartment, she said she was looking for her mailbox. This was remedied by installing a mail slot in her front door. Another person, who was wandering around her apartment building knocking on her neighbor's doors, admitted that she was trying to find the bathroom. Her family made bright signs labeling all of the doors in her apartment, with the biggest one on the bathroom.

In the majority of cases, if you have a simple discussion with the impaired person, they will usually let you know why they are wandering. A paranoid older woman felt that someone was breaking into her apartment when she heard the leaves rustling outside of her bedroom window. She said she needed to run outside to escape these intruders. Her family bought her a large flashlight that she could shine outside the window so she could see the leaves making the noises. As you can see, a simple discussion can lead to fairly easy solutions. Remember the parrot.

Sometimes an older person will say that they wander because they feel afraid, bored or restless. After a more thorough examination it could be discovered that some of these individuals may be suffering from depression or anxiety, which as you already know, can be treated. At other times, an older person may report that they are trying to get some type of exercise. They just happen to get lost. One family member solved this problem when she bought a used treadmill at a flea market and gave it to her father, who had always been an exercise enthusiast.

The problem of wandering often occurs when a person is exposed to a new environment. The anxiety of the situation can further contribute to a person's confusion. This wandering can start as a problem when a family member takes the confused individual into their home. It can also begin when a mentally impaired person starts to attend a daycare center or enters a nursing home. Typically, the individual is trying to find a way back home. This wandering becomes more problematic if the individual becomes combative or aggressive when an attempt is made to stop them.

These confused individuals need to be thoroughly oriented when they enter a new environment. You must explain the reason why they are in a new setting, such as a nursing home or a partial hospital program. It is helpful to have a familiar and trusted family member stay with the individual on repeated visits to the new environment. Reiterate in simple terms the reason for these visits. Tell the individual why they are in this new place and help orient them. Maps of their new environment can be helpful.

Some experts believe that it is important to introduce a confused person into a new situation as early in their illness as possible in order to prevent wandering. I prefer to look at the person's total situation before making any such decision.

Lewis was a 75-year-old man who had early signs of dementia. His family doctor recommended that he attend the local geriatric day treatment program. It was his doctor's opinion that the program would provide the stimuli needed to slow down the dementing process. When the family took Lewis for a visit, they were excited about the program that was presented during the orientation. There was a wide variety of activities, including road trips, that he could participate in while in this program. Unfortunately, when Lewis saw the other persons in the program he became very upset that he was not like them. Almost all of them were women. They were much more confused than he was. Most importantly, he would have been by far the youngest person there. Lewis was so upset that he refused to visit any type of program that his family suggested over the next year.

Even if a person is referred to a high quality program to prevent wandering, that program must match the needs of that individual. It is important to investigate a particular program ahead of time. An individual who is already having a problem with wandering, does not need additional complications.

If a confused person must go to a new setting, it is important to use some of the interventions we have already described above. Simple notes to explain the situation that the person can keep in their pockets are helpful. Remember to provide repeated orientation during the initial part of the transition. Consistent reassurance and being available to talk to the person by phone or in person can make the transition much easier.

WANDERING WITHIN THE HOME

Daytime wandering prevention is based on the premise of keeping the individual involved in carefully structured activities throughout the day. Give your loved one some simple but meaningful tasks during the day that are both mentally and physically easy to carry out. If the wandering continues, then have some interesting back-up jobs they can perform to distract them from wandering.

Wandering at night can be a particularly distressing problem for the family member who is the caregiver. It is difficult to get a good night's sleep when you are worrying about what trouble your family member will get into that night. This problem is even more complicated by the fact that older individuals tend to require less sleep. Confused, paranoid or psychotic individuals can become particularly upset during the night when they cannot identify their environment. For example, if they try to go to the bathroom at night they may become lost and enter the wrong room. They may even forget that they originally got up with the intent to go to the bathroom and then try to do other things such as cooking or going outside. It is not uncommon for a family to be awakened by a smoke alarm after the impaired individual tried to cook something in the middle of the night.

Some impaired individuals will misinterpret their environment at night. In the darkness, they may see or hear things that are not there. These misperceptions may upset them, causing them to become disruptive in the middle of the night. It is helpful to leave a night light on in the person's bedroom and the nearby bathroom. Nightlights in hallways are helpful in preventing the people from injuring themselves when they wander. Posters and signs, which are made up of reflective tape or glow-in-the-dark paints, are useful in guiding a confused person through the home during the dark hours.

The first step in trying to prevent night wandering is to have the older person sleep throughout much of the night. The best way to achieve this is to make sure that the older individual gets tired during the day, so he or she will want to sleep at night. Keep the person occupied with energy burning activities during the daytime hours. Physical exercise, in some form, is extremely helpful during the day, along with mental exercise that can make the brain tired by nighttime. Even though all of these suggestions sound easy, it is important to try to structure them, so that they occur routinely on a daily basis. This is why day treatment programs are designed to keep the elderly stimulated during the day and, hopefully, asleep at night. Part-time jobs, even volunteer positions provide the structure needed to keep impaired persons busy during the day.

Naps should be strongly discouraged for those individuals who are up at night. If an older individual wants to sleep during the day, try to find out why they are tired. Are they involved in too strenuous an activity? If so, can these activities be limited or spaced out over the day? Is the person taking some form of medication that is causing fatigue as a side effect? There are numerous medications that can cause this problem, particularly if they are taken during the daytime hours. It is important to discuss with their doctor the alternative of taking these medications at another time during the day, such as bedtime. Other medications, which do not have the sedating side effects, may be another option. Remember to ask your family member what over-the-counter medications or herbal remedies they might be taking that can also cause sedating side effects.

There are a number of interventions you can take to prevent wandering at night. For example, if the confused elderly person gets up at night to go to the bathroom, try having that person go to the bathroom right before they fall asleep. This may reduce the wandering somewhat.

Individuals who are mentally impaired often respond to stimuli that we do not even notice. The stimuli may wake them in the middle of the night causing them to get up and wander. Try to make their sleeping arrangements as calm, quiet and comfortable as possible. Adjust the temperature of the bedroom so that they are not likely to get up in the middle of the night because they are too cold or too warm. Make sure that their mattress is comfortable and is not causing some type of backache, which could also awaken them. Try to eliminate all unnecessary noise that may disturb the individual. However, sometimes, soft background music will help calm people and keep them asleep. Once again, remember to talk to the individual and ask why they are getting up in the middle of the night. They will often bring up a simple problem that will usually have a simple solution.

Once a person is up at night, there are a number of things you can do to minimize any disturbance. They are all based on the idea of trying to redirect the individual back to bed or a safe activity. In other words, make the idea of going back to bed more inviting. You can do this by having a warm beverage available when they awaken. There are containers available that will keep a liquid warm for several hours. Keep a light snack available by the bed. This may prevent them from wandering into the kitchen to make a meal. Have a television or radio near the bed so that the person can stay in the bedroom watching or listening to some show until they become tired again and fall asleep. At times, an elderly individual may prefer to sleep in a chair. It would be wise to keep one in the bedroom.

Do not try to argue your family member back to bed. This will only serve to upset the individual, as well as you, and more than likely will keep him or her awake. They may also be angry and frustrated because they were unable to sleep through the night. Approach the individual in a calm and quiet manner. Reassure them that it is nighttime and that you want them to go back to bed so that they can get all of their sleep. This kind and caring approach will often work in helping the patient go immediately back to bed. I know that this is sometimes difficult to do when you are tired but any antagonistic approach will surely backfire, causing more problems for all concerned.

In general, try to tailor your response to any night wandering by trying to identify what the individual's needs may be. Remember that talking to your family member is an important component of mapping out a plan to minimize the wandering.

We talked earlier about the person who becomes agitated when they wander. Sometimes these people appear to be driven to pace. They may physically resist any efforts to stop them from walking. The best way to handle these individuals is to distract them by giving them something else to do. I often recommend to families to ask that individual to help them with some job like folding clothes or moving items. Depending on the mentally impaired person's physical strength, I will also advise families to try to find a substitute activity that would burn the same amount of energy that they use in walking. If these interventions are not successful then medications may be required. Please consult with your physician.

THE USE OF MEDICATION
FOR WANDERING

If reasonable measures fail to prevent or minimize night wandering, medications, used judiciously, can prove to be helpful. Sedating medications can help the impaired individual fall asleep and stay asleep at least for several hours. The problem with these medications is that they can cause side effects that can be serious. For example, certain medications can actually worsen confusion at night. A sedated wandering individual can be at risk of falling and injury.

Wilbur was an 82-year-old man who had difficulty staying asleep at night. His daughter, with whom he lived, complained that Wilbur was going into various drawers and shelves during the middle of the night, making such a racket that he would wake everyone in the house. She accompanied him to his family doctor and demanded that something be given to help him sleep through the night. He was given a commonly prescribed sedating drug to help him sleep. Wilber was now able to sleep five hours straight each night. Within a few days, however, he became much more confused and agitated during the day. He even developed a staggering gait. Because of these problems, his physician stopped the medication, and within a few days, Wilbur was back to his baseline. A week later another sedative was prescribed, and Wilbur seemed to tolerate it without any significant side effects. A number of non-medication interventions were also suggested to the family to help prevent Wilbur from wandering at night.

These sedating medications can cause the individual to be more prone to falls, accidents and the loss of bladder control. In addition, they can interact with other medications that person is taking, increasing the chance of additional side effects. The two most common side effects of sedatives are tiredness during the day and a hangover the morning after they take the medication. The bottom line is that medication should be used as one of the last steps in managing the wandering person. Therefore, do not be surprised if the family physician initially refuses to prescribe a medication. Instead, the doctor will prescribe a number of behavioral interventions, many of which have been described above.

DANGEROUS DRIVING

Giving up the privilege of driving is one of the hardest decisions for an older person to make. The elderly highly value their ability to drive in order to maintain their independence. Just put yourself in their shoes. How would you feel if you could not get into your car at this moment and drive to the local supermarket, the movies or your friend's house? Having no license to drive will restrict anyone's lifestyle, no matter how old or young you are.

The situation is worsened when you are forced to take the keys away from your relative in order to prevent him or her from harming themselves or others. The implementation of this decision can cause significant conflict and consequent hard feelings between the family and the impaired elderly individual. Older persons do not like having their adult children tell them what to do, particularly when it comes to taking away their car keys and their independence along with it.

The best way to handle this issue of dangerous driving is to have the older person voluntarily give up his privilege to drive before an accident happens. It is also better for them to stop driving of their own free will, rather than being forced to do so.

The first step to prevent dangerous driving is to have conversations with your loved one about their driving abilities long before there are any problems. What you say during these early discussions can make a difference between safety and injury. Make sure they understand that you want their health and safety to come first. They need to know that you care about them, and this is the reason for your discussion.

Some of the elements of this initial conversation should include the possible effects of medication on your loved one's driving, as well as any physical or mental handicaps that the individual might have. It can also be helpful to bring up news reports about car accidents involving older persons. Some families find it useful to talk about how other elderly people in the family came to make the decision not to drive. Keep these early topics general and non-threatening. Weave this discussion about driving into your normal everyday conversation with your loved one. An ongoing, matter-of-fact dialogue on this topic should be educational and thought provoking to the point that they will understand and accept the decision to stop driving when the time is appropriate. Give yourself ample time to accomplish this.

It is a good idea to educate the older driver about the warning signs that could cause safety problems. This way you, other family members and the older driver can be on the lookout for possible changes in their driving habits and abilities. Some of the trouble signs include not turning around when backing up or not looking into the rearview mirrors, as well as becoming easily distracted while driving. Other warnings include hitting curbs, becoming frustrated when driving, and getting lost or confused in familiar places. Family members and friends may often notice other signs of poor driving habits. The older relative may incorrectly use their turning signal or not stop at stop signs or red lights.

Be on the lookout for the consequences of poor driving such as scrapes or dents on the car or garage. A damaged wheel is often the sign of hitting curbs. The older person may speak of minor accidents or the fact that people seem to be honking their horn at them more often than in the past. Remember, you want to have these discussions about their driving early on so that a major accident does not occur.

The second step is to assure yourself that your older relative is driving safely is by riding along with them from time to time. This way, you can see firsthand if they are having difficulty driving. Using this approach, you might see that they lack confidence while driving. They may make bad judgments in certain situations, such as making wrong turns or not waiting before going through a stop sign. You might notice that they fail to observe important traffic signs or drive at inappropriate speeds. They also may react very slowly to dangerous situations. Other obvious miscues include moving into the wrong lane or confusing the gas and brake pedals. Sometimes impaired older drivers, for no apparent reason, continue to ride the brake because they are trying to be overcautious.

If you are riding along with your older relative and see any of these warning signs, this gives you the opportunity to begin, or better yet, continue a discussion about their driving habits. For example, if you saw that they were almost involved in an accident while you were riding in their car, you could point out the fact that it was a close call and you are concerned about their safety. This may lead into a discussion about what would happen if they could no longer drive. If you bring up the subject early on, you might, over time, be able to convince them of the transportation options that are available for them if they have to give up their keys.

There are alternatives with certain advantages when one can no longer drive. For example, public transportation such as the bus or a taxi has the positive aspect of no parking worries. There is also the benefit that people can save a great deal of money if they sell their car and no longer have to pay for gas, taxes or insurance. Try to be supportive during this phase of your conversation. Assure them that you would be willing to arrange to drive them around or have other family members and friends transport them.

Let your loved one know, most of all, that you are concerned about their safety. Your honest expression that they could be seriously injured or die may make the difference in their willingness to give up their driving without any argument. Older individuals also may be moved to make the right decision if you tell them that you or other family members, such as their grandchildren, are afraid to ride with them. These latter two reasons often help even confused individuals realize the true danger of the situation, not only for themselves but also for their loved ones.

Patients who have dementia or other mental disorders may not recognize their poor driving habits and may even deny that they are having any difficulties. An early sign that a person with dementia is having a difficult time driving is when they get lost in familiar places. They may even come up with bizarre explanations for their accidents. For example, an older woman I once knew claimed that the only reason she hit the barrier island was that it was recently constructed.

Sometimes adult children have a difficult time setting limits on their mother or father. This role reversal can be quite uncomfortable. Get help from outside resources and discuss the case with them. It might be helpful to have people outside of the family, such as doctors, talk with the older individuals. Older persons value the opinions of authority figures and may come to the right decision regarding their driving after a thorough discussion with these outside experts. Hopefully, after extensive conversation and education, the older driver will know when it is appropriate to stop.

What happens if the problematic older driver refuses to stop driving? If you have come to the conclusion, after thorough discussion, that they are a high-risk for an accident, then something must be done promptly. Your loved one's safety and those around them come first. Merely taking away their driver's license or car registration will not work. You may need to disable the car or file down their car keys so that the car is unusable. Automobile mechanics can provide you with a number of ways to safely immobilize their vehicle.

I would like to give you one word of caution. Just because a physician has called the department of motor vehicles, and they have decided to take away an individual's license, does not mean that the older person will not drive. A number of impaired elderly drivers will still try to drive without a license, registration or insurance. Remember, if their judgment is already impaired in terms of their driving, that same judgment will likely be impaired in terms of this decision to drive.

In summary, you will need to have an early and ongoing conversation about the warning signs of dangerous driving. Second, try to observe their driving habits at the first sign of even the smallest problem. Talk with them in a positive and caring manner regarding the possibility of giving up their driving. Let them know that you love them and are concerned about their safety, as well as the safety of others. Use outside experts if necessary. If you know that they are driving in a dangerous manner, you must promptly stop them by taking away their keys or disabling their vehicle.

This chapter addressed the four most common dangerous acts in the elderly, the physically aggressive, suicidal and wandering behaviors, as well as dangerous driving. Because they can lead to such harmful consequences, these behaviors need prompt intervention. Professional consultation is a must. Yet, no matter how much you do to prevent such behaviors and their consequences, there is no guarantee that these problems can be avoided 100% of the time. So, do not feel guilty if you have tried your best.

CHAPTER ELEVEN
Sex

Nothing may be more misunderstood than sexual behavior in the elderly. Many people believe that old folks no longer have sex. This is not so surprising in our culture. When young children come to the understanding of how they are conceived, they find it hard to believe that their parents were ever involved in such an act. It is also not surprising that in this same culture, when a seventy-year-old male admires a younger woman, he is referred to as a dirty old man. Without speculating why we hold these beliefs, let us agree that most people feel that sex is not for the elderly.

The fact is that men and women have sex well into their seventies, eighties and beyond. They are doing so as you are reading this sentence. I do not want to debate the numbers or percentages, but I can easily say that it is not uncommon. In fact, regular sex in the later years of life is usually a sign of good health, both physical and mental. As the musician Pablo Casals once said, "As long as you can admire and love, then one is young forever."

Now here is the not so good news. Sex can become more difficult as one grows older. Yet, there is a silver lining to even that dark cloud. Many sexual problems in the elderly can be helped with a variety of interventions, which we will discuss later in this chapter.

First, we need to talk about what is normal sex for the elderly. To put it simply, sexual behavior that is normal for the adult is normal for the older adult. For example, an 80-year-old man who is masturbating in the privacy of his own room is expressing normal sexual behavior. If that same man is masturbating in the hallway of his daughter's house, then that is unacceptable behavior. The same would be true if the person was 20 years old. The various types of sexual acts must follow the same general rules in all age groups.

It is normal for older individuals to have more sexual difficulties in three main areas. Some elderly persons may notice a decrease in desire for sex as they get older. Others may have a difficult time becoming excited during the sexual act. Finally, there are those individuals who are finding it more difficult to have an orgasm as they grow older.

IDENTIFYING SEXUAL PROBLEMS

Many older individuals can benefit from the therapeutic interventions available for these difficulties. The problem is that many elderly persons have not benefited from the recent sexual revolution and are still unable to talk openly about sexual matters. Ironically, some older folks are also hampered by the false cultural belief that sex in the elderly is rare. Therefore, they think that their sexual difficulties are a normal result of growing old, and they do not seek help for these problems. If these older folks do not want to talk about sex, then it is difficult for family members to know that they are having concerns in this area. Sometimes an elderly individual may hint about the problem or even joke about it. Pay attention to this. They may be giving you a clue.

Too often the older person just keeps these sexual issues secret. How do we get them to open up? First, you or other close family members need to have an ongoing open dialogue about a variety of issues. If the older person does not feel comfortable talking about other private subjects, such as finances or emotions, then it is unlikely that they will be able to talk about sexual problems.

It is not unusual that the person having difficulty taking about sex is the younger family member. If that is the case, talk with a peer or professional. If you do not feel comfortable talking about the topic of sex, it is likely the older person will sense this and also feel uneasy.

Once you have an open communication process, then you may try discussing sexual issues in general terms that may be more socially acceptable to them. Try to use phrases such as "making love" or "being romantic" instead of "sexual intercourse" or other even more graphic expressions. Sometimes using medical or clinical terms to describe body parts and actions may be more acceptable than lay terms. If you are close to this older individual you may have an idea of what might be acceptable language. It may make it easier for your loved one to open up if the person having the discussion is close to his own age.

Another technique to foster a dialogue is to expose the older person to books or magazine articles, which discuss sexual issues in the elderly. A friend of mine, who felt that his elderly mother was having some sexual issues with a new boyfriend, would, from time to time, leave magazines in her mailbox as if they were free samples. They were publications that would appeal to the elderly population and oftentimes had articles regarding sexual difficulties.

The hope was that his mother would read these publications and then talk about some of the issues as they related to her. It took a while, but finally his mother was able to talk to her doctor about her love for this boyfriend. At the same time, she was able to talk about her lack of sexual desire. She certainly went to the right person for this problem. Her doctor evaluated her medications and found that one of them may have been decreasing her sexual drive. When this medication was stopped, her sexual desire noticeably improved.

Sometimes it is easier for these individuals to talk to their friends or another outside person, such as a medical practitioner or a member of the clergy. If you suspect a problem, encourage this discussion. It is also helpful if you truly are at ease when talking about sexual issues. This sends the message to your loved one that is okay for them to talk about these topics.

An older individual with a sexual problem should have a comprehensive physical evaluation. Many sexual problems are related to medical causes, such as certain types of illnesses or medication reactions. The added advantage is that the elderly person often finds it easier to talk to a medical professional about sexual issues. This can also take the burden off family members who may feel uncomfortable talking about such topics with their elder relatives. Let's turn our discussion to the three basic categories of sexual disorders mentioned earlier.

DECREASED SEXUAL DESIRE

An individual who is having a problem with sexual desire does not feel the need to have sex and usually has a decrease in sexual fantasies. As a result, this person will tend to have a decrease in sexual activity, which can be harmful to a relationship. He or she will act openly disinterested or use a variety of excuses to avoid sex.

As stated previously, a decrease in sexual desire is often seen as a side effect of medication. The list of offending drugs is too long to be cited here. Such medication adjustments should only be carried out under the supervision of a physician. I would strongly discourage anyone from abruptly stopping a medication without professional consultation as that drug may be vital to the person's well being.

Beverly was a 72-year-old woman who I had originally treated for depression. Her initial symptoms included problems with sleep, appetite and sexual desire. She had two sisters who had the same symptoms of depression in the past and benefited from antidepressants. After six weeks on medication, she resolved all of her symptoms except for the decrease in sexual desire. She did not feel it was a problem since she thought that it was just due to old age. Her husband, who was still sexually active, was upset about her lack of desire. Beverly got his message. A few weeks later, Beverly picked up a refill of her high blood pressure medication. She noticed in the handout that was given along with the drug that it could cause a decrease in sexual drive. Beverly had taken this medication for years and noticed no significant difference when she accidentally skipped a dose. So she stopped taking it. Two weeks later she had to go to the emergency room because she was in a hypertensive crisis, which means that her blood pressure was extremely elevated. Beverly was immediately placed back on the blood pressure medication. She explained to the emergency room physician why she had stopped her medication, and he referred her to her family doctor. This physician and I developed a plan to carefully adjust her medications. After we modified her medication regimen, she was able to experience an increase in sexual drive, much to her satisfaction.

Depression is a common cause of decreased sexual drive in both men and women. So, if your loved one has symptoms of depression, you should ask how their love life is going. Do not let that individual assume that significantly decreased sexual desire is natural for someone who is growing older. Ironically, some of the antidepressant medications that doctors prescribe can cause a decrease in sexual desire. In these instances, most symptoms of depression will disappear, but the person's desire may still be low due to the medication. So, be sure that your relative discusses this with their physician. Most medications used for depression, however, will actually increase sexual desire, as the other symptoms of depression are resolved.

The other common cause of decreased sexual desire in the elderly is a physical problem. If an older person is suffering from a physical disorder that is sapping their energy and strength, they may not have the pep needed to have an interest in sex. Some individuals who have had a heart attack will be fearful of having sex and, therefore, lose interest. Women who find sex physically painful can also lose their interest in sex. This pain may be due to the aging process of a woman's sexual organs whereby they are unable to produce enough lubricant in order to make the sex pleasurable. Instead, the tissues become irritated, and intercourse is painful. There are numerous medical conditions that can cause a decrease in sexual desire, and a full physical evaluation is mandatory to diagnose and resolve the problem. As a caring family member, you should make sure that your loved one receives a regular physical examination. It is surprising to see so many elderly individuals consider medical problems as a normal part of aging, and therefore, they do not seek treatment.

A colleague of mine told me that his seventy-year-old father was not expressing the usual affection toward his mother. These were the exact words his mother used to describe the problem. This is a euphemism for the fact that he was not having sex with his wife. Fortunately, his father was comfortable talking about these issues. This elderly gentleman told his son that his mother was feeling depressed because she felt that he did not care for her. He went on to tell his son that he was unable to have sex because it was so painful for him the next day. Over the last decade he had been suffering from increasing arthritis that was limiting his movements causing him to be stiff and sore every morning. The day after sex was particularly painful for him. Even though his family members knew that he had arthritis, they never realized the degree of his pain and limitations. This was because he figured that arthritis was just a part of getting older and nothing could be done to help him. Consequently, he did not complain. I told my friend to encourage his father to go see a physician for an evaluation of his arthritis. A couple of months later, he told me that his mother was happy.

This type of situation occurs far too often. If an older person finds sex painful or uncomfortable, it is likely that they will not look forward to it. Thus, their sexual desire decreases, and at times this can have a negative impact upon their relationships.

PROBLEMS WITH SEXUAL PERFORMANCE

The ability to perform sex can also be affected by medications and physical disorders. For example, one of the most common causes of erection problems in an elderly man is prostate surgery. There are other physical causes of erectile dysfunction in the elderly. Common examples include hypertension, heart disease and diabetes. Treating the illness and bringing it under control can sometimes help re-establish proper sexual functioning. There are also medications, that are too numerous to mention here, that can decrease a man's ability to perform. A thorough medical evaluation is helpful in determining the possible causes of erection problems.

Unfortunately, erection problems become more common as men age. Successfully treating the medical illness does not always result in improved functioning. The good news is that there are now distinct drugs that can specifically treat erection problems. These medications, however, should only be used under the supervision of a physician because they can cause side effects that are rather problematic for an older man. In addition, these drugs can interact with other medications that an individual is taking. It is not wise to buy these medications over the Internet or through some other process that bypasses the physician. Only a physician should prescribe these medications, and only after a thorough medical assessment is made. Once the medication is dispensed, the elderly individual should receive ongoing monitoring so that any further problems can be immediately addressed.

Medication is not always required to improve erectile functioning. There are professional therapists that can teach new techniques for improving sexual activity. This therapy usually requires participation of both partners. It is important to note that having an available sex partner is related to better sexual functioning. Regular sexual activity, even in older individuals, can also improve overall sexual functioning. The great thing about this therapeutic approach is that it rarely produces side effects, which is important for older individuals.

Older women can also have performance problems during the sexual act. The sensitivity of sexual areas may diminish. There can be a reduction in the lubrication of vital areas that results in painful intercourse. Often there is a medical cause for painful intercourse. Medications also can play an important role by causing side effects that decrease lubrication and make sexual activity uncomfortable. Even some over-the-counter medications, like certain cold preparations, can produce these side effects.

Eliminating the medical cause can often reduce the woman's performance problems. Stopping or adjusting certain medications can also be helpful. Artificial lubricants that are recommended by a physician can improve the quality of sexual intercourse. Some lotions or creams can actually be irritating or harmful and cause more problems with sexual activity. Thus, it is important to obtain professional advice to determine what specific remedy is appropriate for you.

PROBLEMS WITH ORGASMS

A third area of sexual problems in the elderly occurs during the orgasm phase. Painful sexual activity or any other difficulties during the sexual act can prevent an orgasm from occurring or cause an orgasm to be less intense or unsatisfying. This can happen in both men and women.

Orgasm problems in a woman may be related to painful sexual activity, an infection, increased tension, irritability or fatigue. Eliminating the pain or infection often requires a medical intervention. Eliminating tension, irritability or fatigue may require further exploration as to why these elements are occurring during the sexual act. Sometimes only one negative element needs to occur during the sexual act, and it can cause a domino effect that snowballs to a point where an orgasm will just not occur.

A woman in her mid-sixties came to see me because she was afraid she would never be able to have another orgasm. Sex had always been pleasurable for her, and she had regular orgasms. A month before she came to see me, there was a night where she and her husband tried to have sex but were interrupted by some unidentified noise outside. She became anxious and slightly jumped. All of a sudden, she felt a pain in her genitals that lasted for about a second. Her tension increased, and she was fearful that her partner might accidentally hurt her during the sexual act. Within a couple of minutes, she noticed an irritation and was now worried that something was wrong. She stated that she desperately wanted an orgasm but just could not continue the sexual act. Over the next few weeks, she and her husband tried to have sexual intercourse on several occasions. She failed to achieve an orgasm during these times because she was worried that the pain might come back and signal that something was indeed wrong with her. It seemed like the harder she tried, the less success she had. Since she had not had a physical evaluation in two years I suggested that she see her primary care doctor. After she reported that she had a clean bill of health, I suggested that she and her husband come in to discuss their situation. The first thing we talked about was the importance of having an orgasm. It was clear that having an orgasm was the gold standard for her in terms of the quality of sex. I asked her if she enjoyed the sexual activity prior to an orgasm before she had these difficulties. She stated that it was very satisfying. I then encouraged the two of them at least for the next few weeks just to have gentle sexual foreplay without trying to have an orgasm or attempting intercourse. About a month later I saw them again, and they both agreed that this type of sex was surprisingly enjoyable. I then instructed them to try intercourse in a very gentle manner but do not bring it to a climax. I saw them in another month, but they stated that they failed. They were able to follow my instructions for the first week, but then after that they could not stop the orgasm. During the next three weeks they still tried to have gentle intercourse without an orgasm but continued to fail, with both having orgasms on a regular basis. I asked them that if they could have sex like they had had over the last three weeks for the rest of their life, would they be happy. They both enthusiastically stated yes. Except for a couple of postcards telling me that they had the time of their lives while vacationing, I never had contact with them again.

As you can see, it does not take much to upset the apple cart when it comes to sex. At the same time, sex therapy can be quite effective. This is especially true if physical problems are completely ruled out. It is absolutely necessary for an older person to obtain a thorough physical examination before sex therapy should be attempted. The number of medical illnesses that can impair sexual functioning in the elderly is quite high. For example, there are over numerous medical disorders that can lead to erection problems alone.

Once the medical cause of sexual dysfunction is discovered, it often can be treated to the point where improved sexual functioning can occur. There are occasions when medical treatment is not possible or is unsuccessful. That is when sex therapy can often help.

This chapter will not attempt to cover all the various sex therapy techniques that can be used in older individuals. There are many books on this topic that can be helpful. However, I would certainly not suggest that family members attempt sex therapy with their elderly relatives. There are experts available in this area who can help the older folks. On the other hand, family members can be on the lookout for any changes in the relationships between their older relatives. Be observant for any words or phrases that can imply that there are some sexual difficulties. Remember, the elderly tend not to use specific graphic sexual jargon as younger adults do. More than likely they will complain that their partner does not love or care for them as they had in the past. Sometimes you will hear the comment that their partner has lost interest.

If you suspect that your relatives have problems in the sexual area, it is important to convince them to seek help because many of these problems can be treated. Before you can talk to them about such issues, it is important that you have already established an open and honest communication process. You will also need to use general sexual terms that will be acceptable to them. It may not be a bad idea to have them read the chapter in this book. Many older individuals have a difficult time talking about sex face-to-face. It could be helpful if you were able to provide them with a list of physicians or therapists who can perform the proper physical evaluation, as well as the potential therapy. Older individuals sometimes can find it embarrassing to track down such resources.

Lastly, you need to follow-up with this process. You may need to have several discussions in order to convince your family member to get help. Do not give up after your first try. It is not unusual that it may take some time to convince older folks to seek help in this area.

After they begin treatment, make sure that they continue throughout the entire process. It is not unusual for some older individuals to become embarrassed during the initial phase of the treatment process and drop out of therapy. Let your family members know that you are truly concerned about their relationship, and you would like to see them live happily together as they had in the past. This is the reason an ongoing discussion about this process will more likely lead to a positive result. Explain to them that you are not trying to pry but are only trying to make sure they are successful.

INAPPROPRIATE SEXUAL BEHAVIORS

The other side of sexual problems in the elderly occurs when these behaviors prove to be embarrassing for the family, friends or the community. It is not unusual for an older person, who is showing early signs of dementia, to leave the bathroom door open and accidentally expose him or herself. Some individuals who have memory problems can often forget simple things like closing the bathroom door. This, obviously, can be embarrassing for anyone who walks by.

Similar problems include undressing in public or going into the community only partially dressed. Extremely confused individuals may not realize where they are and urinate in a public area because they believe that they are in a bathroom. For example, a colleague of mine told me that his grandfather went into a dressing room at a local store and thought it was the bathroom. Needless to say, he caused quite a scene.

At times, older individuals, who have brain damage or some type of mental illness, will behave in a sexually inappropriate fashion. They may speak in a crude or sexually vulgar manner. Some of these individuals are described as oversexed. They may talk incessantly about sex. Others may be involved in repeated sexual behaviors such as excessive masturbation.

The best way to handle most of these individuals is to calmly redirect them to another activity that is more appropriate. For example, if they are exposing themselves, have a robe or other piece of clothing that can be quickly put on so that they can be fully dressed as soon as possible. Above all, do not get upset as this never helps.

If the older person is involved in excessive sexual behavior, try to redirect them into some other type of behavior that they may find interesting. For example, an older person who masturbates to an extreme degree may just be doing so because it is the only thing that feels good. Try to identify other pleasurable acts, such as eating or listening to music, as that may divert his or her attention.

Individuals who are involved in excessive sexual behaviors are sometimes very difficult to redirect. They may require a professional who is an expert in behavior modification therapy. Local psychiatric or psychological organizations can provide the names of such experts. Medications can sometimes be helpful. Psychiatrists who work with brain-damaged individuals know about drugs that can decrease the sexual drive or impulsive sexual behaviors. These medications should be used as a last resort.

Some older people may act in what appears to be a sexually inappropriate manner but are actually responding to some type of physical problem. For example, a person who has a urinary tract infection or a rash in the genital area may be touching himself or herself in a way that appears as though they are acting out sexually when they are just trying to relieve some noxious stimulus. Once again a physical evaluation is a necessity.

Another area of particular distress for the family is when the older individual acts out sexually in front of a child, such as an accidental exposure. It is important to calmly and matter-of-factly redirect the older person and remove the child from the situation. Explain to the child that this person does not know what he is doing or that he forgets where he is. Children usually understand when simple and calm explanations are provided.

A similar situation can occur when the older individual acts inappropriately with an adult. For example, if a demented father makes an inappropriate advance toward his daughter, it is likely that he is confusing his daughter with either his wife or some old girlfriend. It is best just to redirect this behavior and try not to be rattled by it. Sometimes it is helpful to talk with other family members about such a potentially distressing event so that you can receive some support and reassurance.

Family support is particularly helpful for the spouse of a demented or psychotic person who is acting in a sexually inappropriate manner.

Henry had been residing in an assisted-living home for demented persons for the last two years when his wife noticed that he was trying to have sexual contact with another woman in this facility. This obviously was quite upsetting for his wife. The nursing staff at this facility arranged a meeting with the significant family members. The head nurse explained that Henry was trying to strike up a relationship with a woman whom he felt was his old girlfriend. This other woman was so confused that she played right along. The staff outlined to the family a plan to separate the two individuals. Unfortunately,

Henry became very upset because he could not see his "old girlfriend" anymore and constantly complained to his wife about this. When his wife tried to convince him that she was married to him he denied this. He felt that his real wife was his mother. This led to numerous arguments every time she visited him. The wife was now even more distressed by this turn of events. At this point, various family members talked with her in order to convince her that this was just part of her husband's dementia that could not be helped. She required a great deal of reassurance, as anyone in her position would. Because she did not like that her husband was always angry with her now when she visited, she agreed that the nursing staff should allow him to talk to this other woman. She also vowed that she would not argue with him regarding this issue. At the same time, she wanted him to be redirected by the nursing staff if he became sexually inappropriate. Because she was willing to make this difficult compromise, her visits became more pleasant. Surprisingly, a few weeks later Henry would ignore the other woman when his wife came to visit, even though Henry thought his wife was his mother.

Because I knew the family in the above case, I knew that they were extremely supportive of their mother. They also wanted to see their father get the best care. The family refused to have their father medicated in order to stop the problem. Sometimes a family member wants their loved one medicated in order to inhibit such behavior. There are some medications that can reduce sexual drive and others that can decrease impulsivity. Yet, these medications can cause side effects in the elderly, and their success rate is at best mixed. These interventions are usually reserved for severe behavioral problems.

Older individuals who have a brain injury or other type of brain disease will sometimes become hypersexual or sexually overactive. This can cause great stress for the spouse. Family support with some professional education will help explain to the affected family members that this behavior is caused by a neurologic problem, a problem that the person cannot help. It is by no means a criticism of the marital relationship. Nevertheless, the spouse will require constant support and reassurance that it is not him or her who is the problem.

If the hypersexual individual is constantly demanding sex, then there are several options that can be used in order to decrease the problem. For example, sometimes it is helpful for each partner to sleep in a separate bedroom. Giving hypersexual individuals a strenuous daytime schedule in order to tire them out will usually decrease their energy and desire to have sex later in the day. Even if the impaired individual has a deficit in cognitive ability, it can be helpful to have the spouse tell them that it is difficult for them to have sex as much as he or she desires. At the same time, the spouse should verbally reinforce that they still love their partner. Even demented individuals will try to keep their spouse happy by cooperating. It is often frustrating for the spouse to handle these situations because, if they kiss or hug their partner, then this may be misinterpreted as a desire for sex. Counselors who are expert in the area of the elderly may be consulted in order to guide a family through such difficult times.

Conducting a normal sexual relationship with a demented individual who has a normal sex drive can be problematic. Often the spouse is also the caregiver and is tired and depressed regarding the situation. That person is just not interested in sex. For this reason and numerous others, it is often helpful to have some respite time for the caregiver. This is time that they should use for their own benefit as a break from the daily stress of care giving.

Going shopping, taking a trip or having a night out can help clear one's mind and enable the caregiver or family member to return with a fresh attitude. That person might even be interested in sex.

Arranging respite time will take some additional effort, but the payback is well worth it. Do not be embarrassed to ask for help from other family members, friends or religious groups. The primary caregiver deserves some time off. Professional nursing staff is available for temporary employment. You can look for these individuals in the phone book or call the local government office on aging for a list of resources. Most importantly, try to have a regular schedule of respite time for yourself. Based on experience, this approach works the best by far.

At times, the impaired individual can have a lower sex drive, either due to a brain disorder or medications, and cannot satisfy demands of the spouse. Persons who are demented or have some elements of psychosis may misidentify their partner and sometimes not recognize them at all. Any of these scenarios can be quite difficult for the spouse to handle. These individuals need to talk to someone. Friends, family members or professional counselors can really help. It is important to recognize that, if a normal relationship is deteriorating because of a person's mental state, it is necessary to develop new and strong relationships that will build an emotional foundation for the future. Family members and friends need to provide this support and reassurance. Remember, your loved one is essentially beginning the grief process. As the wife of one of my patients once said, she felt she was actually beginning the funeral process while her spouse was still alive. As you can see, this is a very difficult time for these individuals, and they require the care and concern of all.

Let me summarize some of the major points. Try to have the best possible communication process amongst all the family members including the impaired individual. This will allow you to talk about sex in a much more comfortable fashion. Next, make sure that the impaired individual receives a thorough physical examination so that any medical problems causing sexual difficulties can be identified. Try to deal with any inappropriate sexual behavior in a calm and matter-of-fact way. Finally, keep your communication channels going in a concerned and caring way. The affected individual and his or her partner will appreciate all of the support that you can provide.

CHAPTER TWELVE
Sleep Disorders

Sleep problems not only affect the person with a sleep disorder, but the family members and caregivers around them. Lack of sleep can lead to decreased energy, weakness, daytime sleepiness, irritability and the potential for accidents, such as falls. These symptoms can make it difficult for the caregiver to help the patient function throughout the day. Persons with dementia, delirium or other mental disorders may have problems thinking and other decreased cognitive functioning, secondary to lack of sleep. Chronic sleep problems can affect a person's attention, memory and overall performance.

Beatrice was an eighty-year-old woman who was brought to my office by her family because she was not getting enough sleep. She would be up all night, walking throughout the house, opening the refrigerator or moving furniture because she was so restless that she could not fall asleep. Her family reported that she would often sleep during the day taking up to five or six naps. Because of her noisy, late night activities, family members were also losing sleep. First, I asked Beatrice to stop her daytime naps. I had the family members watch her during the day and encourage her to stay awake. We then scheduled a variety of activities to keep Beatrice busy during the day. Initially it was difficult for her to stay awake throughout the day, and she did complain about this approach. Beatrice and the family ultimately persevered, and she returned to a normal sleep schedule without the use of medications.

First, let us talk about normal sleep and the elderly individual. As we age, our capacity to sleep deeply and for prolonged periods decreases. When we pass through our fifth or sixth decade the number of awakenings during the night tend to increase. In later years, the number of naps people take during the day increases. As a result, our ability to sleep efficiently decreases as we age.

Sometimes our internal body clock is altered as we grow older. For example, if an older person feels sleepy early in the evening and goes to bed at 8 p.m., he may wake up at 3 or 4 a.m. feeling that he has not slept through the night and therefore did not get the proper amount of rest. In reality, he slept for eight hours but it was the wrong eight hours.

To correct the problem of sleeping during the wrong hours of the day, you need to plan structured activities throughout the daytime so that the person will be tired at the right time in the evening and sleep throughout the night.

Having the individual take a carefully timed nap during the day may alleviate the early evening tiredness allowing that person to stay up to 10 or 11 p.m. and then sleeping until 6 or 7 a.m. You need to be careful using these naps as sometimes it may complicate the problem. People respond to naps differently, naps can help certain persons stay awake until the right bedtime. On the other hand, they may keep other people up later than desired, and this may disrupt the sleep schedule. Recent research has shown that bright light may keep some individuals up later so that they can get to sleep at a more normal hour. Often a combination of these interventions will be needed to correct the problem.

INSOMNIA

Insomnia is the lack of adequate sleep. The amount of sleep needed varies with each individual. Some elderly people can function well on five hours of sleep while others may require as much as nine hours. The best way to determine the amount of sleep needed is to ask the individual what is the minimum number of hours of sleep required in order to wake up relatively refreshed and able to function. That number would be the normal amount of sleep for that individual. I would only like to give one word of caution. It may be difficult for an elderly person, who has a number of medical problems, to feel refreshed no matter how much sleep he gets. You should take this into account when you talk to someone who says they are not getting enough sleep.

Decreased sleep in older adults is often related to medical problems. Persons with physical problems, such as heart or lung disease, as well as mental disorders such as depression and anxiety, are all at a higher risk of having sleep problems. Individuals with dementia also tend to have more sleep problems than the average older person. Sleep disorders are also common in patients who have pain secondary to medical problems, such as arthritis or cancer. Neurological problems, such as restless leg syndrome, can cause sleep difficulties.

Side effects due to medications are often the cause of poor sleep. Some drugs may cause a patient to be hyper and restless at night when they need to calm down and fall sleep. Other medications can make a patient drowsy during the day, causing that individual to take naps and leaving him wide-awake at night when he should be sleeping. It is important to have a physician evaluate these persons so that the offending agent can be discovered and, hopefully, eliminated by substituting one medication for another which may not cause sleep problems. In other instances, the medication may be given at a different time of day. For example, if a medication is known to cause tiredness, it can be given at night. A stimulating medication can be given early in the day so that its effects wear off by evening. Consult your doctor before making any such changes.

TREATING INSOMNIA

The first step in dealing with a sleep disorder such as insomnia is to make a chart outlining when an individual goes to bed, falls asleep and awakens. If a person gets up several times during the night, they should record in the chart the specific times that they awoke. This chart is called a sleep diary. It will help measure the progress made with any intervention. It is helpful to have a person write down the next day if there were any disturbances through the night such as sounds, bathroom trips etc. that broke up his sleep. This sleep chart should be kept near the bedside so that it requires a minimal amount of effort to be completed.

Self-treatment of a sleep disorder begins with good sleep hygiene. Make sure the elderly individual follows these rules. Set regular times to sleep and awaken. Stick to this schedule on a consistent basis. Reduce any noise or light stimulation that might cause one to rouse. Keep the sleeping environment comfortable, not too hot and not too cold. Use a quality supportive mattress so that you can sleep in comfort throughout the night. Sometimes soft music or a hum from a fan or air purifier can be hypnotic and can help a person fall asleep.

Avoid taking daytime naps as they can disrupt the sleep-wake cycle. Do not drink a beverage with caffeine for at least six hours prior to going to sleep. It would be better to avoid caffeine altogether. Do not exercise or participate in other stimulating activity for several hours prior to going to sleep. Try not to eat a large meal or drink excessive fluids before bedtime. Avoid spicy food and alcohol, which can cause indigestion that can disrupt your sleep. Stimulating medication such as decongestants should be avoided during the evening hours. Be careful of over-the-counter sleep medications that can cause serious side effects. Consult your physician before you try any of these preparations.

Behavioral treatment should be the next intervention tried when one has a sleep disorder. Psychiatrists and psychologists are skilled in this type of treatment. Some components of this therapy include the prohibition of naps during the day or lying in bed only when one is sleepy. The specifics of this intervention will depend on the pattern of sleep as outlined in the sleep diary.

Treatment using the behavioral approach has two advantages. First, it eliminates the use of medications, which may have their own side effects, particularly if used over a long period of time. Second, a behavioral approach can result in long-lasting gains, even after the therapy is finished. Medications, on the other hand, usually lose their effect once the person stops taking the drugs. The disadvantage is that a behavioral approach takes more time and is often more expensive.

Pharmacological treatment of a sleep disorder is the most common method currently utilized. The advantage of this approach is that the medications usually work immediately. This is consistent with the current "fast food" approach of medicine.

If a person has a psychiatric disorder that may be contributing to his sleep problems, then that disorder needs to be treated with the appropriate medications. Depression, anxiety, psychosis and bipolar disorders are some common illnesses that have sleep problems as part of their symptom spectrum. We have already discussed some of the medication management of persons with these diagnoses in previous chapters.

Older persons with no mental disorder can be treated with some of the same medications. Antidepressants and occasionally anti-psychotic medications are often prescribed for sleep problems because they are not generally addictive. The sedating antidepressants are typically used. Unfortunately, some of these medications can cause daytime sleepiness or decreased energy because their effects may last too long. It is important that they are taken at the proper time and at the proper dosage to reduce this possibility. The elderly are particularly susceptible to other side effects of these medications including low blood pressure, a higher risk of falls and shakiness of the legs. Physician monitoring of these medications is required.

Another category of sleep medications is the antihistamines. These are the medications found in cold preparations that cause drowsiness at bedtime. Older persons often use these drugs, as they are easy to obtain without a prescription.

Sleep medications called benzodiazepines are commonly used in the elderly. There are several choices of medications in this category. An important common factor in these medications is that they are short acting. Their effects only last a few hours. Therefore, a person can take these medications in order to fall asleep, continue sleeping for a few hours and then awake refreshed. These medications can cause increased confusion or delirium in the elderly. Tolerance to these medications may develop after a few weeks of use. Essentially, this means that they stop working after a period of time. Increasing these medications will only cause further side effects. Therefore, these medications should only be used for short periods of time in order to help the impaired individual regain a normal pattern of sleep. Once this occurs, the medication should be tapered and discontinued. Again, physician monitoring is strongly recommended with the use of any medication. Side effects of the benzodiazepines include memory problems, falls and trouble breathing particularly for those persons who already have problems with their lungs. Therefore, these medications should not only be given for a short period of time, but also at the lowest effective dose.

There are newer medications on the market that act like benzodiazepines but have a better safety profile. It is believed that they do not have any tolerance problems. That means they can be effectively used for longer periods of time. It is also believed that they may produce a more natural sleep. These medications, however, can cause nausea and dizziness. The dizziness obviously can lead to an increased risk of falls. These medications have only been the market for the last few years, and it is still too early to guarantee that they are much safer than their predecessors. Whatever category of medications you or your elderly relative choose, you should first consult a physician and thoroughly discuss the pros and cons of their use. It is also essential that the physician monitor the medication therapy on an ongoing basis.

HYPERSOMNIA

At the other end of the spectrum is the older individual who is suffering from hypersomnia. This disorder of sleeping excessively is less common and usually has a physical cause. The most common reason for older people sleeping excessively is a side effect of one or more medications the individual is taking. Other common causes of this disorder are serious physical illnesses that drain the person's energy leaving them listless and sleepy all the time. Cancer, heart failure and lung disease are the usual suspects, but there are many medical illnesses that can cause this problem. Depression can also cause this symptom.

Too much sleep can produce a number of complications. Memory problems and confusion can be seen in any person who is sleeping far too much. Due to their inactivity, individuals with this disorder can become progressively weaker. Older persons with this disorder are more prone to have falls and broken bones.

A thorough medical assessment is required in order to find a cause of excessive sleeping. This symptom may actually be the first sign of a serious problem in the older person. Thus, the underlying medical illness needs to be identified and treated. A comprehensive review of person's medications should also be undertaken. The physician, once he identifies the offending agent, can substitute another medication. There are also instances in which the problematic medication is no longer needed and can be eliminated.

NIGHT TERRORS

One final sleep disorder seen in the elderly is known as a night terror. Night terrors are often ascribed to younger children who wake up screaming in the middle of the night as if they experienced an extremely disturbing nightmare. This similar behavior can occur in older individuals who are confused, paranoid or demented. This condition often occurs when the older individual has to sleep in a new environment.

When these individuals wake up screaming, they often cannot recognize their environment. Remember, these persons already have distorted thinking or perception because of their mental illness. Sometimes they have a difficult time determining what is real and what is not during that in-between state of being fully awake and asleep. They often are unable to recognize their own room and perceive their environment as threatening and scary. This screaming behavior in the middle of a night can be quite upsetting to family members as well. It is not unusual for the affected person to wake up in the middle of the night and not even remember why they screamed.

Non-pharmacological interventions should be tried first. Keeping a light on in the room can help them identify their surroundings when they awaken. This is often enough to reassure them and reduce the chances of night terrors. Other techniques include having large pictures of family members or familiar objects around to help them orient themselves. I have seen family members leave the television or radio on which acts as a familiar stimulus that helps orient these individuals.

At times, however, some of these interventions just do not work. In that case, there are medications that a physician can prescribe that can help the patient sleep better and also decrease the brain's ability to dream. This seems to help older individuals with night terrors. These persons need to be monitored carefully because some of these medications can actually make the person more confused and more susceptible to night terrors. Remember, medications are not always the best answer.

As you can see from our discussion on sleep disorders, there are a number of interventions that do not require medications. If possible, they should be tried first. If all else fails, then careful use of medications can be helpful, but only under the guidance of a physician.

CHAPTER THIRTEEN
Annoying Behaviors

In previous chapters we have talked about the major areas of behavior problems in the elderly. Elderly individuals with mental problems can, however, display a wide variety of behaviors that are difficult for the community, friends and family to handle. I wish I could say that by the end of this chapter we will cover all the possible conduct problems an impaired individual can have. Having been in the business of treating these persons for the last 25 years, I periodically come into contact with new and unusual problems that require creative and challenging solutions. So, I cannot guarantee that we will be able to cover all possible situations as new ones arise every day.

DEPENDENT BEHAVIOR

Dependent or clinging behavior is a common problem that occurs in the impaired elderly individual. This conduct can occur in a person who has never shown signs of a dependent personality disorder. It is easy to understand why these behaviors originate. Depressed, demented or psychotic individuals have to depend on others to carry out some of their functions when they cannot. To some extent, this behavior is to be expected. Sometimes these people will expect you to help them with tasks that they should be able to handle. This is a sign that the person is displaying dependent traits that could cause problems. It seems that the more these individuals rely on people around them, the more dependent they become. They may become so dependent that they will follow the caregiver around from room to room and never let them alone. If the person is bedridden, they may call for help throughout the day. This repetitive behavior can be particularly stressful for the caregiver.

The basic solution for this problem is to try to redirect the individual with some activity that the impaired individual may find interesting. I have found that elderly women like to dust or fold clothes. Sometimes they like to arrange items in the house or perform some other household activities in order to make themselves feel useful. Give them some of these tasks.

Men like to putter. They will enjoy taking things apart and putting them back together. I often tell family members to find something simple for the man to fix. Do not give an impaired person a task that requires the use of dangerous items such as power tools or an iron.

Family members often ask me what type of jobs they can give to their family member that would interest them. I recommend that they take a look at the interests their family member had in the past. Specifically, I ask them what kind of jobs or hobbies they had in years past, and if there was a simple task in that job that they could repeat at this time.

Carlin was 84-year-old man who was brought into my office by his family because they said that he was getting into everything at home. He had been in a state psychiatric hospital for the last 20 years with a diagnosis of schizophrenia, but his daughter felt that he should come home to live with his family during the last years of his life. Carlin would always follow people, even into the bathroom. This became quite a nuisance as the family members had a difficult time maintaining their privacy around the home. Carlin would also go around the home and unplug every appliance. I met with the family on a few occasions, and we tried all kinds of activities in order to redirect Carlin. Nothing seemed to hold his attention for more than a few minutes, and he was back to pulling plugs or following people. He had been diagnosed with schizophrenia over 50 years ago, and communicating with him was almost impossible. He could express some simple needs, but he could not carry on an understandable conversation. Therefore, no one could reason with him. Then I met with Carlin's younger sisters, and they were able to tell me that when he was young he had a coin collection. The family members made a project of collecting all coins possessed by the immediate family. In addition, they went to a local coin shop in order to purchase some collection books where the coins could be actually stored. The project was a success. Carlin would spend hours on end collecting the coins, stacking them and sorting them. He would put them in the storage books and then take them out and do it all over again. His clinging, following and unplugging behaviors were reduced to a minimum. Most importantly, he had the biggest smile while accomplishing this task.

Redirection of an elderly impaired person is a common intervention that is used to reduce abnormal or dependent behaviors. Yet, as I said in an earlier chapter, family members need to be good detectives. If the usual interventions do not work, do not give up. Keep analyzing the situation. Brainstorming among family members is an effective way of finding solutions.

REPETITIOUS BEHAVIOR

Another common problem is the repetitive behavior of an individual with a mental disorder. This was seen in the story of Carlin outlined above. Sometimes doctors use the term "perseveration" to describe these repetitious actions. Carlin liked to unplug. Other elderly individuals will dust furniture over and over again. Others may wash the same item repeatedly. These repeatable behaviors often seem to calm the individual. This is based on the fact that sometimes, when you try to interrupt these behaviors, the person will become quite agitated. Do not try to abruptly stop these activities even though they may be quite annoying. Also, do not force them to stop their repetitions, nor should you try to argue with them. This will only upset them and lead to more problems.

Some family members feel that, at times, these repetitive actions can actually be useful. They can help the elderly person feel content. If the behavior is not annoying, these repetitions can keep the person busy and keep him or her from other negative activity.

Because redirection is a useful tool to reduce these behaviors when they become annoying, it is best to use this technique in simple and subtle ways. Gentle touching to get the person's attention and then leading them to another more productive activity is often a successful approach. For example, instead of telling a person to stop washing a specific area it may be better to grasp their hand gently and lead them to another area where they could wash something that needs to be cleaned. This will not work if the impaired person does not like to be touched. You will usually know this based on past experience with the individual.

People who have mental disorders and have a difficult time communicating can respond positively to this touching approach, but this may not work for everyone. Some patients who are psychotic, demented or paranoid may interpret touching as some type of physical aggression. Hopefully, by the time you are ready to use this technique you will know if your loved one likes to be touched. If you are unsure, be careful with this intervention the first time you use it and observe the person's response. Explain to them what you are doing so the touching does not take them by surprise and is not misinterpreted.

If your loved one does not like to be touched, it might be useful to hand that person an item that might distract them. A woman who repeatedly tried to dry dishes and dropped quite a few was given some unbreakable plastic dishes which kept her busy and out of trouble. A man who would repeatedly write on every surface in the house was given an artist's brush without paint, which he continued to use, even though it did not make a mark.

VERBAL ABUSE

Insulting or verbally abusive behavior is another common problem seen in elderly persons with a mental disorder. This is not only an issue in demented individuals but also in persons with bipolar illness, schizophrenia or narcissistic personality disorder, as well as some other diagnoses. For example, the person with a bipolar illness may feel that he or she is far above everyone else and may say things that belittle others. A schizophrenic person may be out of touch with reality and insult a relative believing that person is someone else. Another example would be a woman with a diagnosis of paranoid schizophrenia who called her sister a prostitute, because she did not believe that her sister was related to her. Instead, she believed her sister was a woman who was having an affair with her husband.

These verbal outbursts are embarrassing for the family, particularly if they happen in public. At other times, these comments are just hurtful. There are also instances when the impaired individual accuses his family members of doing something mean to him, such as stealing or lying. The natural human response is to defend oneself by getting into an argument about the comment that is being made. Yet, this is rarely helpful. Arguing usually upsets both individuals and almost never leads to an ideal resolution.

I usually tell family members to first ask the individual who made the claim to explain what it means. Believe it or not, the individual may just be upset and may have made the statement out of frustration. Even normal people say things that they do not mean when they are angry.

Florio was a 76-year-old man who was being treated for depression. His sister, who routinely brought him in for his appointment, asked to speak to me at the end of an office visit. The sister, who was his major caretaker, was upset because Florio accused her of being mean and uncaring. I told her to go home and ask him what he meant when he accused her of being mean and uncaring. At the next visit, she told me that Florio had been upset because his children were not visiting him. He explained that he was not upset with her but with his family in general. This provided some sense of relief for her.

A person with a mental illness may have a difficult time stating exactly what he means. He may use the wrong words and phrases, and what comes out is not what he wanted to say. Some persons who have had a stroke can suffer damage to the language area of their brain. This can make it difficult for them to choose the right words. Instead, they may speak words that they do not intend to say, words that can have negative connotations and could be insulting.

Damage to the front part of the brain can cause a person to say mean or inappropriate things. This area of the brain functions as our internal censor. Let us say that someone cuts us off while we are driving on the expressway. We may think of certain expletives that we would like to say, but we refrain from doing so. A person with damage to the frontal lobe of the brain may lack this good judgment. This could lead them to blurt out curse words and other inappropriate statements, which could cause a volatile situation. An individual with this type of brain disorder might lose the ability to be tactful. If he or she did not care for a certain relative, they may blurt out that they do not like the individual.

It is difficult to prevent all possible inappropriate verbal outbursts in a brain-damaged individual due to the fact that these behaviors are often unpredictable. It is important for family members to understand that they do not exactly mean what they say. It is equally important for these relatives to explain to other people, who have contact with the impaired person, that they are unable to speak appropriately, secondary to the brain damage or a mental illness. They should be told not to take their comments personally. If the outburst occurs in a public area where there are strangers around, it might be best to redirect this individual away from that setting.

There are a number of strategies to handle this problem. First, we have already talked about the intervention of asking them to explain their negative comments. If these individuals still have some normal brain functioning, they may be able to realize the inappropriateness of their statements and hopefully explain them in a more positive manner. In the example where the impaired individual made the statement that they did not like a relative, they may later modify their statement to say that they did not like a certain quality of that individual. Help them find the right words to explain their situation.

If they do not have this capacity, sometimes it is helpful to simply ignore their inappropriate statements and not take them seriously. This can take some practice because repetitive complaints can hurt, no matter what the source. Remember we are only human. If anyone has a difficult time ignoring these complaints or insults, it is helpful to talk with other family members or health care professionals for support.

You have seen the term "redirection" used in a variety of ways in order to handle problems in the impaired older individual. Elderly persons who are being verbally abusive can be redirected by simply talking with them in order to change the subject. If an individual is constantly complaining about how their son does not visit them, it might be helpful to talk about why these visits do not occur. An alternate response might be to ask the person what can be done to motivate the son to visit. This will change the tone of the discussion to a more constructive one, which may lead to positive change.

Sometimes a confused or psychotic person can make serious complaints, such as they are being physically abused. Because there have been numerous instances of physical abuse in the elderly, many of these claims need to be investigated. This is often a heartbreaking and embarrassing experience for innocent family members.

Keep in mind that such an investigation does not mean that you are automatically being judged as guilty. These are routine inquiries mandated by law to protect the elderly at risk.

If the impaired older person, who is severely confused, continues to make false complaints of abuse, it is useful to change the subject or distract them by asking them to help you with a task. If they have some thinking ability left, ask them directly why they are making such statements. Do not be afraid to gently tell them that these complaints are hurtful. Above all, do not argue as this always leads to a worse scenario.

SCREAMING

A variant of unacceptable verbal behavior is screaming. These outbursts may occur occasionally or constantly. They are very disturbing to those around them. If the screaming person is living in a nursing home or an assisted-living facility they are often referred to a hospital for treatment, because it is it difficult to tolerate their behavior. A mentally impaired older individual who screams is a treatment challenge for even the most astute professional.

The first step in dealing with such an individual is to provide a thorough medical workup. Screamers are often quite confused. Some of these people are trying to communicate their needs by screaming. They may be in pain or discomfort but are unable to state exactly what is wrong. A comprehensive physical evaluation may provide a diagnosis that could be the cause of the patient's screaming.

Anthony was an 86-year-old man who had been the victim of numerous strokes, which ultimately led to a significant amount of confusion. He had been living in a nursing home for the last four years. The administrator of this nursing home asked me to see this individual because he was constantly screaming day and night over a several week period. Just before I saw Anthony, the primary care doctor of the nursing home evaluated him. As a part of the medical workup a number of x-rays were taken. A number of newly fractured vertebrae were identified. Anthony was placed in a supportive device and within a few days the screaming stopped abruptly. I never did have to see him.

If a person screams only periodically, it is important to identify what is going on within the environment at that specific time that might be stimulating this behavior. For example, a paranoid individual might be screaming because they are fearful of a certain person. A dependent person might be screaming in order to get attention or have their needs met. Family members and friends will need to observe what was going on at the time when the screaming started.

Berta was a 78-year-old woman who was living with her daughter since she broke her hip. Every few days Berta would wake up in the middle of the night and scream as loud as she could. By the time the daughter arrived at her bedside, Berta could only state that she had a nightmare of someone breaking into the room. After a few episodes of screaming, the family wanted to put her in a nursing home. The daughter called their family physician and asked what she needed to do in order to make this happen. He told the daughter to bring her mother in for an evaluation. The doctor, who was a friend of mine, performed the evaluation and could find no reason for this behavior. He then gave me a call. I instructed him to tell the family to put a tape recorder by her bedside and turn it on when she goes to sleep. After two or three screaming episodes, the family was able to identify certain sounds in her room just prior to the scream. They were able to recognize sounds of wind rustling through the trees with the branches scraping her window on those nights when she was screaming. Berta was later able to confirm this by stating she heard in her nightmares someone outside the window scratching the glass. Once they contacted their family physician with this information, he was able to prescribe the cure. He told them to put an air purifier in her room and turn it on at high speed. Also he told them to trim that particular tree. The noise from this appliance blocked out all of the outside sounds, allowing Berta to sleep peacefully throughout the night. Careful observation is the key in determining what is happening in the environment that may be provoking problem behaviors.

Unfortunately, many people who have this problem are unable to tell people why they are screaming. Screamers tend to have brain damage or dementia that impairs their ability to restrain themselves from shouting. Because of their mental condition, they are also unable to express why they are screaming. This makes it frustrating for family members or professionals to determine the cause of this behavior. Once again, everyone needs to be a detective to find the reason for the screams.

Here are some tips you can try to prevent your loved one from screaming. Move your loved one to a different room or location. They may be over stimulated by sounds or sights in their environment and need to be in a quiet place. Conversely, they may be screaming because there are no stimuli and they are essentially bored. Thus, they are using their own sounds as self-stimulation. In this case, you might try keeping a radio or television on in their room.

Sometimes persons who scream are scared of being left alone. They are trying to get attention, as well as your company. It is unreasonable to expect that you can be with them around the clock. You may try a television or radio as a substitute. Yet, if they really want your presence, then it might be helpful to try to provide an alternative such as a tape recording of family members or even a video. If this does not work, then it might be helpful to have family members take turns staying with your relative. However, it will be important to wean your loved one away from this type of physical presence, because over time it may become an overwhelming task. One way to do this is to use the old redirection technique. While people are spending time with your relative, have them do things that might interest that individual. Knitting, playing solitaire or performing some other simple activity may be able to take the place of the screaming. Try as many activities as you can. Hopefully, one or a combination will work.

There are cases when nothing seems to help decrease this behavior. This is when professional help is needed. A psychiatrist or a physician with expertise in the area of geriatrics may offer as a last resort the option of providing medications that could decrease or eliminate the screaming. Unfortunately, these medications have had mixed results and a number of them cause significant sedation. For this reason, many of them are given at night so that families can get some sleep.

A few patients with this problem do not respond to any intervention. If a house is large enough, a room distant from the normal household traffic can be selected and soundproofed with materials readily available at a building supply store. This plan should be used with caution. If this method is chosen you must establish some type of communication process to assure that your loved one can be monitored. Should any serious problems occur, you would need to know about them as soon as possible. This may include a sound or video monitoring system as well as regular in-person checks. You can use the same devices that are used for infants. Since this limited monitoring carries some risk, you should consult a physician or psychologist who deals with this kind of elderly patient.

Nursing homes or other long-term care facilities have the same problem with these few patients whose screaming does not respond to the usual treatment methods. These providers will also tend to segregate the screamer from the rest of the population. You want to make sure that "out of sight", or should I say "out of sound is not out of mind." If your loved one is in this category, ask what measures are being taken to treat the screaming and what is being done to observe the patient so that their other needs will be met.

Every such facility must have a treatment plan to address all of the problems of each patient. The staff at the facility will have regular treatment planning meetings to construct an individualized plan that addresses all of the patient's problems, medical and psychiatric. Family members should be invited to such meetings. I strongly encourage you to attend these meetings on a regular basis. This can be a great opportunity to provide input in this process so that you learn exactly what is being done for your loved one, particularly if they have behavioral problems including screaming. You may also be able to provide valuable information to the staff, such as what causes this behavior or what interventions you have tried in the past that have worked or failed. This data can then help them design a plan to minimize this problem in the nursing home.

STEALING

People who are confused due to dementia or some other mental disorder such as schizophrenia may often steal things without realizing what they are doing. It is important, however, to determine exactly what is causing the stealing.

Mona was a 77-year-old woman who was brought to my office because she had embarrassed her family recently by taking some lingerie out of the local department store. She walked out of the store with these items in her pocket only to be stopped by a security guard. Her family members did not see her take them. She had never done this before, even though they knew she had a diagnosis of dementia that was made a few years earlier. I asked Mona directly why she did this. She insisted that these were her items of clothing that she owned for a number of years and did not know what they were doing in the store. Therefore, she decided to take them. As always, I asked the family members to be the detectives to see if she was confusing some of her clothing at home. Indeed, they found a number of items in her drawers that she had taken from other sources, including her daughters. I provided a number of simple suggestions for the family. First, and most obvious, they needed to watch their mother when she went out shopping. Fortunately, she did not go anywhere without her daughters. I also suggested that they needed to frequently talk with their mother while out shopping so that she would be distracted from taking anything. If possible, they should give her shopping bags to carry so that she could keep her hands busy. Finally, they were going to check her pockets and bags before she left the store.

The general suggestions in the above example are the basic techniques that are used in dealing with patients who inadvertently steal. If a family member is caught stealing by a store's security guard, then a simple explanation of their condition and their inability to understand what they are doing usually resolves the situation. There are rare instances, however, when store management is not so forgiving. They may threaten to press charges. Carrying a copy of a physician's letter explaining the patient's condition may help resolve this scenario.

There is another less common condition caused by damage in the front part of the brain that could prompt an individual to steal. That particular area of the brain controls a person's judgment. A stroke or trauma in that region can cause a patient to make poor or impulsive decisions. They may steal, expose themselves or behave inappropriately because of their poor judgment. If the rest of the brain is healthy, they may show no symptoms other than their lack of common sense. A physician can make this diagnosis with the proper neurologic evaluation. They can be treated with the same interventions that were used above.

Greta was another story. This 75-year-old woman would occasionally steal a book or magazine from the local library. The library personnel never caught her. Her luck changed when she tried to steal an item from a local bookstore. She tried to justify her behavior because she felt she was entitled to steal from the library since she had paid taxes for many years. When she stole from the bookstore, she used the excuse that they were making excessive profits and they would not care if an elderly lady took something. She rationalized that no person would have a little old lady arrested. Greta was wrong. When she went to court the judge gave her probation with an order that she never go into that particular bookstore. The judge warned that if she were arrested again she would receive a stiff fine.

Some elderly persons with personality disorders will feel entitled to break the law. Remember that antisocial personality disorder we discussed in chapter eight. Those individuals understand exactly what they are doing but just don't care. They feel that people owe them something because of their old age. You can try to reason with them and explain the consequences of their behavior, but if they have been antisocial all their lives, it will be difficult for them to change. What they will need is a good lawyer.

THE UNCOOPERATIVE PERSON

Helping an elderly person with a behavioral problem requires teamwork. Professionals, family members, friends and even the patient himself are a part of this team. It can be extremely frustrating when the older person does not cooperate with the evaluation or treatment process. This individual may refuse to see a professional for an assessment. They may not cooperate with the entire evaluation or refuse certain tests. Later in the treatment process, they may refuse to collaborate with the professionals or family members trying to help them. They may initially agree to do something, but later refuse to do it. Family members may become frustrated because they see these individuals as stubborn and refusing the help they need. Sometimes these persons demand to be left alone. It is not unusual to see family members give in to this demand because they are discouraged with the entire process of helping their loved one.

Do not give up. This is a common situation that has been faced by numerous families in the past. In most instances, you will be able to get your loved one to cooperate if you consistently try different approaches until you find one that works. Keep plugging away and remain calm and patient.

In chapter two we discussed the problem of getting an elderly person to see a professional for evaluation. I suggest that you read that chapter again, as it outlines a variety of techniques to convince your loved one to get an assessment. You can use the same techniques if they refuse to have tests performed or refuse to cooperate with the treatment process. Let me give you a few more suggestions if they still refuse to cooperate with you.

First, thoroughly discuss with them the reason why they are being uncooperative with a particular task. They may have valid reasons.

Lucretia was a 66-year-old woman who was brought in by her family because they felt she was trying to kill herself. She had been diagnosed with diabetes two years before and had been in the emergency room on several occasions recently with extremely high blood sugars. Her family thought she was depressed and was trying to passively commit suicide by not taking care of herself and her diabetes. Lucretia was embarrassed to tell her family members that she would become extremely anxious when she was trying to give herself the insulin shots. She was afraid she would accidentally inject insulin into a vein and kill herself. As a result she, would skip some of her injections because of this anxiety. Sometimes this did not cause any problem, but at other times she had to be taken to the emergency room because she became medically unstable. We developed a plan where a nurse would visit her and give her the injections on a daily basis. After a few months of observing the nurse giving her the injections, Lucretia tried to do it on her own again. She was much more successful this time around.

Just because an older person has a mental disorder, do not presume that every time they refuse to cooperate they are being unreasonable. Talk to them first. They may provide you with a simple answer and an easy intervention.

Sometimes the older individual will provide an explanation that does not make sense. This may be based on their underlying mental disorder and may be an indication that they require further treatment in order to stabilize their condition. Medication or therapy might be needed in order to overcome this resistance. Talk to their doctor.

KEEPING A POSITIVE RELATIONSHIP

Uncooperative behavior is often due to a poor relationship with the caregiver. Let's be honest. Working with an impaired individual over the long haul can be quite frustrating. You might find yourself losing your temper or saying things that you do not mean out of annoyance. Even mentally disabled individuals can perceive your negative emotions. It is a part of human nature to be uncooperative at times with individuals that we perceive as being mean to us. If you sense that this is the reason for the person's resistance, talk about it. Try to identify the issues as specifically as possible. Once you do, the answer may be readily apparent.

Horatio, an 82-year-old stroke victim, was brought to my office by his family because they felt he was constantly fighting with them whenever they tried to provide him assistance when dressing or feeding him. The left side of his body was paralyzed, and he also had a difficult time swallowing. The patient's daughter had been taking care of him in her home since his stroke eight months earlier. The family was a particularly busy one. The daughter's husband was a physician who worked 70 hours a week, and she was raising four teenagers. Horatio was frustrated with his inability to dress or feed himself. He was also perturbed by the fact that he felt that his daughter, while assisting him, was always rushing him through these tasks. At times, he would become so frustrated that he would push her away and refuse to cooperate. His daughter felt that he was just getting old and stubborn. She never asked him directly why he was behaving in such a fashion. After a long talk in my office, they agreed that if she took her time and was pleasant he would cooperate with her request. This worked only temporarily because the daughter was overwhelmed with the challenges of running the household. I arranged a meeting of the extended family in my office. Luckily, the family was motivated to keep Horatio out of a nursing home. They were willing to divide some of the care giving so that the daughter could get some time off, which quickly improved her morale. I suspect that Horatio also needed a break from his daughter. Over the next several months, he was much more agreeable with his daughter, as well as the other caregivers.

If you are overworked in your job of care giving, change the structure. Talk with family members or friends who may be able to provide some of the care. Friends of the impaired person are often willing to assist on a regular or short-term basis. These individuals realize that it may not be long before they require some help themselves, and they hope that someone will do the same for them in the future. Local towns and counties usually have agencies geared toward providing services for the elderly. Call your local government or go on their Internet site for further details. There are usually groups affiliated with churches, synagogues or mosques that volunteer to assist the elderly with certain tasks. Some will only sit with an older person, but this may give you the time to take a break, do other activities and hopefully come back to the role of caregiver invigorated.

Please do not be embarrassed to ask for help. Providing care for an uncooperative person is no easy job. Nobody expects you to handle this burden all by yourself. That is why we have the previously mentioned groups and agencies. Talk to someone you trust.

Another way to restructure your care giving and make it more palatable is to set your priorities. You do not have to be superman or superwoman. So, do not try to be the perfect caregiver. After all, if you overwhelm yourself trying to do everything, you may burn out and ultimately be of no use to your loved one. Your attitude may change for the worse. Even a mentally ill family member will likely notice this change and act out further by resisting care.

Samantha was a 47-year-old woman who came to see me because she was feeling quite depressed. Her mother died a year earlier, and she was now taking care of her elderly father. She promised her mother on her deathbed to do everything for her father, as her mother had done when she was alive. Her father had been bedridden over the last three years due to severe arthritis. Samantha granted his every wish. If her father had a yen for a certain kind of ice cream, she would immediately go to the store to buy it. She even quit her job in order to be with him, literally, around the clock. Samantha was the perfect daughter. As the months took their toll on Samantha, depression set in. She started to become irritable with her father and then felt guilty about it. Often, she would go into some distant room in the house and cry for hours. Then she would feel guilty about leaving her father alone for that period of time. The father then became angry because of her lack of attention and started to become uncooperative with simple tasks, such as dressing or feeding. He felt that she no longer cared about him, and this made her feel even more guilty and depressed. I first asked Samantha to make a list of all the specific care-giving activities that she provided for father when she first started. She gave me a list of 122 tasks. Then, I asked her to pick from the list only those jobs that she needed to perform in order to keep her father healthy. The list was now down to seven. Next, I asked her to select several additional items from the original list that she could do to make her father comfortable. After much discussion, she was able to select 14 additional items making a new combined list of 21 jobs she could perform in order to keep her father healthy and comfortable. I was able to convince her, after much persuasion, that this was a more reasonable goal. She did not have to be the perfect caregiver. We then met with her father to outline the situation. Her father came to the understanding that his daughter was trying to do too much. We agreed that the new list of jobs would give his daughter the opportunity to provide good care without becoming overwhelmed and depressed. He was much more cooperative from that point onward. I had to see Samantha for a few more sessions so that she could work through the issue that she was not able to carry out the literal meaning of her mother's final wish.

She was ultimately able to ask for help from other family members, and her depression finally resolved.

Setting priorities is a helpful way of restructuring the care-giving process so that one is not overwhelmed with the job, particularly with an uncooperative patient. As in the above example, make a list of all of the tasks, and then determine which ones are essential for the person's health and welfare, as well as a reasonable amount of comfort. Run this list, or any other ideas you might have, by a third party who can give you an outside and objective opinion. This could be a friend who has been through a similar situation, a medical professional or a member of a mental health or dementia support group. Remember, you do not have to be perfect. Organize your priorities, and try to get some outside assistance. You will be in a better mood and so will your loved one. This will decrease the chance of any uncooperative behavior.

Another reason for uncooperative behavior may be based on the impaired individual's perception that you are trying to harm him or her. This can be the result of the confusion related to dementia or delirium. A paranoid person or a schizophrenic person of the paranoid type can also believe that you are trying to hurt them. For example, if you are trying to help them put on a shirt you might need to hold their arm. They may feel that you are trying to grab their arm in order to hurt them or break it. Hence, they may become uncooperative and may even fight with you.

With such individuals it is best to explain to them ahead of time what you are about to do and why. Keep your explanation short and simple. In fact, as you continue providing care, keep explaining exactly what you are doing. For example, tell them that you need to hold onto their arm in order to help it go through the sleeve of the shirt. Tell them that you are going to be gentle and will take your time. You may want to explain to them why you are doing what you're doing. For example, if you need to dress them in order for them to go out, tell them where they are going and why they need to be properly dressed.

In cases of extreme confusion or paranoia, rational explanations may not work. Pick your battles, or as I said in the previous paragraphs, establish your priorities. A friend of mine wanted to take her mother to church. She gave up because her mother was so confused that she could not dress her in her church clothes. She would fight with her mother for several hours in order to try to dress her for this occasion. Since it was wintertime, I suggested that she just find a big coat to fully cover her mother and not spend time trying to dress her in her fine clothes.

The bottom line is that when you deal with a confused or a paranoid individual, you should pick the basic tasks that need to be done. If you cannot rank these priorities, run your ideas by another person whom you trust. Most importantly, as I have said before, try not to argue. It only makes the situation worse.

Another way to handle these resistant individuals is to try a simple behavior modification program. Try to find something that the individual likes and reward them with this item if they cooperate. For example, if your loved one likes cookies, have some readily available where they can see and smell them in order to motivate them to cooperate. Even a very confused individual can respond to this approach. More discussion about behavioral modification will occur in a later chapter. The important theme to remember is to keep trying different rewards and approaches. As recorded in the Koran, "God helps those who persevere".

LEGAL HELP FOR THE RESISTANT PERSON

There will be times when reason and reward will fail. That is the time to get professional help. Perhaps your loved one has a mental disorder causing uncooperative behavior that can be treated with medications. Consult a physician. Sometimes legal counsel is needed in order to provide treatment that the patient refuses. Certain individuals can become so confused that they are unable to comprehend the fact that their uncooperative behavior may cause them harm. In these cases, a lawyer should be consulted in order to use legal means to allow the provision of care even if the patient refuses. Attorneys who specialize in "elder law" will be qualified to handle such situations. Your physician may know an attorney who handles such affairs, since doctors are often called upon to provide a statement regarding the patient's state of mind as a part of these legal procedures. You can also find these lawyers in the phone book under the heading "elder law."

Ideally a document called a "durable power of attorney" can be drawn up before an older individual loses their ability to understand critical situations. When the older person is still competent, they can grant this authorization to allow an individual to act on their behalf in case they lose their capacity to make rational decisions. This power of attorney can be drawn up in a way that can give broad powers to the specified person, or the specific power or charge can be limited. For example, a limited power of attorney may give the managing person the authority to make only certain types of medical decisions.

The two most common types of power of attorney are medical and financial. The first document gives a person the right to make medical decisions on another's behalf. The latter allows a person to make decisions regarding another's assets and finances.

Often older persons do not have the foresight to complete a durable power of attorney. When they get to the point where they cannot make the appropriate decisions and are refusing necessary care, then a "guardianship" of the person should be obtained. Usually the closest family member will consult an attorney and petition the court to grant this guardianship request. The appointed guardian can handle the affairs of the impaired person. Most lawyers can handle these proceedings.

I would like to give you a bit of advice. If possible, try to obtain a power of attorney rather than petition to be a guardian at some future date. The latter process is typically more complicated and expensive.

If an uncooperative elderly person is in a crisis situation, which poses an imminent threat of harm to themselves or others they should be taken to the nearest emergency room immediately. The legal interventions mentioned above will take some time. Do not wait to intervene if there is a question of safety.

I am often asked whether it is legitimate to hide medications in a patient's food. This approach is used if a person is unwilling to take the medications they absolutely need. Obviously, this is a controversial question that has no simple answer. If possible, this approach should be avoided. It can seriously damage a trusting relationship. However, there are times in which a lawyer may need to be involved in order to accomplish this legally through a guardianship procedure as outlined above. Get some legal and medical advice so that you can weigh the risks verses the benefits of such an intervention.

A doctor's evaluation will be required as part of the process of obtaining a guardianship in order to determine whether the person is competent. Often, that same physician will be required to outline the specific treatment that the patient needs. Once the guardianship is in place, the managing family member should consult their relative's physician to determine the best way to provide their family member the care that they need. Just because the guardian is authorized to force medications or other treatments does not mean that the uncooperative individual will automatically become cooperative.

Anne Marie was a 74-year-old woman who was diagnosed with dementia when she was 64. After she turned 70, she started to have a number of medical problems, including a couple of minor strokes and heart failure. She was on a total of six medications but stopped taking these medications because she thought these drugs were causing her heart to fail. The irony was that these were the medications she needed in order to keep her heart condition stable. Her family was concerned that she would develop cardiac failure. They consulted a lawyer and were able to obtain a speedy guardianship. Armed with these legal papers they told Anne Marie that she had to take the medications. After a couple of weeks of bitter arguing, they tried to physically force her to take the medications by holding her down and opening her mouth. She easily spit them out. Needless to say this entire series of events was quite traumatic for all parties. At that point, they called her family physician, who in turn called me. A conference call was setup between the cardiologist, family physician and myself in order to map out a plan to make sure that Anne Marie took the medications. We were able to alter her list of medications so that all of them could be given in liquid form. The family was able to mix these medications with her food and drink, thereby avoiding any verbal or physical confrontations. Anne Marie is now 81, and her cardiac condition remains stable.

A number of medications are available in a variety of different forms. Liquids, concentrates or powders can easily be combined with food and drink. There are even forms available that are tasteless and colorless. Coordinating a plan with different providers and family members is not that difficult, as seen in the above example.

At times, psychiatric medications may be required to reduce the person's paranoia or anxiety about taking medications. If the impaired individual is willing to take these drugs, they may become calm and more compliant with other treatment interventions. This may eliminate the need for any kind of legal proceeding. Remember, forcing medications or trying to trick the patient into taking medications should only be done if the patient is incompetent, and there is legal authority to do so. If you are unsure about this process, please consult an attorney or physician. Laws often differ from state to state.

For those who are reluctant to contact an attorney because of the cost, there are other options available. The office of the attorney general of a particular state can be contacted for a general legal opinion. These offices usually have specialists in elder law and are able to provide written or verbal answers to your questions. Nearly all states have advocacy groups for the elderly population. In most states and local governments, the titles of these groups may vary, but if you look in a phone book under your local government, check for words such as aging, elderly etc. These organizations often have brochures that explain the resources that are available for the elderly, including legal services. Support groups such as the Alzheimer's Association or the National Alliance for the Mentally Ill can also provide advice regarding laws and policies related to the impaired elderly population.

CHAPTER FOURTEEN
The Basic Plan

In previous chapters we have discussed a number of behavioral problems, their possible causes and suggestions for interventions to manage them. This chapter will outline in some detail the process of creating a behavioral management plan. There are several reasons why this chapter is needed. First, I realize that I could not have covered in the previous chapters every possible behavior problem that an impaired elderly person could have. Therefore, I want to present a framework to address the problems that I have not mentioned in previous chapters. Second, some impaired older individuals will present with difficulties that do not appear exactly like the ones we have discussed. Problematic human behavior can be quite variable, and so may be their solutions. This chapter will help you develop a treatment plan that will address these variables.

Another reason for this chapter is that there will be cases in which the suggestions and recommendations provided in previous chapters do not lead to a successful outcome. By developing a comprehensive treatment plan, you should be able to address these failures by learning from them, so that you can adjust your strategy. Hopefully, a new approach will produce a positive outcome.

A potentially successful treatment plan includes the following components. First, you must detail the problem, describing the target behaviors in specific and measurable terms. Second, you will need to develop reasonable and measurable goals in order to determine your progress. Third, you will choose your interventions based on your observation of the pattern of behavior and its relationship to any stimuli in the environment. Next is the implementation phase, where you will try out your interventions and specifically record their effect. Lastly, there is the analysis phase. Here, you will determine which interventions worked, and which did not. Based on that information you will move to the strategy adjustment phase, where you can modify your approach based on previous successes and failures.

If you are lucky, and your intervention is successful, you need go no farther, as you have already achieved the outcome you want. If you did not succeed the first time, then you return to the analysis phase where you can reformulate your strategy. Do not consider it a failure if your first intervention did not work. This commonly happens and provides you with a learning experience that you can use to modify your approach, hopefully achieving success the next time.

A COMPLETE AND CONSISTENT APPROACH

Before we begin a discussion of the various components of a basic treatment plan, I would like to provide a piece of advice. Take the time to develop a specific plan. It is only human nature that we try shortcuts, but especially in our American culture, we want to be successful immediately. Most behavioral plans that do not work fail because people try to save time and cut corners. The result is a sloppy process that does not produce the desired result.

Marvin, an 84-year-old man, caused his family to be so frustrated that they wanted his doctor to sign papers to put him "in a home." That physician referred the family to me for some guidance. It seems as though Marvin would always get into everything. He would rummage through drawers, wander away from the house and take apart small appliances. As his family put it, "He gets into everything." Because the family was so upset with Marvin, they wanted something done immediately. For this reason, I prescribed a small amount of medication in order to decrease Marvin's restlessness. At the same time, I told the family that we needed to formulate a behavioral plan to eliminate or minimize these problematic behaviors. I asked the family to list the top five behaviors that they wanted to change and record how many times these behaviors occurred during the day. When they came back for the next session, they did provide the list of the top five behaviors, but they did not take the time to estimate how often these behaviors occurred. They told me that they would know if the behaviors had improved. Besides, they were busy with their own lives and did not have the time to perform this observational process. This made it somewhat difficult to suggest interventions, but we did come up with some approaches. A month later, when I met with the family, they continued to be frustrated because they thought nothing was working. When I questioned them about their approaches, it appeared that they were rather inconsistent in carrying them out. For example, I asked them to select a specific person to be responsible to see that Marvin received his medication on a daily basis. Instead, they stated that they would all be responsible for this task. However, it appeared that they did not watch Marvin take his medication 50% of the time. They also did not follow through with the suggestion that a designated family member buy Marvin an old appliance for him to dismantle, so that he would leave their possessions alone. Since they did not take the time to measure his problem behaviors, we had no idea as to his progress or lack thereof. We met for two sessions that week and outlined a detailed treatment plan. I basically told them that if they followed my suggestions to the letter and they saw no measurable progress, I would not charge them for these two sessions. A month later the family reconvened and reported that the top five problem behaviors decreased between 60 to 80%.

It is true that, when developing a comprehensive treatment plan, you must take the time and make an effort. Look at it this way. Think of all the time you may have wasted already with approaches that failed. I know a family who spent over 20 hours per week trying to redirect their loved one from problem behaviors. When I saw them in my office, they complained about the fact that it might take a few hours to set up a detailed course of treatment. I told them the choice was theirs. They could continue to waste more than 20 hours per week or spend three hours developing a good plan, and perhaps another two or three hours per week implementing and monitoring it. They chose the latter and found out two months down the road that they only spent one hour per week to carry out the plan, which proved to be quite successful.

I hope I have convinced you to take the time to carry out each of the following components that we will discuss.

I can only tell you from experience that this philosophy is an important one that will determine your final success.

A crucial part of any strategic approach is to make it so efficient that it requires the least time and effort in the long run. Thus, it is important to have as many supportive family members as possible working together in such an approach. This way, the burden will not fall solely on one person.

It is important to gather all the interested family members, friends or other helpers to assist you in the development of the plan. Do not create the course of action all by yourself, and then expect others to help you out. Other persons may have new and creative ideas that would make it a better plan. In addition, it is better for all people involved to have ownership of the plan, rather than to order others to carry out a plan that has been implemented by one individual. You will find that you will receive more cooperation if the people involved in the plan are part of it from the very beginning.

Make the planning session inviting. Choose a time that is convenient for the majority of the people involved. Make it a social gathering. If possible have some refreshments available. I have found that people who are treated well and are in a good mood will tend to offer more help.

DEFINING THE PROBLEM

During my years of practice in psychiatry, a nurse will sometimes ask me to prescribe medication because a patient is agitated. My usual response is that I do not prescribe medication for an agitated patient. That is when I get the puzzled look. I then respond that I will only prescribe a drug for specific behaviors. For example, if a patient is hitting or kicking another person, I know exactly what behavior needs to be corrected. If they are hitting their head against the wall, then I may need to try a different intervention. If people are angry and speaking in a curt or sarcastic manner, they too may be described as agitated but will probably require an entirely different approach. Most importantly, agitated behavior does not automatically require medication. Therapeutic interventions can sometimes work better.

I often get agitated waiting in long lines. Luckily, so far, no one has given me any medications. The point is that one must specify the exact behavior that needs to be addressed, so that the right intervention can be utilized. Try not to use terms such as "agitated", "aggressive" or "hostile". They are too general for purposes of developing a detailed treatment plan.

To detail a problem means you have to use descriptive and concrete terms. In other words, choose terms that are visual and paint a picture. Pounding the desk with a closed fist is much more specific than saying the person is angry. You can visualize a person pounding their fist and know exactly what is happening. However, if a person is described as "angry", there are many pictures that could describe their emotion. More importantly, by defining a detailed behavior, you can count the number of times this individual has episodes where, for example, he pounds his fist. If this is the primary behavior that you wish to resolve, you can establish a baseline count, which is the number of times the person is showing that behavior at the time you begin your plan.

For example, if Uncle Joe pounds the table about four times a day because he is angry, you know the exact problem and how often it is occurring. This is important because you can track your progress in resolving this behavior. Once your treatment intervention takes place and the behaviors decrease, you will know that you have achieved a successful outcome.

Sometimes, family members will tell me that they want to resolve their family member's anger and not just the expression of that emotion. I usually ask them how they know they are not resolving the emotional problem. You see, our actions represent how we feel and how we think. It is truly hard to separate them. If we resolve all of the expressions of a particular problem, we are likely resolving the problem.

Another way to look at this would be to ask yourself how do you know the problem still exists. You must perceive some physical expression that makes you think the problem is not resolved. If that is the case, you need to describe that particular action or demeanor. That will be the new target behavior.

Often, you will need to detail numerous problems, as most impaired elderly people have more than one problem. Try not to combine them. For example if a person is hitting, kicking, and spitting, detail each of these problems separately. Establish a baseline count for each of those target behaviors. The reason for this is that each behavior may require a different intervention. If you combine those behaviors and call them hostile or aggressive, they will be generally more difficult to track, and more difficult to approach with a proper intervention.

A CLINICAL EXAMPLE

As we proceed through the rest of this chapter I will use the following example to illustrate how to develop and implement a basic treatment plan.

Crystal was a 77-year-old woman and a former librarian who had no mental health problems until her early sixties when she suffered an episode of depression after her husband died from a heart attack. In her late sixties, she had a stroke, which weakened the left side of her body to the point that she could not perform some usual daily functions such as washing dishes or cleaning her house. During her seventies, she had a number of minor medical problems that left her even weaker. At that point, her daughter's family decided to take her into their household. By the time she was 77, her family was growing tired of trying to help her with her basic tasks. They felt that she would act helpless in order to get their attention. This frustration led to some family arguments, which made all parties feel bad. Crystal would have crying spells related to these arguments, and at other times for no apparent reason. She would also cry out in the middle of the night and bang on the wall. This was quite disturbing for her family. By the time the family came in for an evaluation, they were so frustrated that they felt the only alternative was to send Crystal to a nursing home.

The first step was to define Crystal's problems. The crying spells were easy to measure because they were obviously quite visible. She would cry about three times a day unless there was an argument. It was noted that she would cry almost every time after a family conflict. Family conflicts occurred three times a week. They were defined as verbal arguments that had no satisfactory resolution.

The problem of acting helpless was a little more difficult to define. The family gave the example that Crystal could not, or would not, feed herself dinner. This behavior would occur on almost a daily basis. Yet, she would be able to eat breakfast and lunch somehow on her own. Another example of her helplessness was that she requested assistance to go to the bathroom about three times per day. Yet, she seemed to be able to go to the bathroom by herself other times without requesting any help.

Finally, the family was able to quantify the screaming and banging at night, as well as noticing a pattern for that behavior. It would occur on the average of twice a week, usually on Friday and Saturday nights.

SETTING GOALS

Before we continue with the case of Crystal, we will discuss the two requirements for setting proper goals. First, the goals must be reasonable to achieve. Next, you must specify the goals in concrete and measurable terms. Take the time to satisfy these requirements. If you try any interventions before you establish realistic and specific goals, you will not be able to determine the exact extent of your success and will have a much more difficult time adjusting your strategy.

A family once came to me with the problem that their father was stealing. They were in a hurry to resolve this behavior and only wanted to know what they could do to stop this conduct. As we tried to detail the specific problems and goals, the family just wanted to know what approaches to take in order to rectify the situation. Even though I made them write down the specific problems and goals before leaving my office, it was very clear that they only chose to remember the strategy they were going to use to help the father with his stealing. In fact, at the end of my workday, I found that the son had left the written list in my office. When they came in the next week, they were quite frustrated because they could not tell which approaches worked, as his behavior seemed to improve at times, and at other times there was no change. I had no clue either as to their actual success, because they were not monitoring or recording the frequency of the problem that they had written down the week before. Unfortunately, we had to start from the beginning.

Accurately defining problems and goals provides a framework for monitoring the success of any interventions. You will be able to use this information to adjust your strategy in order to achieve ultimate success. Without it, you are lost.

Let us first talk about establishing realistic goals. There is little doubt that we would like to have our parents conduct themselves as they did when they were younger, in good health and a sound state of mind. Often, families will ask me to help their loved ones act as they did when they were younger. Can you make mom cook and clean like she used to do? Will you be able to do something so dad can drive again?

Before we can establish realistic goals, the impaired elderly person must be fully evaluated and his or her limitations need to be thoroughly discussed. You cannot expect a person to physically or mentally perform a task that they are not equipped to do. If you try to establish an unreasonable goal, it will not only frustrate your loved one, but also the family members who are involved. Goals should be hopeful, but not unreasonable.

A woman once asked me to tell her how she could stop her depressed mother from crying. The mother had suffered a heart attack a year earlier and had been depressed since that time. Her father had also died three months earlier, and this increased her mother's depression. I explained to her that it was reasonable to expect that we could help her mother with her depression, but it would be unrealistic to prevent her from crying. After all, people need to be able to express emotion after a loved one dies.

Therefore, we need to select goals that can be achieved. Know your relative's limitations. Discuss them with other family members or someone who is knowledgeable regarding the elderly. This will help provide you with some objectivity so that you can develop reasonable goals.

Another important factor in defining realistic goals is to know your limitations. An example of this was a relative who came in with a list of about 40 behaviors that she wanted to fix in her father. This would have been an overwhelming task for a family member, or for that matter an entire family. It was much more practical to select the top five problematic behaviors to work on first.

Limit the number of behaviors that you will address. Establish a list of priorities. Obviously, it would be more important to prevent a relative from wandering, than from biting their fingernails. If you are unsure as to what should be the priorities, discuss this with other family members or experts. Use their knowledge and objectivity.

You will also need to know your limitations in order to develop an appropriate approach to the problem. For example, if you set a goal that requires you to be with that person for 10 hours per day, consider your ability to perform that job and how long it would be before you burn out. If your approach is going to be time-consuming, try to keep it time-limited.

Sometimes, goals for the elderly person are intertwined with goals for the providers. Therefore, you will need to know the limitations of your helpers. Many families fail to carry out a strategy because they make promises to do things that they cannot carry out. Make sure that your helpers, whether they are family or outsiders, will be available for a certain length of time to do their job. Also, be sure that they have the skills to carry out their tasks.

A schizophrenic woman who was afraid that her food was poisoned would only eat in the presence of a family member. I helped her family set up a schedule so that people would be able to stop in during mealtimes and assist this woman. She only trusted the family members that she knew. One weekend, her daughter asked a friend to substitute for her while she was away. The mother did not eat the entire weekend. The friend tried as hard as she could to get this individual to eat, and she was afraid to call anyone for help. By Sunday evening, this elderly woman went to the emergency room in a dehydrated state.

Thus, having a goal where a family member was available during all mealtimes is not always as easy as you think. You will need to develop contingency plans that you may have to test before they are used. In the above case, it might have been wiser to have the daughter's friend sit in at a mealtime with the daughter present, before the daughter went out of town. After that, the friend could attempt to assist the patient at mealtime with the daughter not present but also not out of town. This approach may have helped predict the elderly woman's response to a new person.

Once you have established a limited and prioritized set of realistic goals, you will need to put them in measurable terms. Let us return to the example of Crystal.

Initially, I cautioned Crystal's family that they could not expect her to be perfect. Even if the plan worked, there still might be times when Crystal would need to cry. If something upsetting happened to her, this would be a normal response. There were even the legitimate times for Crystal to scream. For example, suppose she were to fall and break a hip. Screaming for help would be a reasonable response.

Next, we tried to prioritize three initial goals. The screaming was the most disturbing conduct for the family, so that was our number one goal. The second most important goal was to have Crystal cry less. Least important of the three goals, according to the family's wishes, was to have Crystal eat her meals independently.

The next step was to construct goals that were measurable and observable. The family stated that they would be able to tolerate Crystal screaming one night per month. In fact, they stated that if they were to achieve that goal, they would be eternally grateful. The second goal was to decrease Crystal's crying episodes to only three times per week. Lastly, it was important for the family to have Crystal eat her meals independently all but one time per week.

Finally, it was important to summarize the goals and make sure that all of the family members were in agreement. This also gave us a chance to discuss the possibility that there might be times in which there would be a valid reason for Crystal to scream or cry, and this should not be counted against her goals. Everyone agreed to this.

OBSERVATION AND INTERVENTION

In Chapter One, I discussed the importance of using observation in order to determine whether a family member has a particular problem. In this chapter, I encourage you to be even more attentive to your relative's problems. With this approach you should be able to determine what is going on in the environment that may be producing the undesired behavior.

Humans are part of the animal kingdom. Therefore, we must deal with the rules of that system. Humans, like animals, respond to the stimuli in their environment. Even though we would like to think of ourselves as rational and civilized creatures, we still respond to what is going on around us. Keep this rule in mind when you are trying to develop an intervention to reduce a problematic behavior. Because we are human and have a higher-level of brainpower, our responses to the environment may be complicated and difficult to understand.

If a three year-old boy touches a hot stove, he will scream or cry. This is a simple example of the rule we have been talking about. In order to prevent this response, we will need to educate this child, so that he will not touch a hot stove, or we will need to move the hot stove from his reach.

When an 83 year-old woman screams, we will also need to determine what in the environment is stimulating her to do so. Sometimes, we are lucky and will find a simple stimulus that is causing the behavior. At other times, the evidence is not readily apparent. Thus, we will need to use our power of observation to search for the hidden cause of the problem behavior. Here are some tips to increase your skills in this area.

First, talk to the impaired individual. Hopefully, they are coherent enough to provide the reasons for their actions. This usually makes an intervention pretty straightforward. Unfortunately, there are times when, for a variety of reasons, a person cannot state exactly why they are behaving in an inappropriate manner. They may be unable to speak or put their thoughts together because of some type of brain injury or mental illness.

Even though they are able to express themselves in only a limited fashion, they might be able to provide you with clues as to the cause of their problem. At times, they will tell you they do not know why they are carrying out their actions. Talk to them anyway. Try to find out what is going on in their lives at this time that might be affecting them. Discuss their relationships, goals in life or other important topics that may provide you with the context in which the problems are occurring. This may give you some suggestions as to what do in terms of an intervention trial.

Try to observe the behavior as it is happening. It is sometimes helpful to look in on the impaired individual without being noticed. If you are seen, you then become a part of the stimuli around them. This may not give you a reliable account of what might be causing their behavior. Also, it is important to be there at the start of the act. Look at what is going on in the person's surroundings. Did anything occur that was new or unusual? Did you notice any sounds or movements nearby or in the distance? Was the person doing anything before the problematic behavior? Were they sitting, standing or lying in bed? Were they moving or were they still? Sometimes older persons will moan or scream if they are in pain when they move. If they have had a stroke in the brain's language area, they may not be able to tell you specifically why they are screaming. Observing their discomfort may lead to an intervention that will make them comfortable and prevent the screaming. Were they listening to the radio or watching television and heard or saw something on the air that upset them?

There will be times when the problem behavior seems to be occurring at random and has no apparent cause. Even in these instances, there may be stimuli in the environment that you have been unable to observe that may be contributing to the problem. Sometimes, it is helpful to have another family member or friend observe the individual to see if they notice anything that might be the cause of the problem. Do not feel bad if they find the cause of conduct when you did not, as we tend to overlook things in familiar surroundings.

I know I have been repetitive with the suggestion that you should not hesitate to involve experts, especially a doctor who has expertise in dealing with elderly. That person might be able to help you better observe and assess the situation and give you ideas as to what to look for based on the specifics of the problem.

The Bible states, "Observe the opportunity." (Ecclesiasticus 4:20). Once you find, through observation, a stimulus that may be provoking a loved one's problem behavior, the intervention is often quite obvious. In the above example of the person who is screaming from pain, we observed that they do so because their movements cause them significant discomfort. Some obvious interventions include some type of physical support to help them move without pain or medications that will reduce the discomfort.

There are occasions in which the cause of the poor conduct is difficult to determine despite a variety of people observing and assessing the situation. Use your best judgment and try a number of reasonable interventions. You can learn from those successes or failures how you will adjust your strategy so that you will ultimately have a successful outcome. We will talk more about this later in our reassessment phase.

Before we move on, I want to note that you may feel that many of my suggestions in the areas of observation and intervention are either obvious or over-simplistic. You would be surprised how many people in these situations overlook problems and solutions that are self-evident. In difficult circumstances it is human nature not to see the forest because of the trees. So, be on the lookout for answers that are right in front of you.

TRIALS AND INTERVENTIONS

I often ask families about the strategies and approaches that they have already taken with a loved one to resolve a difficult situation. You do not want to waste your time on any approaches that have not worked in the past. Make sure that you properly carried out the intervention in the past before you call it a failure.

I was once trying to help a family that was dealing with a mother who was quite verbally abusive and profane, especially when she was communicating with other family members. One of her children read some psychology books about dealing with difficult people. Based on this research, they took the approach of walking out of her room when the mother became verbally abusive. This intervention only worked for a short time. When I was doing my evaluation of the situation, I asked what interventions they tried in the past, so that I would not have them repeat past failures. Walking out of a room when one is confronted with a critical or profane person is not an unreasonable strategy. So, I asked them to explain exactly what they did. It was revealed that, indeed, they did walk out of the room when the mother was being abusive. However, a number of her children would overhear the mother still screaming profanities, and they would re-enter the room within a few minutes to argue with her. They felt that walking out of the room did not work.

It was clear to me that their strategy was not being carried out exactly the way they intended. Basically, they needed to stay out of the room until the mother calmed down. That was the response they wanted. To go back in the room when the mother was screaming was rewarding the screaming behavior. With some reassurance, I told them that that no one should go into the room as long as the negative behavior was still occurring. This simple adjustment of the intervention worked.

Carefully review your previous strategies. Is there any way they can be adjusted before they are rejected as failures? After this review, if you feel that previous interventions will clearly not work, do not waste your time repeating them but instead try to learn from them. We will talk more about adjusting your strategy later in this chapter.

BASIC INTERVENTIONS

There are several basic categories of interventions. Even though they represent different approaches, you may find that you will need to use more than one category in order to resolve a behavior problem.

Manipulating the environment is the first such category. This has to do with the observation process that we discussed earlier in this chapter. If you find that there is some type of stimulant in the environment of the impaired person that is causing the problem, you may need to remove that stimulus or change it. If there is a noxious noise that is causing an elderly person to wake up in the night, remove the sound or mask that it with another, more pleasant sound.

There can be multiple provocative elements in the patient's environment that may be the cause of their inappropriate behavior. You will need to make a number of changes in their surroundings in order to improve their functioning. Sometimes the entire environment is just too stimulating for the patient. This is typically a problem in the case of schizophrenic, psychotic, or demented elderly. They just cannot handle all the stimulation that is occurring around them. In such cases, the impaired person needs to be removed from the situation. I remember an older relative who was extremely uncomfortable in the arcade along the boardwalk at the beach. The various sounds and lights of all the machines would get to him, and he would have to find a quiet place to sit.

At times, there can be subtle items in the person's surroundings that may be affecting their behavior. Even the smallest details that may not be a problem for a healthy individual can affect a mentally impaired one. A patient of mine would wake up multiple times during the night, because the sound of her space heater fan starting up would startle her. She could not sleep for an extended period of time and as a result was always tired and was becoming more confused. Her problem was resolved when her family bought her a quiet convection heater that did not have a built-in fan.

It is important to ask about even the smallest stimulation in the environment. Your powers of observation need to be refined to the point that you can notice these minor facets. It sounds simple, but it takes practice, perseverance and experience.

Providing positive rewards to obtain the desired behavior is the second basic approach. We often think that we only use this specific type of intervention with infants and younger children. The fact is that this approach is used for people of all ages. Adults are compensated for their work behavior because they receive enjoyment from their job or they get a paycheck. Therefore, the payment or job satisfaction motivates an individual to do a good job. The same approach works for an elderly person. For example, if we want an older person to eat their entire dinner, rewarding them at the end with a dessert they like may motivate them to complete their meal.

In most instances, it is not difficult to find what a person likes, in order to use it as a reward. Food, trips, visits and gifts are the usual motivators to change an individual's behavior. For some mentally impaired people such as a depressed person, it may seem as if nothing will motivate them. This is where it becomes harder to find the right type of reward. If they cannot tell you what would be enjoyable for them, try to review their history. What did they like in the past? Do they ever smile? If so, what are they doing at that time? Ask other family members and friends if they have any ideas as to what could be used to inspire them to change. Make sure the reward is simple and reasonable and that you will be able to use it repeatedly. A trip to Hawaii would be nice, but it would be difficult to implement.

Once you have found the reward that you think will work, tell your relative in advance what you will do when they perform the behavior you desire. Hopefully, this will motivate them. The key to using this approach is to state clearly to the individual the specific action that they need to perform. Keep it simple. This approach will fail if you make the behavior so complicated that they cannot understand it. For example, if you tell your family member that he needs to go upstairs, take a bath, change his clothes and go to bed, that may be too many commands for him to understand or even remember. Give him one simple command and then give him his compensation. In the above example, it would be better to break it up into four separate commands, each with its own reward.

If you want to stop a certain behavior, the best way to use this approach would be to reward your loved one after a certain amount of time passes in which they did not exhibit the problem behavior. During the time that they act appropriately, it is good to remind them that the reward will be given to them at the end of a certain time period, should they continue to do well. Be specific about the behavior that you want to them to avoid and be reasonable about the time period in question.

The following statement best summarizes this approach. "Mom, I am glad to see that you're not wandering out of your room. If you stay in your room until 7 p.m. I'll read a chapter of your book to you." In the above statement, you have told your relative the specific action she should avoid and also exactly what she needs to do in a certain time in order to obtain the specific reward.

One of the common mistakes that we make in using this approach is that we expect the individual to do too much in order to get their compensation. For example, it may not be possible for the mentally impaired individual to control their actions over several hours. You may need to reward them for behaving appropriately after only a few minutes. Later in this process, you can try extending the time period during which they need to act properly in order to receive their reward. In summary, keep the reward approach simple, specific and time-limited.

The negative consequence category of intervention is one that I tend to avoid. It is often perceived as a punishment. For example, if you were to tell your mother that she would not be able to see her grandchildren if she wandered away from her room, that would be a negative consequence of her behavior. She would feel that she is being punished. This approach tends to create guilt and hard feelings.

The only time that I suggest using this approach is if the person is involved in some type of dangerous behavior. You would clearly have to outline any harmful actions that would result because of their inappropriate behavior. An example of this would be to take your relative's car keys away and explain to them that you are doing so because you are afraid that they may harm someone or themselves.

While providing a negative consequence in order to control behavior may work in the short-term, in the long run it may destroy a positive relationship. No one likes to be punished, and that person may resent you for doing so.

The educational approach is another category of intervention that is often overlooked. Sometimes, when we deal with a person who has a mental disorder, we think that they do not understand issues like normal people.

For example, depressed people may look as if they have a puzzled expression, but that does not mean that they are unable to understand a logical discussion. Even people who are delusional can still relate in a coherent manner. Therefore, we should make the effort to explain to them how their negative actions affect other people. Their inappropriate behavior can also impact negatively on their own health and well-being. This should be explained to them.

An example of this approach would be to explain to an older person who has a skin infection the simple reasons why they need to be seen by a doctor, in order to have this condition treated. You may need to read about the consequences of an untreated infection, and then explain it to them in simple terms. For example, an untreated infection can lead to gangrene and possible amputation. It can also lead to an infection that spreads throughout the entire body and can be lethal. With this specific information, you can educate your family member in order to motivate him or her to see a physician. You can also explain how this would affect the people who care about them.

When using the educational approach you need to keep your discussion simple and concrete. What do I mean by "concrete?" Use words that can paint a picture. Tell the individual what gangrene looks like. Explain how they will function if they lose a limb. Use simple terms. Try not to be overly dramatic, as the listener may no longer pay attention because it is too upsetting. Use a simple matter of fact, but caring, approach.

I realize that I have been focusing on keeping the intervention process simple. This, unfortunately, carries the implication that a person with a mental illness is somehow less intelligent than the average person. This is not so. In fact, such individuals can be quite clever.

A friend of mine worked as a groundskeeper during his college years at a local psychiatric hospital. One day, as he was leaving the facility, his tire went flat. He pulled over to the side of the driveway to change the tire. First, he took the hubcap off and then the lug nuts that were holding the tire. Then he put the lug nuts in the hubcap. When he took off the tire, he stepped back onto the edge of the hubcap and sent the nuts flying down the hill into a fast moving stream. As he was deciding what to do now that he was stuck with no way to attach the spare, he heard a voice coming from a window in the nearby hospital building. The man told him to take one lug nut from each of the other three tires and use them to attach the spare. As my friend paused with a smile, he heard the voice one more time. "Just because I'm crazy doesn't mean I'm stupid."

Do not assume a person with mental illness is automatically stupid. Certainly there are those individuals who have impaired thinking, but with reasonable discussion they will usually be able to understand this process to some extent. Try to determine their level of understanding and then communicate at that level.

It is often helpful to have educational materials that you can give to the impaired person. There are brochures that explain many of the issues affecting the elderly in simple terms. You can find them in physicians' offices, local health departments and agencies that deal with the elderly. Even churches may have informative articles to help their elderly members.

Such educational materials are particularly helpful for two reasons. First, they give credibility to the discussion that you had with your relative. Your loved one might have some doubt about some of the information you shared, but if they see it in writing from a legitimate source, they will tend to believe what you had to say. Second, your relative will have something in hand that they can mull over while they are trying to decide what they need to do. Hopefully, this will save you some time in repeated explanations to them.

Using some of the basic interventions that we discussed here, let us go back to the original example of Crystal. After careful observation, the family was able to determine that Crystal would wake up screaming about the time that the family's teenagers came in after their weekend dates. It appeared that the noise they made at that hour scared their grandmother and woke her up. She thought that someone was trying to break into the house, so she would scream and bang the walls to get the attention of her daughter and son-in-law. They instructed the children to be as quiet as possible when coming in. This reduced her screaming episodes to only two nights per month. This environmental manipulation was a partial success. This was just short of the one episode per month goal we had set.

The intervention that we used to decrease her tearful episodes was to explain to Crystal that it upset the family members to hear her crying. We used the educational approach. The daughter explained to her mother that her crying upset the entire family, and that if she was upset, she should talk about whatever issues were bothering her. In addition, using the reward approach, the family went into her room to talk with her when she was upset in order to calm her. They felt that this would provide a brief reward and hopefully decrease her tearful behavior. Unfortunately, this approach caused Crystal to now have five tearful episodes per day. We were headed in the wrong direction with this reward intervention.

The last problem to be addressed was Crystal's need to be fed by her family, which occurred at the rate of one meal per day. We again used the reward approach here by telling Crystal that, if she ate all of her meals using her own power, one of the family members would spend five minutes talking with her during that meal time. This was a complete success. After a month, Crystal was eating all of her meals by herself, except when she was physically ill and truly needed assistance. Crystal just wanted some attention. Now that she got it, she did not need to pretend that she could not feed herself.

Do not be afraid to try any intervention that seems reasonable. Using this approach, any failure is, in one sense, a success because it will provide you the additional information needed to modify your strategy, as you will see later in this chapter. However, try one intervention at a time. If you try to use too many at the same time you may get mixed results and will not know which approaches were effective and which were not. While I am encouraging you to use a variety of interventions, use them in a methodical stepwise manner.

In previous chapters, I have discussed a number of interventions related to specific diagnoses or behavioral problems. Give them a try if your loved one has a similar condition. You might need to modify the interventions slightly to suit your particular situation. If that particular intervention does not work, vary it somewhat and give it another try. Once again, you will gain further information even if the specific approach fails.

IMPLEMENTATION AND OBSERVATION

Implementation of your intervention and the observation of the outcome are critical to adjusting your strategy in order to achieve ultimate success.

One of the main points of this section is to emphasize that you must make sure that the intervention you plan to use is the one that you actually implement. Earlier in this chapter, I talked about a family who was trying to decrease their mother's verbally abusive behavior by ignoring it. But that was not the approach they implemented. If you recall, they would re-enter her room if she continued her criticism. They did not consistently ignore her verbal abuse. Though they developed the proper intervention, they did not implement it correctly. Therefore, you need to make sure that the intervention you use is one you choose. Ask yourself if you are exactly carrying out the intervention that was discussed or if you deviated in any way.

When I meet with a family for the first time, I ask them what steps they have taken to resolve their relative's problem. Many times they have tried approaches that seem to be reasonable and should have worked. When I ask them how they carried out the specific approach, I sometimes hear techniques that were inconsistent with what they were trying to do. Then I ask the family to make sure that they carry out their plan exactly as planned. A consistent second try may succeed.

In order to implement a strategy correctly, you must be consistent with your approach over a reasonable period of time. In other words, do not give up immediately if your initial attempt does not appear to be working. Maintain some consistency. After a reasonable length of time of trying that approach, analyze your implementation technique. In the example of the verbally abusive mother, if the family members noted that some people were not ignoring the mother's behavior, they would counsel these persons so that all would be consistent in ignoring their mother's verbal abuse. All individuals involved in implementing the plan should agree in detail how to carry it out in the same manner.

Make sure that when you implement the plan, you try only one approach at a time for a single problem. Some patients come to see me asking for a medication for depression, another for anxiety and yet another to help them sleep. If I were to give them three medications at that first visit and they were to develop side effects, it would make it more difficult to determine which medication was causing the side effects. The same is true for implementing your interventions. If it all possible, try one at a time for a certain period to see what positive or negative effects result. I realize you are dealing with a variety of behaviors that need to be brought under control as soon as possible, but this methodical approach works best. If you do need to implement more than one step at a time, make sure the two approaches are used for entirely different problems. This will make it easier to monitor the outcome.

Monitoring the outcome of your intervention is often overlooked. Counting the episodes of a problem behavior takes time and can be boring. It is, however, essential to the entire process. You might think a strategy is working because the behavior has decreased. This often happens in the early implementation phase. This is called the placebo effect. We expect that the approach will work, and therefore we convince ourselves that it has. Without counting the exact episodes of the problematic behavior, we will not have an objective measure of whether the intervention is successful. Our subjective measuring stick is often not accurate.

It is important to measure the target behaviors throughout the implementation process. If the approach worked for the first week, we may notice that during the second week the impaired person's conduct begins to deteriorate. By measuring the target behaviors each day, we can discover exactly when things start to go downhill. Once we know the specific time, we will be able to take a look at what was happening in the person's environment, or in the implementation of the approach at that time that may have caused the person's behavior to become worse. This will allow us to modify the intervention so that it can be more successful.

I often ask families to draw a chart or a graph so that they can easily document the target behaviors over a length of time. This is not difficult to do and saves a great deal of time in the long run. On the vertical line of the graph you will document the number of episodes of the target behavior. On the horizontal line of the graph you can keep track of the days or weeks depending on the time period that you are monitoring. Families often find it rewarding to see on paper the progress that they have made.

Let us return to the case of Crystal. We counted her target behaviors. During the first month there were no episodes of Crystal requiring assistance when eating her meals. Her screaming episodes occurred only twice that month and both of those episodes occurred during the last weekend of the month. Lastly, her tearful episodes increased from three to five times per day. With this data in hand, I, along with the family, moved into the analysis phase of the treatment plan.

ANALYSIS AND ADJUSTMENT

In this phase, we examine our interventions and adjust them so that we can try again in the hopes of achieving a better outcome. If we have carefully followed the first few steps of the plan, we now have some data, which will tell us which interventions worked and which did not. In addition, if we were careful observers, we may be able to determine why the intervention did not work.

Regarding the example of Crystal, her daughter noted that when her son came in from a date during that last weekend of the month, his girlfriend was giggling and laughing loudly enough to wake up Crystal. The adjustment made here was to ask her son to keep the noise level down at that hour of the night. The son also needed to tell his girlfriend the same. Essentially, the adjustment in the approach was to include the teenager's friends in helping to keep the environment quiet for Crystal. This seems like an easy resolution to the problem. Yet, if it were not for the observational skills of Crystal's daughter, who noticed the stimulus, the solution may not have been so apparent.

Other questions to ask in order to assess your trial intervention should also be based on careful observation. Why did the strategy work only at certain times? Was there any difference in the implementation of intervention? Did the intervention work better if carried out by a certain individual? Did the impaired person respond better at specific times of the day? Was he or she alert, sleepy or for some reason more confused? How was his mood? Do you know why he was in a bad frame of mind? What was your mood or the mood of the person carrying out the intervention? Older folks can sense negative feelings and may not cooperate, no matter what intervention you use. Try to examine every aspect of your intervention and its implementation. If you are a good detective and use your powers of observation, the adjustments you will need to make become self-evident. In the case of Crystal, her daughter was able to identify the stimulus that caused her mother to scream during that last weekend. This led to an easy fix.

Another way to analyze the impact of your approach is to carefully monitor the impaired person's response. If you followed the directions in the previous section, you already have some information related to the person's reaction to your approach. To use the example of Crystal, I asked the family members to observe Crystal's demeanor when they tried to talk with her in order to stop her crying. Surprisingly, the granddaughter noted that her grandmother would begin crying when she heard someone near her room. This led the family to speculate that perhaps this was a grandmother's way of getting people to talk to her. The grandson added his observation that

Crystal would often display a brief smile in between her tearful sobs.

Using the above information, the family tried a completely different type of intervention in order to stop the crying. They developed a schedule whereby they would go into the grandmother's room when she was not crying and spend a minute or two just chatting with her. Crystal did not know about the schedule, but she was aware that the family was paying more attention to her.

When the family implemented this approach, their grandmother's crying episodes decreased to one or two per day. They were headed in the right direction. The family members analyzed the situation again after trying this approach for three weeks and noted that Crystal would cry if no one stopped in her room, when she heard them in the vicinity. This usually happened if the family members were rushing to do something and could not spend a short time with Crystal. They realized their intervention of scheduling brief talk time could not be fully implemented all the time.

After some family discussion, it was decided that they would buy Crystal a bookshelf stereo system along with a collection of CDs with music from the forties. This setup was able to pleasantly distract Crystal from sounds in other rooms. Using these latter two approaches, the music and the scheduled talks, Crystal's crying spells decreased to about two to three per month, a goal they considered acceptable.

Carefully monitoring a person's response to an intervention can help you adjust your strategy, leading to a new approach that will provide a better outcome. Again, your ability to observe carefully is crucial. Here are some sample questions you should ask yourself and other family members who are implementing the approach. Did your family member's mood change after the approach was carried out? If so, what exactly happened? Did he become more uncooperative? Did his facial expression change? Was his behavior different after the intervention? Did he make any specific comment? It is perfectly acceptable to talk simply and directly with the impaired individual and try to make sense out of their reaction to your approach. Did he find your approach offensive or condescending? This pattern of questioning should allow you to collect some useful information in order to alter your strategy.

Do not be afraid to try several approaches in a methodical fashion. Even if you are not sure your approach will work, you will gain some valuable information by reassessing your actions. Trust your inner feelings. They are often correct in determining the appropriate strategy. As long as you intervene in a safe and caring manner, you always have a reasonable chance of producing the positive outcome you desire. Keep trying, and do not give up. If nothing seems to work, talk with an outsider such as a physician or someone who has experience with the elderly.

Once you have decided on a new approach, go back to the implementation phase and try again. If your new strategy does not produce the desired result, go back to this analysis and adjustment phase and reassess the situation. The more you repeat this cycle, the more information you will have to improve your chances of a successful outcome.

Before we end this chapter, I would like to give you one final caution. It is not unusual to have some negative feelings toward your impaired relative. Their behavior can be very frustrating for you and all those with whom they come in contact. Do not let these negative feelings spill over into the planning process. You do not want to use an intervention out of frustration or anger that may do more harm than good in the long run. The best advice that I can give is to formulate your plan of action when you are in a friendly and charitable mood. Your chances of success will be much higher

CHAPTER FIFTEEN
The Secret To Success

If someone were to ask me the most common reason for failure when working with the elderly with behavioral problems, I would say a broken spirit. To succeed you must maintain a positive attitude. I realize this may be difficult at times, because dealing with some mentally ill individuals can be quite challenging and frustrating. By the time I see some families, they are literally "burned out" trying to deal with their impaired relative. Often, they have waited to the last minute to get help. You see, many people consider it a failure when they have to seek professional help, and so they tend to put it off as long as possible. By that time, they are often emotionally and physically exhausted.

My first bit of advice is to seek help after you have made some good faith efforts to resolve the problem but, for whatever reason, your interventions are not working. Remember, you are not the only one who has dealt with these problems. If you wait too long before you see a professional, you risk losing hope and that is a problem that will need to be addressed before you can focus on your impaired relative.

SHARE THE RESPONSIBILTY

I cannot over-emphasize the fact that you are not alone. Even though you might consider yourself the primary or sole caregiver, there are a number of resources that can help you with these issues. Ask family members to provide assistance. The worst they can do is refuse.

You may get a better response if you court your helpers and set the foundation for your request. Ask them over for coffee or tea. A home-cooked meal also has its advantages. Familiarize them with your relative's situation. This is very important, since many people are reluctant to help because they fear the unknown. Emphasize the positive aspects of care giving, for example, the internal reward one gets for helping someone. I know when I help an older person and see them smile or thank me, I feel good. Another positive aspect would be the development of a closer relationship with their loved one.

When you ask them to help, select specific jobs that they can do that are not overwhelming. They may not be able to help you out for an entire day, but they might be able to go to the market for you or sit with your relative for an hour or so.

I often tell the primary caregiver to list, in writing, a variety of jobs that need to be done during the day. If at all possible, the caregiver should try to delegate whatever jobs they can to relatives or friends. You would be surprised how many family members say that if they were asked to help they would gladly give their time. It is often helpful to give out jobs that are interesting and fun. For example, ask a family member or friend to take the impaired elderly person on a brief trip, or to stop by for a visit. This should free you to take a well-deserved break. Hopefully, this can be fun for all concerned. You can then use this time period to become reinvigorated. Use some of these breaks to do something rewarding for yourself. Do not use this extra time solely to catch up on other tasks. You should try to work out some type of consistent schedule so that you can have this respite on a regular basis.

When you delegate tasks to family, friends or neighbors, pick small jobs at first. Educate them briefly about your relative's limitations and what you are trying to accomplish. Try not to overwhelm them with jobs that are too complicated or inconvenient. You will risk losing them as helpers. Once your helpers gain some skills and confidence, they might be able to take on more challenging tasks, giving you more free time.

TAKE CARE OF YOURSELF

To keep your spirits up, you have to take care of yourself first. If you burn out and give up, your loved one may not have anyone to take care of him or her. Do not try to do all the work by yourself, if it at all possible. No one expects you to do it alone.

A 50-year-old woman once came to see me because she was depressed to the point that she did not want to get out of bed. She was feeling guilty because she was not taking care of her bedridden mother. She found herself in a vicious cycle of becoming burned out and depressed, leaving her with less energy to take care of her mother, which made her feel even more guilty and depressed. Before we could even develop a plan for her mother, I had to see this woman for a few visits to help her reorient her attitude and redefine her care-giving role. She put herself in this position by following her father's dying wish, which was to take care of her mother. Her interpretation was that her father was telling her that it was her job alone to be the caregiver. After some discussion, she was able to understand that if she were to continue with her current role as the sole caregiver she would become useless and not be able to help her mother at all. Obviously, this would not fulfill her father's request.

If you are overextended in your role as caregiver, look at the reason for putting yourself in this position. You are not a failure if you ask for help. Some family members either consciously or unconsciously believe that if they do it all, they will be seen as a martyr and other family members will have to help. This approach rarely works. Ask yourself why you have to do everything for your loved one. Talk to other family members and friends about your role. Are you being fair to yourself? Sometimes, it is helpful to talk with a professional such as your family physician, a psychologist or psychiatrist.

Besides family members, seek out your relative's old friends. They might be more willing to help out because I am sure that sooner or later they hope that the favor will be returned. I have found that nothing will brighten up an older individual more than to see an old friend. You can also use this friend as a source of information. Talk to them. Remember, they have years of experience. They might be able to tell you how you can help your loved one in a more efficient manner. They can provide the insight you need and do not have, because you are younger than your impaired relative.

Talk to clergy. Not only can they improve your attitude, but also they might provide resources to assist you in your care-giving role. There are many volunteers and religious groups who are looking for ways to help in the community. It is not surprising that many of these individuals are in the same age group as your loved one. People are often helpful in communicating with a person of their same age. They might be able to provide you with some insight into your relative's problem and suggest some solutions. In many instances, you do not need to be affiliated with the religious group in order to get help. Look for these organizations in your local phone book.

Talk to groups that work with the elderly population. In almost every city or town there is an agency that has the specific function of assisting the elderly with their problems. They can also improve your overall perspective by providing the assistance you need and giving you some relief. Volunteers from these organizations can talk with you about the difficulties you are facing and direct you to support groups of individuals who are dealing or have dealt with the same issues.

In the back of this book you will find a brief listing of agencies that can be helpful. First, however, I would suggest that you look in your local phone book under the words "elderly" or "aging." In this era of computers, it is also fairly easy to put the same words in your search engine along with the name of your town or city. This should give you a reasonable list of available agencies or groups that might be able to provide some assistance. Many phone calls or contacts with these agencies come from individuals like you. Caregivers tell me that once they reach out to these groups they feel a real sense of relief. They now know that they are not alone. Sometimes, just talking to a representative of these groups will help you reorient your feelings and put them in a more positive light.

SUPPORT SERVICES FOR THE ELDERLY

If you have some financial resources, consider hiring someone to help you so you can take a break. A person called a "home health aide", "sitter" or a "personal care aide" can assist your loved one with dressing, eating and using the bathroom. Because they have these skills, you can leave your relative with them for significant periods of time, allowing you to take care of your own life. You may need to interview several such people because their skills can vary greatly as do their personalities.

Do not feel guilty about leaving your family member. Sometimes you both will need a break from each other. There are numerous resources available to help you accomplish this.

A geriatric day program, or adult day care can provide several hours of structured activities during the daytime for an elderly person in need. Meals are sometimes included. Like paid caregivers, these programs can differ widely in their quality and philosophy. These programs usually encourage the impaired individual to visit before they enroll. This is a great idea for elderly persons who are somewhat wary of new things. It is important that there be a proper match between the person and program. Some things an adult day program can provide that are difficult to match at home are the various activities and socialization opportunities. This is very important for people who are depressed, withdrawn or demented. For them, this type of setting can be quite therapeutic. Without overstating the obvious, having your loved one in such a program gives you the time and opportunity to do the things you need to refresh yourself.

You can learn about the available geriatric day programs from your local mental health department, office on aging or equivalent. Many of these programs are either free or ask for a small contribution. Some of these programs will have arrangements for transportation. Others may ask you to volunteer some of your time in the program. Giving some service is not a bad idea. This provides you the opportunity to observe your loved one in a new setting, as well as note the overall quality of services provided. You may also learn a few tips in managing behavioral problems from some of the staff. It is a good place to meet members of other families. This will help you expand your support network.

Respite care or short-term residential care can be used if you need to get away for a while. Even caregivers need vacations. Assisted-living facilities may offer this type of service. Once again, your local health department or office on aging can point you in the right direction. You will need to plan in advance for the exact dates that you will be away in order to use these services. A few of these programs can help on a last minute basis in case of an emergency.

Some caregivers and programs just do not work out. They may not be the right match for your loved one, or the quality of service they provide is not up to your standards. Shop around. While finding a good provider may initially take some time, in the long run it will be worth the effort. I do want to caution you that no program or provider is perfect. They all have flaws but we need to balance them with their strengths. I ask that you do this with the programs and providers you seek.

A patient who had a long history of schizophrenia became quite dependent in his old age. His family hired a number of sitters before they found one who was able to deal with his verbally abusive behavior. This new sitter developed a chemistry with this older man and was able to get him to behave. They got along famously. The daughter and son-in-law, who both worked during the day, sometimes came home during the afternoon to find the sitter watching soap operas. The son-in-law wanted to fire the sitter but the daughter was able to convince him that her father was still receiving good care and no harm was being done. She also reminded him of the long list of sitters they had interviewed before they found one that worked.

As long as your loved one is being cared for appropriately, consider yourself lucky. Look at the pros and cons of any caregiver or program before you make a change. Most importantly, remember, nothing is ever perfect.

THE SUPPORT NETWORK

Another way to keep up your spirits is to establish a support network. Talking with other family members is the first step in the process. Even if they are unable to help out in the care of your loved one, they can provide you the moral support or advice needed to keep going. Try to find someone who has already gone through the same type of issues. Is there another family member who is dealing with mental illness in their immediate family? Are other family members dealing with older individuals?

Next, try to find friends or neighbors who are dealing with issues of mental illness or aging. They may have the same feelings as you, since they are dealing with their family's problems. Mixtures of emotions such as anger, frustration and guilt are difficult to handle alone. You will need to talk with someone about your feelings, so that you will be able to resolve them and move on, not only in your role as caregiver but more importantly with your life. Remember, as I said above, if you cannot take care of yourself first, you will not be able to take care of your loved one.

Do not feel guilty, if you harbor angry feelings. It may seem unfair that you have to be the primary caregiver or that others do not want to help out. Sometimes, you feel that you are the only responsible person that cares about your loved one. Having feelings of anger and resentment is normal. Sometimes, your anger can spill over and you may say things to others that you later regret. If you feel that you are getting to this point, talk to someone about your feelings. As I said in previous chapters, it will only make matters worse if you express your anger inappropriately toward your impaired relative. To prevent this, you will need to find another outlet.

You do not want to feel overwhelmed as the responsible care provider. You can avoid getting to this point by developing your support network early on. There are people and agencies that can help you. Do not be afraid to tell people that you need help, because many organizations can provide it. It is important to remember that you are not the first person going through this difficult scenario.

People often feel guilty because they believe that they are not doing enough. This often happens when a caregiver asks for help. For some reason, certain persons believe that they should be the sole person responsible for the impaired individual. They feel that asking for help is a failure on their part. Nothing could be further from the truth. Look at it this way. I have already explained the need to maintain a positive and caring attitude in your work with your impaired relative. A benevolent and caring approach by you is the key to your success. You do not want to feel guilty for having a negative relationship with your loved one, so you will need to maintain a positive attitude. This means you will need to take breaks from your care-giving role, and to do so, you will require assistance. To look at this another way, getting help will relieve you of some of your stress. This will help give you a positive attitude. This attitude will improve your relationship with your impaired family member, which is likely to lead to his or her cooperation in the management of the behavioral issue.

Persons who have a mental illness are usually very sensitive to negative feelings in others. When helping them with their problems, you need to have them on your side, and they need to know you are on their side. Maintaining a healthy spirit is a win-win situation for you and your relative.

SIGNS YOU MIGHT NEED HELP

The best way to maintain a positive attitude is to identify your need for help early in the care giving process. Do not wait until the situation is so bad that resolving the negative issues could be much more difficult. Develop your network of support from the very beginning.

Some of the clues that you need help include feelings of sadness or depression that last for several days. It is normal to feel down when you are dealing with an impaired individual who may be frustrating your efforts and taking much of your time. But, if the feelings are persistent, take some corrective action. If you notice that your appetite is decreased or you are losing weight, this may be another sign of depression. Ask yourself if you are feeling alone and overwhelmed. Do you find yourself crying often? If you are having thoughts of suicide, get help immediately.

Another sign that your emotional state is in question is a problem with sleep. Are you able to sleep through the night? If you are consistently having difficulty falling asleep because you are worrying, or you are waking up too early in the morning and cannot get back to sleep, you could be suffering from an emotional disorder. Are you noticing that you feel tense or anxious? Signs of anxiety include muscle aches, tiredness, tremor or persistent headache.

Other clues that may indicate that something is wrong would be excessive drinking or shopping. If you need to perform these activities to feel better this could be an indication that you need help. Are you using over-the-counter medications or prescriptions without your doctor's advice in order to help you with your mood? That would be another warning sign.

Previously, we talked about how it is normal to feel frustrated or angry at times, particularly when you are dealing with a person who is acting inappropriately. You have to be aware of these feelings, so that you do not cross the line and let your anger get out of control. Seek help if you are yelling or screaming with any frequency. Do you have the feeling that you could lose control? Most importantly, if you believe that you might become physically aggressive with your relative, you need to obtain some assistance. This also applies if you find yourself handling your relative in a rough manner. Are you handling them with more force than is reasonably required?

Pay attention to these clues so that you will be able to recognize your need for help as soon as possible. More importantly, try to establish a support network at the beginning of your care-giving role. If this is in place you will have a readily available group to talk to if you have any problems.

This network should consist of friends, family members and professionals whom you can count on to provide guidance as you proceed through the difficult process of working with a behaviorally disturbed individual.

Do not hesitate to contact support groups and organizations such as the Alliance for the Mentally Ill or the Alzheimer's Association, when you take on the role of caregiver. You may not think you need help at that time, but you would be surprised as to the amount of helpful information these groups can provide to make your job easier. They will also be able to refer you to counselors or support groups in case you run into trouble with your interventions or your emotions.

COUNSELING

Let's talk about counseling. Many people avoid such help because they feel that they are not sick or crazy. In an earlier chapter, I talked about how the impaired individual refuses treatment or an assessment for the same reason. Do not get caught in this trap. Even though many people who are in the care-giving role do not need professional counseling, you should not see it as a failure if you require some assistance. One of the saddest situations that I see in my practice is the individual who puts off counseling until they are at wit's end. First, they have lost all of that time that they could have been feeling better, had they sought help early on. Second, when they come for assistance and are at the point of feeling overwhelmed or are giving up hope, it makes the counseling or treatment process more difficult. The bottom line is that, if you feel you need counseling, get it. Do not wait.

I often hear the excuse that the caregiver cannot afford the time to go to counseling. While an initial investment of time is involved, in most circumstances, counseling will enable you to become a more efficient provider. In the long run, you will actually have more time available not only to provide care, but also to take care of your life in a more positive fashion. You can obtain counseling through some of the groups we have already talked about. In addition, there are clergy, social workers, nurses, psychologists and physicians available to talk with you about your difficulties and provide guidance.

If you are still afraid to seek counseling, ask some of your relatives or friends if they ever sought such help. You will be surprised to find out that many people have received some type of assistance. They can help educate you and hopefully motivate you to seek help. Also, you should ask them who they saw and if they were they helpful. You may want to see the same counselor.

Let me give you a brief description of the counseling process, because it is quite simple, and certainly not scary. These professionals will talk to you about the problems that you are having in straightforward terms. They will provide practical advice as to how you can cope with your issues. Counselors are normal people who have experience not only as a result of their training, but also the experience they have obtained in dealing with similar problems through the years. They know about your problems. They can help. They typically are concerned and caring individuals who truly want to help.

THE BOTTOM LINE

First, I would like to point out to you that everyone makes mistakes, and no one is 100% successful. I do not want to mislead you. The examples that I have presented in this book talk about positive outcomes. Believe me, there were numerous cases that were difficult for me to handle and even some cases that were out and out failures.

When I ran into a roadblock, I sought help. At those times, I would ask for a consultation from my colleagues. Many times this proved to be quite helpful. Yet, there were still a few failures, even though I refused to give up. There would have been many more negative outcomes had I, or the family members, given up. At the same time, there was no question that I, like many family members, needed to maintain a positive attitude in order to produce a successful outcome. That is the key ingredient to success. With that philosophy, failures will come few and far between.

I have attempted to cover various types of clinical situations in this book along with suggested solutions. In addition, I have outlined a process to address numerous other situations. In spite of this, I am sure there will be many cases that differ somewhat from the clinical examples given. There will also be situations that seem similar to the cases seen in this text, but have different circumstances or complications. Remember, this book is a guide. If your approach is not working, or you are not absolutely sure of your intervention, seek help from a professional. You should ideally consult with a physician familiar with the treatment of the elderly.

I hope my message is unquestionably clear. Most elderly individuals with emotional and behavioral problems can be helped. Do not assume that these issues are just part of the normal aging process. Spread the word. Tell family members, friends and other associates that many of these problems do have solutions. Recognizing these disorders and developing a methodical care plan can be, not only, life improving, but at times, life saving. We will be old folks one day. I am sure we would want the same.

Finally, do not forget to ask for help for both you and your loved one. Remember, the secret to making any plan work is to implement it in a constructive and caring manner. To do this, you must be a person with a positive attitude. So, take care of yourself so that you will be able to take care of your loved one. Good luck.

APPENDIX I
Resource Organizations

The AGS Foundation for Health in Aging – Depression in older adults.
http://www.healthinaging.org/
public_education/tools_depression.php
Phone: 1(800) 563-4916 Toll Free

ALZBRAIN.ORG – A site for Alzheimer's information
http://www.alzbrain.org/index.htm

Alzheimer's Association
http://www.alz.org
Phone: 1(800) 272-3900 Toll Free

American Psychiatric Association
http://www.psych.org_info/elderly.cfm
Phone: (703) 907-7300

American Psychiatric Foundation
http://www.psychfoundation.org/
publications/mhfacts.cfm
Phone: 1 (888) 35-Psych Toll Free

Depression and Bipolar Support Alliance
http://www.dbsalliance.org
Phone: 1 (800) 563-4916

Elder Web
http://www.elderweb.com
Phone: (309) 451-3319

Geriatric Mental Health Foundation
http://www.gmhfonline.org/gmhf/default.asp
Phone (301) 654-7850

Internet Mental Health
http://www.mentalhealth.com

Resource Organizations

Mental Health and Aging
http://www.mhaging.org
Phone: 1 (800) 688-4246 Toll Free

National Alliance for the Mentally Ill (NAMI)
http://www.nami.org
Phone: 1 (800) 950-6264 Toll Free

National Institute on Aging (NIA)

http://www.nia.nih.gov

Phone: 1(800) 222-2225 Toll Free

National Institute of Mental Health (NIMH)

http://www.nimh.nih.gov

Phone: 1 (800) 615-6464 Toll Free

National Mental Health Association

http://www.nmha.org

1 (800) 433-5959 Toll Free

APPENDIX II
Technology Resources

Activity Compass Device
http://www.somersetmedicalcenter.com/18483
This device detects that a wandering patient might be lost and will prompt him or her to return home by pointing out the right direction. It also has a built in alarm.

The Alzheimer's Store
http://alzstore.com
Phone: 1 (800) 752-3238
The Alzstore is a great source for numerous devices that help persons with memory and wandering problems. It also has a fine listing of books on Alzheimer's and related disorders.

American Medical Alarms
http://www.americanmedicalalarms.com
Phone: 1 (800) 542-0438
This company handles alarms that enable a confused, lost or injured person to signal for help by pressing a button on a wristband or pendant.

GPS systems for Alzheimer's and other confused patients
http://alzheimers.upmc.com/gps.htm
This website explains how the GPS navigation system can work for the confused person who wanders.

Love Connection Patient Monitors
http://www.loveconnectionmonitors.com
Phone: (706) 829-2544
This is a resource for alarms that notify the caregiver that a patient is starting to wander. The patient can also sound the alert if they need help.

Technology Resources

National Alzheimer's Association
http://www.alz.org
NAA has periodic articles on new technologies as well as a wealth of information on Alzheimer's disease.

Project Lifesaver
http://www.projectlifesaver.net
Project Lifesaver is a tracking system available in several states for patients who wander.

INDEX

INDEX

INDEX

INDEX

INDEX

ABOUT THE AUTHOR

Thomas F. Krajewski, M.D. is the former Chief Physician for the State of Maryland and Assistant Secretary for Health. He has also held the position of Assistant Secretary for Addictions, Mental Hygiene and Developmental Disabilities for Maryland and was the Director of the Springfield Hospital Center, which was, at that time, the largest psychiatric hospital in the state. Twice named "Top Doc" by Baltimore Magazine, he has lectured nationally and internationally on topics such as Patients' Rights, Psychological Aspects of Aids and Family Therapy as well as Geropsychiatry. He has also appeared on programs such as the Charley Rose Show and Ted Koppel's "Nightline". Dr. Krajewski, who is better known as "Doctor K" to his colleagues, is currently an Associate Clinical Professor of Psychiatry at the University of Maryland School of Medicine, Coordinator of Geropsychiatric Services for the Mental Hygiene Administration of Maryland and he heads the Medical/Psychiatric Program at the Spring Grove Hospital Center.

CPSIA information can be obtained at www.ICGtesting.com
Printed in the USA
LVOW13s0358100214

373034LV00001B/313/A